Love Across Difference

Love Across Difference

Mixed Marriage in Lebanon

Lara Deeb

STANFORD UNIVERSITY PRESS
Stanford, California

Stanford University Press
Stanford, California

Printed in the United States of America on acid-free, archival-quality paper

Library of Congress Cataloging-in-Publication Data

Names: Deeb, Lara, 1974- author.
Title: Love across difference : mixed marriage in Lebanon / Lara Deeb.
Description: Stanford, California : Stanford University Press, 2024. |
    Includes bibliographical references and index.
Identifiers: LCCN 2024003547 (print) | LCCN 2024003548 (ebook) |
    ISBN 9781503640054 (cloth) | ISBN 9781503640757 (paperback) |
    ISBN 9781503640764 (ebook)
Subjects: LCSH: Interfaith marriage—Lebanon. | Sects—Social
    aspects—Lebanon. | Lebanon—Ethnic relations.
Classification: LCC HQ1031 .D39 22024 (print) | LCC HQ1031 (ebook) |
    DDC 306.84/5095692—dc23/eng/20240205
LC record available at https://lccn.loc.gov/2024003547
LC ebook record available at https://lccn.loc.gov/2024003548

Cover design: Daniel Benneworth-Gray
Cover art: Jana Traboulsi
Typeset by Newgen in Guyot Text 10.25/15.5

Contents

Introduction

Love Across Difference

Nina opened the door to her apartment in a beautifully renovated old building in Beirut. "Welcome, come in, it's so nice to meet you!" she exclaimed, with an infectious smile. We greeted one another with the customary three air kisses on alternating cheeks. I followed Nina to the living room and sat on one of the white sofas while she went to the kitchen to make us Arabic coffee.

The sofas were framed by a massive, white, elegantly decorated Christmas tree and a backlit black canvas with the phrase *Bismillah al-rahman al-rahim*, which means "In the Name of God, the Most Gracious, the Most Merciful," written on it in glowing calligraphy—ubiquitous fixtures in Christian and Muslim homes, respectively. Across the room, I saw two paintings, one of a Christian saint and the other depicting the names of the Rashidun Caliphs, leaders of the Muslim community after the Prophet Muhammad.[1] Nina returned and sat across from me, tucking one leg underneath her. A domestic worker appeared a moment later and set a silver tray between us with the coffee, glasses of water, dried apricots, and thin sesame seed crackers.

As Nina poured the coffee and passed me a cup, I explained my project. An acquaintance had connected us, and our small talk led us to discover several other mutual friends. Nina's parents are wealthy Roum Orthodox, one of Lebanon's major Christian sects; my father's side is also Roum, from a different region of the country.[2] Nina grew up in the heterogeneous neighborhood of Ras Beirut, as did many of my relatives, and we share family and friendship connections to the area's elite educational institutions. Once we had placed one another on Lebanon's social map, with her permission, I turned on my digital recorder, setting it as unobtrusively as possible on the table.

"Just tell me your story," I said. "However you want to tell it. How did you meet Ali? What happened then? From meeting him to marrying him, however you want to tell me."

"Well," Nina began, "we met through a common friend when we were very young, or at least I was. I was nineteen, I was at university, and he was twenty-eight. And just like that . . ." She started laughing. "Just like that, we fell in love, like right away, we knew! Like I remember from the moment of our first date, we went out for dinner, and I came home and told my mom, 'I think I met the one.' My mom said, 'Hmm, interesting, what's his name?' I told her his name, and it is obviously Muslim, obviously Shi'a, and she said, 'Forget it, he's not the one.'"

———————

Lebanon may well be the most complicated place in the world to be a mixed couple. It has no civil marriage law, eighteen official sectarian (religious and ethnoreligious) groups with fifteen religious personal status laws (laws for marriage, divorce, child custody, and inheritance), a political system built on sectarian difference, and a history of fraught politics and periodic violence. Until relatively recently, as compared to Europe or the United States, most marriages were family approved if not orchestrated. Plus, Lebanon is tiny, a condensed country with a compressed social space. Six degrees of separation is a stretch—more often it's only two. Compressing social space can turn it into a pressure cooker of status anxieties.

Lebanon is also the country in the Middle East with the most mixed marriages per capita. In this book, I use "mixed marriage" to refer to interreligious couples, meaning marriages between two people from Lebanon's major religions: Islam, Christianity, and Druze, an eleventh-century offshoot of Islam.[3] At times in Lebanon's history, marriages between Christians from different sects (e.g., Roman Catholic, Maronite, Roum Orthodox,

Syriac) or Muslims from different sects (Sunni, Shi'a) have been considered mixed, but I will call those "intersectarian."

To say that Lebanon has the "most" mixed marriages is relative, as they likely represent between 2 percent and 5 percent of all marriages among Lebanese.[4] In the US, according to a 2001 survey, 22 percent of marriages were interfaith.[5] Still, having the most makes sense given Lebanon's relative religious diversity within the region.[6]

As a point of comparison, when I asked family and friends in Jordan if they knew of mixed couples—other than Jordanian Muslim men married to European or North American Christian women, which is more common—few could list more than one or two. Some people recalled elopements that ended in disownment or violence. One person told me interreligious couples have to emigrate. A few people came up with a handful of couples, mostly elites. And indeed, in Jordan, Muslim-Christian relationships are "the classic examples of star-crossed lovers" and rarely end in marriage.[7] Egypt is similar, and the rare nonelite Muslim-Christian romance leading to marriage can foment sensationalist speculation about bride abduction and forced conversion.[8]

In contrast, when I asked Lebanese strangers about mixed marriage, they usually mentioned a recent media story about it (George Clooney's marriage to Lebanese-British lawyer Amal Alamuddin, whose family is Druze, was a popular one), talked about civil marriage instead, or told me it was once rare but growing more common. Older men sometime recited a saying that roughly translates to "A person who marries outside their religious group will die with their predicament" (*Li byekhod men gher melto, b mout b 'elto*)—meaning that they are stuck with the consequences, and those consequences will be dire. People assume mixed marriage will be difficult, not necessarily for the couple, but for their families, and they're right. When two Lebanese from different sects decide to marry, more often than not, drama ensues.

Parents have cried, pleaded, feigned heart attacks and other health scares, reasoned, argued, called on extended family or clerical pressure, used the silent treatment, threatened disownment, embarked on avid matchmaking efforts, badgered their child's partner, restricted their child's movement, and, rarely, threatened violence—all to express their opposition to mixed marriage. Most of these parents aren't particularly religious. Most have friends or coworkers from other sects. So why does mixed marriage trigger intense resistance? As the following chapters show, at a fundamental level, mixed marriage disrupts parents' expectations for their families' social and literal futures and challenges dominant social ideas about love, patriarchy, sectarianism, discrimination, and difference.

―――――

Undaunted by her mom's reaction, Nina dated Ali anyway. "My parents knew I was going out with him. And the whole time they were asking me, 'What's going on, Nina? What's happening, Nina?' Like, 'You know this isn't gonna end up anywhere, why are you going out with him?' And the whole time I kept saying, 'I'm just having fun, I'm just having fun, I'm just having fun.'" When she graduated from university, Nina and Ali's relationship continued, on-again, off-again, for a decade. Even during the "off-agains," they stayed in touch. "We broke up and got back together, broke up and got back together about five hundred times because my parents weren't agreeing to it."

During those years, Ali tried talking to Nina's dad, explaining that he was serious about the relationship and wanted to marry his daughter. Her dad refused him, telling him to "forget about" Nina, that they were "not made for each other." Nina's parents had done some digging into Ali's background and didn't like what they found. Aside from sect, he was too far from their expectations for a son-in-law. Although Ali attended elite schools, had a promising professional career, and came from an educated family, they held less wealth and lower social status than Nina's elite clan.

Nina's mother regularly brought up the relationship. "Who is this family? What social circle do they come from? How can we not know anything about the family you want to marry into?" At the same time, she understood her daughter wanting to marry for love. "I married for love," she would say, "and I wouldn't have wanted anyone to stand in my way, and I'm not trying to stand in your way. All I'm trying to say is, try to find someone else. If you go out with a bunch of people, and you come to me and say, 'You know what mom, I still love him,' then that's it, do what you want, but just try first."

So, Nina tried. "I had a lot of fun," she told me. "And I laughed a lot. But I never took anyone seriously." Nina even allowed her parents to set her up on dates with eligible Christian bachelors from families they knew, accompanied by her mother or another relative. She went back to her mom and said, "You can see that I'm trying, but seriously, you've seen these guys, would *you* go out with them? Would *you* say, 'Yes, they interest me?'" Her mother conceded the point, agreeing that none would have interested her either. "There you go," Nina retorted. "It's not like I'm not *trying* to meet someone else."

When I asked her why she had spent years complying with her parents' wishes rather than eloping with Ali, Nina explained that she didn't want to marry without her parents' approval because she had a great deal of compassion for the hardships they had faced raising children during Lebanon's 1975–1990 civil war. "Our parents' generation really had a hard time raising us, they really had a shitty life in this country, you know? They didn't have anything other than war and stress. And now I think about it, like *I'm* stressed, what the hell am *I* stressed about? My parents lived through the war. I don't know how they made money. I don't know how they worked every day. I don't know how they got up every day. I don't know how they did this. I don't know if they were on medication. They would take us to school, then bombs would drop so they would run back to pick us up from school."

Nina's deep appreciation for her parents' sacrifices ruled out eloping, even though that was the path some of her friends had chosen. "It was a red line for me. I knew I wanted to marry him, but not in a way that hurt my parents, or upset them, or defied them."

––––––––––

While Nina spent years discussing Ali with her parents, dealing with their disapproval, Ali's parents stayed out of it. This was expected. Some Lebanese men must fight their families to marry the women they love, but their battles are less frequent and intense and are typically short-lived. Mixed marriages must contend with patriarchy because they involve women trying to make marital choices against the grain of their families and society. My interviewees wanted to marry, to take part in that heterosexual and patriarchal system, but they wanted to do so on their own terms.[9]

The generational conflict between children fighting for love and parents doing what is best for their children out of love is a symptom of an incomplete shift from arranged or family-mediated marriage to companionate or love marriage. The first questions most parents ask—"Who are they? Do we know them?"—are a holdover signaling their discomfort with the unfettered choice some young people assume comes with companionate marriage. Marriage grafts families together, not individuals, and those families are supposed to be similar. Even as many people described their marital choices as based on romantic love, like Nina, they told me about the pull of broader kinship connections in their lives.

In Lebanon, mixed marriages also run headfirst into patriarchal and sectarian family status laws that add legal discrimination to the sexism Lebanese women face. Take fifteen personal status laws and multiply by two—because the laws are different for males and females—and you end up with thirty legal categories.[10] Differences in rules for marriage, divorce, and child custody mean that the details of the sexism Christian, Druze, and Muslim Lebanese women experience vary, but no group has it uniformly worse than the others. The combination of this legal system and social norms shapes decisions about how to marry for women of all sects in the country.

The forces of patriarchy weigh more heavily on women, but men are far from immune. I heard nearly as many stories about parental pressures on sons of all sects as on daughters. Sons carry parents' expectations for their family's future; patriarchy is a hierarchy of generation as well as sex. Factors like class, education, and even personality can alter dynamics in ways that disrupt gendered religious or legal limitations. Just because religious and state authorities regulate families in specific ways, social practices and ideas don't necessarily follow.[11]

Some of my interviewees named patriarchy and sexism as the source of their struggles, railing against these forms of discrimination. Others searched for legal loopholes, seeking ways to ensure their rights within a system stacked against them. Yet others acquiesced to social norms, whether by upholding patriarchy themselves or feeling stuck, with no other options.

————

While Nina was empathetic to her parents' position and spent years trying to make them happy, she also brooked no compromises when it came to marrying for love. She insisted her ideas about love came from her parents' romantic story; people still referred to them as "lovebirds." So, a few months after meeting Nina, I went to meet her mother, Salwa. Salwa told me she and her husband had fallen in love as young teenagers. They exchanged secret glances and letters for a year until he dared call the house and she heard his voice for the first time, then braved years of clandestine meetings until she was old enough to date. They finally married, a decade after their first glance, with their parents' blessing.

This experience weighed on Salwa. "If a groom had showed up and asked for Nina's hand, I don't know what we would have said," she told me, thinking back to those years of conflict with her daughter. "People were asking to introduce Nina to their relatives. And we thought, if we pressure her and she marries someone *we* choose, someone Christian who we consider good socially, and then she comes to us one day and says, 'I'm not happy,' we will never ever forgive ourselves."

On the one hand, Salwa struggled to accept Ali because he didn't fit into her dreams for Nina's future, from the decorated church steps for the wedding photos to the extended family Christmas gatherings. On the other hand, she said, "I couldn't stop her because I know what it means to marry for love. I couldn't imagine my daughter marrying someone who doesn't make her heart beat faster every time he puts his key in the door."

Eventually, on one of her breaks from Ali, Nina met a guy she could imagine falling for. She called her mom to share the news. Again, the first thing Salwa asked was, "What's his name?" Nina told her his first name, which assured Salwa that he was Christian. Then Salwa asked for his last name.

After a brief pause, Salwa responded, "Wait a minute, where is he from?"

"He is European."

The phone went silent. "Go back to Ali," Salwa finally said.

As Nina told me this part of the story, she collapsed into another round of laughter. "In the echelon of bad to worse," she laughed, shaking her head at the absurdity of the situation, "it turned out marrying a foreigner and never moving back to Lebanon was the worst thing that could happen." That new relationship ran its course quickly.

Then one day, she was talking to Ali on the phone. "He called me. Or maybe I called him," she told me. "I forget. But I had just left that other guy. And I started crying on the phone, like, 'Fuck my life, like this one guy I meet after a million years who seems right and it doesn't work out.' So, Ali says to me, 'I don't understand, like I'm living god knows how far away from you, and I'm still in love with you, and you're crying over some guy who came from who knows where!'" He booked a flight, stayed with Nina for a while, and then relocated to be closer to her. Soon after, Nina made her decision. "That's it, it's Ali. Ali is the one."

She called her parents and told them the news. "You know what," she said, "I dated a lot, and I tried, and it's still Ali. And you are going to get to know him, because I have decided this is it, he's the one.'" I asked her how they replied. "They were like, 'Okay, that's it,'" she answered, "but, like, after ten years! It took *ten years*."

————

Most of the parents in this book who opposed mixed marriage wanted the best for their children. They wanted them to be happy, and even to marry for love, but they also wanted them to fall in love with an appropriate person. Being a loving parent means working toward your child's well-being, and many believe that well-being hinges on a harmonious marriage and that harmony grows from similarity. And most Lebanese—like most people around the world—marry people who they see as similar to them. "We have a lot in common" competes with "Opposites attract"—and the former saying is more likely to be heard about a successful marriage than the latter. The catch here is that most of my interviewees saw their spouses as similar to them. With a few exceptions, most don't see their marriage as "mixed."

In 1941, sociologist Robert Merton defined intermarriage as the "marriage of persons deriving from those different in-groups and out-groups other than the family *which are culturally conceived as relevant* to the choice of a spouse."[12] A mixed marriage is a marriage between people who society *believes* differ from one another. Most Lebanese today believe that religion—down to the specific sect—is the most important feature defining those in-groups and out-groups. But where parents, society, and the Lebanese state see difference, most mixed couples do not. As one person told me, "Other people see religious difference, but all we see are the things we have in common. We grew up in the same neighborhood. We were born at the same hospital. We've both lived outside the country for periods of time. We feel the connections, the similarities. We never felt like strangers, or like we were worlds apart from one another."

My interviewees aren't naive. They understand perfectly well that society and their families view them as a mixed couple because they are interreligious or intersectarian. Some love one another because of or despite that difference. But their commonalities far outweigh labels of sect or religion. As we will see, one of the fundamental issues at the root of these family conflicts is a disagreement about what similarity and difference entail in the first place.

Social pressure inflames disagreements about who is marriageable. Lebanon is a small world where families and social circles intertwine and where economic networks may rely on those relational ties. Most parents are terrified of the social consequences of their child's mixed marriage, for that child but also for themselves. Threats of shunning are powerful. Children are supposed to act in ways that maintain a family's networks and social worlds. Love is reciprocal; it carries expectations. The family members or friends pressuring parents, urging them to keep their child in line, to solve the problem of an errant relationship before the wrong person has been admitted into the family tree and social world, are also seeing difference where the couple sees similarity. At these moments, sect often seems like the only thing that matters, the most important characteristic of a potential spouse.

My interviews tell a different story. When I ranked the factors underlying parents' concerns about mixed marriage, religious difference came in sixth. At the top of the list was "What will people say?"—social pressure, in other words, whether from relatives, neighbors, colleagues, or friends. Fifty percent of parents who had opposed a mixed marriage worried about social consequences. The two factors following closely behind amplified this social pressure. One was a difference of social status between families, whether defined by socioeconomic class or some other metric like education, time spent outside Lebanon, local area of origin, or sect. The other factor was a lack of exposure to people from the sect of the potential spouse, accompanied by fear of the unknown plus a reliance on negative stereotypes about that group (e.g., "They are less cultured"; "You will be forced to dress a certain way," etc.). The next factors each came up in only 10–15 percent of parent objections: "The family is unknown to us," often because of geographic difference; "The political situation will make life difficult for you if you marry someone from X community"; "You will not be able to raise children properly together"; "We are too different from them to make this work."

People used the language of sect to describe most of these concerns or objections, but they weren't about religious differences. No one was talking about which prophets a person believes in, or how they cross themselves or hold their arms during prayer. In Lebanon, sectarianism is the dominant script for social difference, the most readily available, tip-of-the-tongue language for talking about it. But it's an empty script that can be molded to any meaning. Everyone assumes sect is the type of difference that matters most, but when people talk about sect as the problem, they are often referring to socioeconomic class, or village versus urban differences, or political disagreements, or some other issue. In that Lebanese saying—"A person who marries outside their religious group will die with their predicament"— the word for "religious group" is sometimes used more broadly to refer to other social groups, like family, region, or class. The fact that people recited the saying to me when I brought up mixed marriage demonstrates the prominence of sect as a category in Lebanon. Other kinds of social difference hover under the surface because sectarian language has already carved an easier path along which words can flow. And deep in the core, it's usually about status—defined by different criteria but subsumed into the category of sect.

Relying on the language of sect simplifies people's lives because it doesn't see them through an intersectional lens, a lens that understands their experiences through the overlap of different identities. Being Sunni Muslim, female, wealthy, and urban is a radically different experience than being Sunni Muslim, male, poor, and rural. The combinations are myriad. Intersectionality isn't simply additive.[13] It isn't enough to list the characteristics, like race, gender, and class, that shape a person's life, identity, and experiences. The characteristics themselves aren't separable; they define one another. Anthropologist Maya Mikdashi coined the term "sextarianism" to capture how sect and sex cannot be understood separately. She analyzes how, at every level—from state institutions like personal status law to practices like marriage or activism—sect and sex *together* shape Lebanese experience.[14] As you read the stories in this book, keep this idea in mind.

Relying on the language of sect hides other kinds of difference from sight. The drama around mixed marriage uncovers those submerged differences, uncovers the taken for granted or deliberately ignored aspects of discrimination and stereotyping and shows us sect doesn't have to be at the center. Seeing these other kinds of difference dislodges sect from prime position, making it one category of difference among many. As parents came to terms with their children's choice of spouse, they too had to put sect back in its place, undoing their own assumptions and learning about the similarities that had drawn their son or daughter to that person. Nina's parents were no exception.

––––––––

Now that Ali was a reality, it was time for Nina's parents to get to know him. Salwa had a long chat with him about the standard of living they expected him to maintain for their daughter. She left that conversation reassured and went to her husband and said, "Don't tell Nina I said this, but I liked him, and if I like him, how can I blame her for falling in love with him? He's a sweet, nice guy, very handsome; it's easy to like him."

Getting to know Ali helped allay one of her father's concerns, which was that Ali would someday grow religiously conservative. "He is like us," Salwa told me. "He has a drink after a long day at work; this makes us comfortable. We don't drink a lot, only socially, but if he stopped drinking, that might bother me. And if I am honest, if his mother were veiled, that would have bothered me, because we don't have such a thing in our family." They did, however, have other mixed marriages in the family, which eased Salwa's social worries. "If my daughter had been the first one in the family, ouf! It would have been too much. But because more mixed marriages were happening, I felt like, okay, maybe some people won't say anything or hold this against me."

It also helped that Ali had built a career that brought him into the Ras Beirut social circles of Nina's family. Salwa and her husband had done their research: "Of course, we immediately started investigating, not only about him, but also about mixed marriages, the law, children, legacy, all those things, but yes, also about him. We asked around. And it turned out that one of my husband's friends knew Ali well, and said he was one of his best students and also a gentleman. And Nina's uncle asked also and came back and told us, 'There is nothing against him, no one says anything bad about him. This person, as a man, as a guy, there's nothing against him.' This all helped."

Key among the findings of their investigation was that Ali could indeed provide financially to allow Nina to maintain an upper-class lifestyle. Salwa was explicit about this point: "If Nina loved someone from a different religion who was poor, of course I wouldn't accept it. Even if he was a Christian, I wouldn't accept it. There are certain standards. It isn't the money. He has to be educated and ambitious and able to give her a good life. And we need to be able to sit with his parents and be able to get along with them. It's okay if they have a little less than us, and it's even better if they have more than us, but it has to be similar." As Salwa continued describing class similarity while insisting that it wasn't about money, it became clear that she associated a certain level of material comfort with how people act at home: "He has to care for her, to treat her the way her father treats me." As she got to know Ali, Salwa grew convinced that he was indeed like her husband in this way.

The moment her parents accepted the match, Nina's extended family embraced Ali. Salwa and her husband threw the couple a huge engagement party. A few distant relatives expressed disapproval to Salwa: "One of my relatives told me that if it were her daughter, she would have committed suicide! Can you believe it? But she is a distant relative, and we didn't pay her any attention."

Ali's family had remained silent until this point, but his parents were unhappy the couple chose a civil marriage in Cyprus instead of a *katab kitab*, a Muslim marriage contract, which could take place in Lebanon without Nina's conversion. They blamed Nina, fearing she would pull their son away from his family and environment. Their discomfort erupted in arguments about the wedding details, like what the invitation cards should say. Nina's father encouraged her to ignore them. He told her that he had gotten to know Ali, that he was a good man who loved her, and that's why he had blessed the match.

By the time they married, Nina was thirty. "Ali always jokes about it," she laughed. "One of his friends said to him, 'You know what, they aren't going to hand her over to you just yet, she's still young, she will still get a lot of suitors, but once she hits her late twenties, if she isn't married yet, her parents will give her to you.' Ali jokes that it's true, that's what happened."

Ali's friend's prediction speaks to double standards that hold only women to ideals of virginity and fertility. With time, not only did Nina grow in confidence, but her age put her at greater social risk for both premarital sex and fertility loss, which may have helped change her parents' minds. Ali was also willing to wait—for Nina to be ready to face her parents and for her parents to see him through more realistic eyes. As Nina put it, "We survived so much, it shows how strong our relationship was, and he waited for me."

Looking back, Salwa is happy that her daughter is happy and confident that Nina's marriage is strong. But once in a while, small things irk her. When she attends a baptism celebration, there's a twinge of envy toward the grandmother. Her relationship with Ali's mother is pleasant but not chummy. "I'm not completely open-minded," she admitted. "Of course, I would have preferred a Christian man, I can't lie about that. But don't ask me why, I know it's silly, and when I think about it, I find it shallow. Saying, 'Ouf, there will be no church, no church decorations,' such silly things. But it was a preference. It was an expectation." Those moments pass, Salwa rarely voices such thoughts, and all is well.

––––––––––

While Nina's parents conceded that love won the day, love alone wasn't enough to have changed their minds. In the end, as they got to know Ali, they could say to themselves and their social worlds, "Although he is Shi'a, he is just like us." But why did they assume he was so different in the first place? Such assumptions aren't unusual in Lebanese society. Whether Christian, Muslim, or Druze, Lebanese parents often react in sectarian ways when their child wants to marry someone of a different group.

Sectarianism is one of the most overused and misunderstood words in US public discourse about Lebanon and about the Middle East more generally. Sect is not a natural category—it's one of the many ways human beings categorize one another. Sect begins as a box into which people sort themselves or others according to ideas about religion, but over time, that box accumulates layers of meaning that have no relationship to religious belief or practice. Think about why there have been so few Catholic presidents of the United States, for example. Do American voters disagree with the way Catholics treat Communion versus Protestants? Some likely do, but for the most part, the problem is whatever else people associate with being Catholic versus Protestant. We could call that sectarianism. In Northern Ireland, the line between the two is staunchly political; the differences are about territory and sovereign loyalties. We do call that sectarianism. In the US, it is more common to use "denomination" to label groups like Roman Catholics, Protestants, Mormons, Southern Baptists, Seventh-Day Adventists,

Methodists, or Jehovah's Witnesses—to emphasize their Christian unity instead of their sectarian differences. To an outsider, the term "sect" makes just as much sense.

The word "sectarianism" has become a semantic mess—an umbrella term that includes the structural, political, institutional, economic, and legal aspects of sect-based discriminations along with the social and interpersonal.[15] In Lebanon, the term carries at least three meanings. It is used to describe interpersonal and institutional discrimination against people of other sects. It also refers to the system whereby the government labels each Lebanese citizen at birth with their father's sect—one of eighteen official religious and ethnoreligious categories counted by the state.[16] That label determines the personal status law that applies to that citizen. To do anything related to personal status—marriage, divorce, child custody, or inheritance—a person must follow the laws of their category.[17] Individuals' official state-designated sect may have nothing to do with what they believe or practice religiously, how they identify, their political views, or even how society views them. Finally, sectarianism or, more accurately, "political sectarianism" refers to Lebanon's political system since its independence in 1943, with those eighteen sectarian groups, none a majority, dividing power in the country. Lebanon is also a parliamentary democracy. Combining political sectarianism with parliamentary democracy means that every elected and appointed public position—from prime minister (always Sunni Muslim) and president (always Maronite Christian) to professors at the public university—is distributed according to sect in a system based on a nearly hundred-year-old census and ratified in the 1943 National Pact among political elites.[18] (If this seems confusing, imagine how confusing the electoral college in the US is to people who understand democracy as a direct one-person, one-vote system.)

Sectarianism has come to exist through historical processes, processes that both lead to and are fueled by bias and discrimination. Antagonism between sects or religious groups is neither natural nor necessary. Relationships between groups take historically specific forms. Like other communal identities, sectarian categories—and even the idea of sect itself as a category—have been created by human beings over time. None of this is primordial or the inevitable outcome of age-old divisions.[19] Lebanese sectarianism in all its forms developed over the course of history. Historian Ussama Makdisi has shown how, in the nineteenth century, interactions between Ottoman Empire reforms, European interventions, and local religious authorities led to sectarian politics and violence to such an extent that sect became the key defining aspect of modern political identity in Lebanon.[20] The French mandate government that held power between the end of World War I and Lebanon's independence in 1943, along with local elites, solidified this nascent sectarianism, began the process of codifying it into personal status law, and created the political-sectarian government that persists today.

Once society is divided by sect and those categories carry political, economic, and social importance, their borders are maintained, not only by the state and institutions,[21] but also by people going about their everyday lives.[22] As a form of discrimination, sectarianism is constantly reinforced by people's actions and words. Writing about racism, anthropologist Ghassan Hage explains how racists imagine their world and try to protect or secure some aspect of their lives by "turning difference into polarity."[23] Once difference has been polarized, the racist works to manage their space or home, however defined, by excluding, eliminating, or controlling the other. If we apply this process to sectarianism, we see how when a parent freaks out because their child wants to marry someone of a different sect, that parent is creating social polarization—us versus them—by packing meaning into the category of sect. By paying attention to how this happens, we can see how opposition to mixed marriage perpetuates sectarianism. When they fixate on sect as the problem with their child's choice of spouse, parents bolster the idea in society that sect matters more than anything else. When other people in those parents' social worlds scold them about their child's marriage or when gossip about their family reaches their ears, sectarianism gains fuel. When people are shunned, or threatened with shunning, for the apparent crime of not stopping a mixed marriage, sectarianism burns stronger.

The couples in this book show us how people push back at these ideas about difference, push back at the idea that everyone has to belong to a sect that defines who they are and who they love. Where their families or communities see only sectarian difference, they often see similarity. In the end, what constitutes a "mixed" marriage in the first place is in flux. Lebanese law thinks certain combinations are "mixed," parents have varying opinions on the matter, and couples' opinions vary even more. Some of my interviewees shook off their society's ideas about sect and difference in their youth, some faced internal struggles before they could marry someone from a different background, and some were raised by parents who taught them the secular ideal that religion didn't matter and then blindsided them when it came to marriage. Their perspectives are the foil for how sectarianism persists in society, revealing why they stand out as unusual, why some people are grafted onto a family tree without a fuss and others risk being pruned. While they understand that their love and persistence won't end sectarianism or sect-based discrimination in society, many of them hope it will contribute to change. The final chapter of this book takes up that hope as a question about the future. And in the best of anthropological tradition, their struggles and hopes can teach us about our own social worlds and about how human beings react when people force a change in their ideas of who is in their family by creating new kin through marriage.

———————

How does one study social worlds? Anthropologists primarily use two methods in their research: interviews and participant observation. The latter is exactly what it sounds like: participating in a social world while trying to understand it not only through your observations but also your own embodied experiences of sharing—to a certain extent—in that world. It sometimes feels like I've been doing participant observation for this book for most of my life. I was born in Beirut to a Roum Orthodox Lebanese father and a Protestant Armenian Lebanese mother. My family fled the civil war when I was young, emigrating to a suburb of Pittsburgh, Pennsylvania. We visited Lebanon throughout my childhood, and as a graduate student in my twenties, I began spending summers, and then two consecutive years, living in Beirut on my own. Since then, and since meeting and marrying my spouse, whose worldview mirrors my own and whose family is Sunni Palestinian, I have continued to spend significant time in Lebanon. Several friends have pursued mixed relationships, and I've heard about their experiences, just as they have heard about mine. This book grew out of my efforts to make sense of the sectarian social worlds that infused my life uncomfortably. It was too easy to simply accuse people of being sectarian or racist or bigoted. I wanted to understand more about what was going on.

First, I had to figure out who I was going to interview. Rather than starting from geography—Lebanon—I started from a sense of identity—being

Lebanese. Multiple waves of displacement precipitated by the civil war, Israeli invasions in 1978 and 1982 and the Israeli occupation of the South until 2000, and economic migration—including the recent wave triggered by the currency collapse—mean that while approximately four and a half million Lebanese live in Lebanon, estimates of the diaspora population range from eight to fourteen million. My interviewees all understand themselves to be Lebanese, no matter where they were born or now live. Many also see themselves as part of a community of strangers connected by the fact that they married someone of a different sectarian group in a context where sect matters. The kinds of social relations they negotiated, the social dynamics that mattered to their families, and the struggles they faced in relation to their marriage choices connects them to each other. Their quintessentially Lebanese stories resonate outward, carrying perspectives and ideas that can teach us about the United States and beyond. Too often, images broadcast in film and media valorize an individualized romantic love that underestimates the degree to which family and society hold sway over many Americans' choices as well, shaping the outcomes of falling in love.

I decided to focus primarily on Lebanese married to other Lebanese because I wanted to isolate sect-based discrimination in order to examine its roots and boundaries. I am keenly aware that many residents of Lebanon are not Lebanese. Whether fleeing violence or seeking work, around half a million Palestinian refugees, over a million Syrian refugees and laborers, many Iraqis and Kurds, and over a million migrant workers from Ethiopia, Sri Lanka, and elsewhere live in Lebanon. Adding the dimension of racial and national categories would require another project. Including marriages to white Europeans, North Americans, or Australians would bring anti-Arab racism, its internalization, and Lebanese desires to view themselves as white into the mix. Including marriages to nonwhite non-Lebanese would add an analysis of the racism rampant in Lebanese communities, including anti-Black racism and intersectional racism against migrant domestic workers. While I understand that the families my interviewees created are defined as Lebanese families by excluding racialized others, in order to hold focus on sect, I didn't include interracial or inter-national marriages. In a nod to the historical porosity of borders between Lebanon, Palestine, and Syria, as well as contemporary population movements, a few couples where Lebanese are married to Palestinians or Syrians make an appearance.

Over a decade after first dreaming up this project, I began formal interviews, shifting from casually interjecting "What do you think of X?" into social occasions to recorded conversations where I asked people in mixed marriages to tell me their stories. The first one was in 2012. I started with friends and acquaintances, and it snowballed from there. Fearing my sample was too linked to Beirut and the university and NGO spheres where my friends clustered, I began asking random acquaintances in other fields and parts of the country if they could help me find interviewees. I placed an ad on Facebook and received a flurry of replies from total strangers. People were eager to share their mixed marriage stories. At the end of each interview, I always asked whom else they could put me in touch with. In the end, I completed interviews with people across a relatively broad swathe of Lebanese society. It took time. I followed many threads and lost some to communication gaps. I interviewed as many people as possible in person, stacking interviews on long days, and spoke to others, especially younger people, via FaceTime or Skype. We spoke in a mix of Arabic and English, depending on their inclinations. Some people interjected French, though I asked them to stick with one of the two languages in which I am fluent. Some interviews were one long conversation, others developed over time and multiple encounters. Most took place between 2016 and 2018, with a few lingering into 2019.

Overall, I recorded interviews with 192 Lebanese. This doesn't include the handful of comparative interviews I conducted with interreligious Arab couples where neither party was Lebanese. Nor does it include the hundreds of informal conversations I have had with everyone from manicurists to close family members since the late 1990s about the subject. My recorded interviews included 158 people in heterosexual interreligious marriages (representing 129 such marriages), 9 in Sunni-Shi'a marriages, and 5 in interreligious queer relationships. Sometimes I interviewed only one partner, sometimes I interviewed each spouse separately, and sometimes I interviewed the couple together. I left it up to them to decide. Of these interviewees, 74 percent were female, and 26 percent were male. All had married sometime between 1962 and 2018; the oldest was born in 1939, the youngest in 1992. Two people had divorced at the time of the interview and six were widowed, and the mixed marriage was a second marriage for two. Among them were nine families with multiple generations of mixed marriages, three sets of sibling pairs, and four other sets of relations (like cousins who were both in mixed marriages).

I also interviewed mothers of people in mixed marriages, from all the major Lebanese sects, plus a handful of other family members. Research assistants helped me gather additional data. Nadim el-Kak interviewed nine unmarried young women, then reinterviewed eight of them three years later. Mariana Nakfour interviewed religious clerics, Christian, Muslim, and Druze, and followed up on other research matters for me, like calling the morgue at the American University Hospital (now the American University of Beirut Medical Center) to ask about cremation rules and checking with lawyers to clarify personal status procedures. Statistics are difficult to come by in Lebanon, and most of the numbers I provide in this book are thanks to Mohammad Zamzam and his creative data gathering and number-crunching abilities.

I collected basic information about more than two hundred additional mixed marriages through stories people told about other people. There was a Maronite woman in the North who married a Muslim army officer who moved into the village and fit right in. There was a Druze man who converted to Shi'i Islam to marry and was disowned. There was a woman whose first marriage, to someone of her sect, failed, while her second marriage, to someone of a different religion, was a great success.

Over the years, I heard more stories about failures than successes—mixed relationships that ended before marriage, often because one or both partners couldn't handle the pressure. Lebanese interreligious couples face family opposition while dealing with laws that confound their efforts to build a life together, snide comments about their partner, myriad stereotypes wielded as weapons, and social norms telling them they are wrong—all on top of the usual stresses of growing a relationship and planning a wedding. Those who make it are rare. Most people don't even contemplate breaking the rules. It may be unthinkable, or their social worlds might limit them to appropriate partners. Or they might suppress their desires, refusing to date someone of a different religion, or end mixed relationships before they get serious. The risks, hassles, and potential damage to family and social worlds simply isn't worth it to them. It's not all romance and kumbaya. Romeo and Juliet didn't make it. Neither did Layla and Qays. The couples who make it to marriage, the couples whose stories you will read about in the pages that follow, are the exceptional ones.

So, who are they? They come from all the major Lebanese sects: Sunni Muslim (25 percent of my interviewees), Shi'i Muslim (12 percent), Druze (16 percent), Maronite Christian (19 percent), Roum Orthodox Christian (16 percent), and other Christian sects (12 percent), including Armenian Orthodox, Roman Catholic, Roum Catholic, Syriac, and Protestant. While Druze may appear to be overrepresented in my interviews because they are estimated to comprise less than 5 percent of the Lebanese population, this is in fact a close approximation of their representation in mixed marriages. The numbers Mohammad Zamzam crunched suggest that as of 2018, 19 percent of Lebanese interreligious marriages involved Druze. In other words, Druze seem to be more likely, per capita, to marry outside their sect than other Lebanese. Similarly, while I interviewed about half as many Shi'i versus Sunni Muslims, our data shows that this is also a close approximation in terms of mixed marriages, as Shi'i marriages to non-Muslims are 60 percent of such Sunni marriages.

My interviewees come from Lebanon's cities, towns, and villages, from the North and the South, the coast, the mountains, and the Bekaa Valley. Most of them (57 percent) spent significant time in their youth in Beirut; others (10 percent) grew up outside the capital or abroad. No matter where they spent their childhoods, like many Lebanese, one-third lived outside the country for a time before marrying. By the time I interviewed them, they lived mostly in Beirut (58 percent) or in diaspora (25 percent).

They were primarily well educated. Two percent had never attended high school. Those who did attended a variety of institutions: charitable foundation schools (2 percent), the not-quite-free public schools (14 percent), relatively affordable parochial schools (24 percent),[24] and private schools ranging from the relatively affordable (20 percent) to the very expensive (29 percent).[25] Nine percent went to high schools outside Lebanon. Over half attended private universities in Lebanon (62 percent), while others went to the public Lebanese University (15 percent), studied outside the country (13 percent), or attended technical school (5 percent). Just under a quarter have graduate degrees in a variety of fields.

These educational backgrounds, combined with where they grew up, what their parents did for work, and their own self-identifications, tell us something about their class backgrounds. Approximately 30 percent hailed from the Lebanese elite or from wealthy families, 45 percent were from families with professional parents or self-described as "upper middle" or "middle class," 10 percent were from families with parents who were teachers or public employees, 10 percent were working class, and 4 percent were from the rural poor. When I interviewed them, they worked in a wide range of fields, including finance/business (14 percent), academia (14 percent), UN/NGO/INGOs (8 percent), health care (7 percent), media (6 percent), the service industry (6 percent), education (5.5 percent), and as homemakers (5 percent), plus a few in advertising, engineering, IT, architecture, law, accounting, politics, sex work, agriculture, manual labor, and a few who were unemployed. These categories don't capture Lebanon's deep class polarization and related social segregation—marrying someone of a lower class is so unimaginable that the language for objecting to it scarcely exists. The categories also don't capture the massive gap between those who are financially secure and those who are not or how wide that gap has grown.

There are no existing studies that would allow me to compare the demographics of my interviewees with the demographics of all Lebanese in mixed marriages. The data Mohammad extracted tells us that mixed marriages are indeed more common in Beirut than elsewhere, though growing up in Beirut doesn't guarantee family approval. It's clear that my interviewees are skewed toward the middle and upper classes. I don't know if that is an accurate reflection of who is intermarrying, but I do know that Lebanese usually meet marriage partners from other sects at university or in their workplaces. Gender norms of employment make this less likely in working-class communities, and since the civil war, the affordable public Lebanese University has grown sect segregated. So, while my interviewees are wealthier than average and are centered in Beirut, it is plausible that so are Lebanese mixed marriages overall.

At the same time, family disapproval cut across geographies and class backgrounds. As one of my interviewees put it, "You'd be surprised; sometimes the people you think are not fanatics turn out to be. The ones who think of themselves as agnostic or secular will say 'No way, no way' to a mixed marriage in the family. Then someone whose family is politically conservative and very religious won't have an issue with a mixed marriage. Sometimes you can predict it. But sometimes people really surprise you."

————

In some places and times, especially when religious difference is linked to political divides, mixed marriage represents the ultimate in transgressive love and the transgression of communal boundaries through love. When Mohandas Gandhi's son Manilal wanted to marry a Muslim woman, Fatima

Gool, Gandhi wrote him a letter asking him to change his mind, for his own sake, the sake of his dharma, and, crucially, "the interests of our society."[26] In twenty-first-century India, Hindu-Muslim couples that persevere are rare and generally part of the urban elite.[27] Islamophobia and anti-Muslim political agendas fuel the Hindu Right's sensationalist allegations that an organized "Love Jihad" is tricking Hindu women into converting to Islam and marrying Muslim men.[28] Northern Ireland is another place where mixed marriages—between Protestants and Catholics—have been met with hostility and are rare.[29] Mixed marriages also lend themselves to imaginations of a more diverse, more peaceful future. Christian women married to Jewish men in pre–World War II Germany famously rescued their spouses through the only major German protest against the Nazi deportation of German Jews.[30] Scholars have asked whether increasing rates of ethnically mixed marriage among the nations of the former Yugoslavia might lead to greater acceptance of one another[31] or whether intermarriage might be "a catalyst for social change" in Northern Ireland.[32] In the US, concerns about Protestant-Catholic marriages (and later, Christian-Jewish marriages) moved from anxieties about the immigration of non-Protestants to evidence of their assimilation into white Protestant cultural worlds.[33]

My interviewees had the capacity to see a future with the person they love despite social and familial forces insisting that such a future is impossible. And they had the capacity to act in ways that created that future. Some of them understood their own battles as part of something larger, part of an effort to change the sectarianism entrenched in Lebanon's laws, institutions, and social dynamics. Others believed that love is blind to sect. Some held that they had the right to marry whomever they want; for them, it was a matter of independence and free will. Others knew they were breaking the rules and did so deliberately. Some struggled with their own defiance of convention, whether for reasons of faith or because of stereotypes or their desires for parental approval or social conformity. Others were caught off guard when their parents rejected their partners. And some refused to even acknowledge the rules they were breaking, denying convention power through their refusal. Their stories ranged from dramatic elopements or decade-long romances like Nina and Ali's to short, intense conflicts or even unflappable family harmony.

Even when it was easier, it was rarely easy. "It was fine, though of course my parents would have preferred a [choose your sect] woman." "We had no problems, but of course my parents would have rather had a [choose your sect] son-in-law." It's worth reading a little more into those statements, as some people hesitate to paint their parents or families in a negative light. Most of my interviews took place years after the stories people told me had ended with some approximation of a happily ever after. Their stories have been shaped and reshaped over time. In their retrospective narrations, they laughed about moments that now sounded absurd but were once painful. Underneath the words are people, relationships, knots of love that are being forcibly reshaped, strained, and sometimes torn in the process.

In some cases, emotions were still raw or relationships still sundered, pain seeping out like sap, even years later. One young woman who was shocked when her father denied her permission to marry her boyfriend began crying as she relived his rejection, reexperiencing both her anger and her empathy for how trapped he must have felt in order to do this to her. Others cried while remembering derogatory remarks relatives had made about their spouses. The most difficult moments were when people spoke about the loss of a parent who had not approved of their marriage—parents who passed away before forgiving their children or before giving them their blessing to marry.

I never pressed the issue. Some people paused the interview or began telling me another part of their story. But in most cases, emotion was in the past, surfacing in the narrative as a simple description: "It was hard." "It was difficult." As you read these stories, place yourself into their narrators' shoes. Imagine what it would feel like to lose a relationship with a loved parent or sibling. Imagine what it feels like to have to choose between the person you want to marry and a parent, knowing that you could lose one of them. That feeling is in all these stories, even when it doesn't appear on the page.

I wish I could tell all the stories I gathered, but there simply isn't space. You'll rarely meet people twice in these pages, and many of their stories fit well in multiple chapters. As you read them, I hope you build a collective sensibility about their themes and patterns, as I did during my research. To protect people's privacy and identities as much as possible in this compact social context where I have to assume that people might know or know of one another, I've done more than change names. (There's one couple in the book who insisted that I leave their names as is, but I'm not telling you who they are.) I blurred some incidental details in ways that don't alter their stories. If I changed a job, I chose something associated with the same class and status. Artists didn't become doctors, nor did pharmacists become rural laborers. I specified only those neighborhoods that matter, using regions of the country instead, or descriptors like "Christian foothill town" or "mountain suburb of Beirut." The length of time between meeting and marriage might have shifted by a year or two. The sofa in the living room might be beige instead of brown. Numbers of siblings might have changed.

I also followed up with people to check how they were doing. In early 2021, I sent drafts of stories to most of my interviewees for confirmation that I had adequately protected their identities. The responses were overwhelmingly positive. Very few asked for changes, most said they enjoyed reading about themselves in the third person, and some found it odd. Two people hated the pseudonyms I had chosen and asked me to change them. Nina chose her pseudonym to echo one of her favorite works of art, a sculpture representing a tragic interreligious love story.[34] A few people asked me to reinsert details I had removed (like the type of work they do) or corrected errors of detail. A few asked me to change additional details. And a few asked me to delete harsh comments their parents had made or the "likes" and "ums" that peppered their speech. I honored all these requests. The vast majority made no changes to their stories.

Many also shared both happy and sad news. Some had lost parents in the year(s) since we had last spoken. One had divorced. Some had been injured or had family members severely injured in the devastating August 4, 2020, explosion in Beirut, though thankfully none of them lost their lives. In the wake of Lebanon's economic collapse, some had emigrated, often with heavy hearts. Others were thinking about doing so or trying to adapt to a new reality in the country. Despite the overall tragedy of 2020, others shared joy: new babies, a child who had graduated, a new job or opportunity, a renewal of vows.

———

December 30, 2020

Hey Lara,

It's been a long time. Much has happened. We left Lebanon and we are now in Abu Dhabi. Actually we are doing our 14 days quarantine. We had to leave. Although I was "thawra" [revolution] to the bone and one of the front liners who used to get beaten up, at the end I decided that as much as I love my country, I love my kids more and they deserve to be pulled out of this abusive relationship that has been going on for generations in Lebanon.

To end the story on a positive note though, this Christmas my parents invited Ali's parents to spend Christmas Eve with us and they came and everyone had a good time. After corona, the crisis, the nuclear explosion in Lebanon we have all learned that other than love and family nothing else matters.

I now sleep next to a few Virgin Marys on my bedside that I collect. Although I used to be agnostic, I have found love and peace in praying and I now do that almost every other night before I go to sleep. I have the Mar Charbel oil that I put on my head, Ali's, and my children's every other day. Ali on the other hand is still a scientist at heart but he allows me to put the oil on his forehead when I pray. It's funny when I read this! So much has changed since I last saw you but I am still in love with my husband and grateful to life and God or spirit for everything it has given me, for protecting my babies when they were at home alone when the explosion happened. True I left Lebanon with no money, uprooted, and that house you wrote about I cried many tears over, as I looked up from the street for the last time remembering all the good times we had there, but Lebanon gave me the love of life, my family, and the resistance to live no matter the circumstances.

Xx from Abu Dhabi,

Nina

––––––

As I wrote this book, many of the people who generously shared their stories with me found their lives upended. Since completing my interviews, Lebanon has undergone a revolution that began in October 2019 (in which many of my interviewees took part) and its subsequent suppression by the state,[35] experienced a massive explosion in Beirut (heard as far away as Cyprus and felt in the mountains), and is in the throes of an economic crisis and currency devaluation so shattering, so deep, that it is predicted to rival the civil war and great famine in terms of devastation wreaked in the country. Salaries in local currency became virtually worthless, medications disappeared from the market, and prices for basic necessities, when one could find them, increased tenfold, practically overnight. When I began my interviews, the poverty rate was 20 percent; as I write, it has jumped to more than 80 percent.[36] Meanwhile, Lebanon and California, where I am located, along with the rest of the world, have weathered the Covid-19 pandemic as well as heat waves, floods, fires, and other symptoms of climate change. And as this book goes to press, the Israeli military is executing a genocidal assault in an effort to eliminate Palestinians from Gaza, and regularly bombarding southern Lebanon.

How does one write from 7,430 miles away from a place that holds a piece of one's heart as that place is shattered by layers upon layers of violence and criminal negligence? When the narrators of the stories you tell have had close calls, relatives hospitalized, homes destroyed? When we are all experiencing tidal waves of shock and grief and disbelief and rage? When couples who once imagined flying to Cyprus for a civil marriage can no longer afford the airfare, and courtships have been delayed or broken because people have died, or can't afford to find a place to live together, or have emigrated, seeking to make a living?

I hold to the idea that these stories of love and family, tears shed over disapproval rather than stitches and wounds, matter—as history, as fantasy, and as dreams for the future. All anthropological research, all ethnography, is always about the past. We imagine that it's about the contemporary moment, and that it's the job of our historian colleagues and friends to take up what came before. But there is no such thing as the present once you try to grasp it, ponder it, write about it. Living in time limits human beings, including anthropologists, to writing about the past. The ideas and interviews in this book grew before the multiple crises that uprooted Nina and many others, but those ideas and desires and problems continue into the imagined future, as discriminations to be dismantled and instantiations of possibility, including kinship possibilities that cut across sectarian identities and assumptions. In these conditions of crisis upon crisis, social networks are more important than ever as a source of support, even necessary for survival. Whether expanding or disrupting the social norms of kinship, the consequences of mixed marriage have only grown deeper.

With that, I invite you into these Lebanese social worlds.

One

Who Counts as Different, Anyway?

I've heard the story many times. When he was almost thirty, Latif asked Nada's father for her hand in marriage. She was sixteen and in high school at the time, the youngest of three sisters. The eldest was in love with Latif's friend. The middle sister was at university, uninterested in marriage. Nada's father agreed to the proposal with the condition that Latif wait a year for Nada to graduate first. The men shook on it.

That evening, the story goes, Nada's mother broke the good news to her. "Latif, the handsome young lawyer who works with your dad, wants to marry you."

"If he's so handsome," Nada retorted, "why don't you marry him yourself?"

But he was a good match, and good young women listened to their parents in those days. The two married a year later, in 1943.

When my grandmother Nada married my grandfather Latif, she relocated from one neighborhood of their Roum Orthodox Christian village in Lebanon to another. Leaving her parent's impressive house with its multiple arches and high ceilings, she moved down the hill into a modest home with her husband, his parents, and his paternal grandmother. The recently built house had a second floor over three barrel-vaulted lower rooms, and its thick stone blocked the humid summer air and bone-aching winter chill sent by the sea winds.

Despite the status difference between their families, Latif was a good prospect, with a sharp intellect, unwavering integrity, and piercing pale blue eyes. He was the first in his family of farmers to have a university degree. Latif's father and grandmother had traveled twice to the US, during a famine at the turn of the twentieth century and again two decades later when a locust invasion decimated crops. Latif's father peddled kitchenware and later had a grocery store; his grandmother worked as a midwife. When the Great Depression hit, they brought home the gold coins they had earned and bought land to farm, built that two-story house, and paid for Latif's education in Damascus.

Nada's family hadn't been farmers for generations. A successful lawyer, her father hobnobbed with French and Lebanese elites. Her grandfather had lived in Brazil for a time and written three books. He had been Latif's teacher at the village elementary school. Seated under a tree, students gathered round, he held a long willow switch. Latif was not a good student and knew the sting of that switch, as it sought anyone whose attention wandered.

Ambition eventually did its work, and Latif's career bloomed. The couple moved out of the village, raising their four children mostly in Beirut. All of them met their spouses without their parents' involvement, at university or work, or through mutual friends. They all chose Lebanese Christians, but none were from the village. Their daughters married Roum Orthodox men from a different part of the country. Their sons married women from different sects, one Maronite, the other Armenian Protestant.

In my generation, only two cousins, women raised in Lebanon during the 1975–1990 civil war, married Lebanese Christians. Thus far, the rest of us, raised mostly outside the country, have broken the rules of national, ethnic, or religious background, plus those of sexuality.

On the one hand, this looks like an obvious story of generational change toward greater diversity, linked to urbanization and diaspora. On the other, it's a story of change in people's assessments of what counts as "mixed." In my generation, no one questions the idea that Lebanese society views a spouse of a different nationality or religion as "different," but what about a spouse from a different Christian sect or region one generation earlier? Or the class difference between Latif and Nada's families? Which of these marriages count as mixed? Who is too different to marry? And what counts as different in the first place?

———————

Everyone knows how to read the ever-expanding concentric circles that make up a social world. We read social worlds like tree rings. The inner circles are the heartwood core, older relations, people whose cellulosic fibers connect through generations. Most people know which rings contain appropriate marriage partners and which are too close or too distant. Children absorb these unspoken rules from overheard snippets of adult conversation. They wonder about changes in their parents' tones when talking about some weddings versus others. Anticipation, pride, envy, disdain, shock, disapproval—facial cues teach youth how to receive news of various engagements. Some parents are explicit, explaining to their children why a particular match is a bad idea, what kind of person they are supposed to marry, what characteristics are desirable, if not required.

Spouses must be both different and similar enough. You do not marry a sibling—unless, of course, you are a figure in Genesis or Greek mythology, or part of some royal lines. But how many degrees of separation must exist for a cousin to be an acceptable partner? Can you marry a first cousin? A second? A sixth? Whatever visceral response you may have to this question, the answer depends on your social context. In Lebanon, through the mid-1900s, many families preferred to keep marriage within the extended family, an arrangement that kept land within the family as well.[1] If a desirable relative couldn't be found, you looked to your village.[2] More recent studies show that consanguineous ("of the same blood") matches—including those with distant relatives like third or fourth cousins—continue to comprise 17–35 percent of marriages in the country, depending on class, religion, and neighborhood.[3] In some rural areas, elders continue to encourage kin marriages because they believe such marriages are more secure and stable.[4]

Latif and Nada's match was facilitated by village proximity and family connections. The man Nada's sister was madly in love with was also from their village. One of Latif's sisters married a distant cousin; the groom being a known entity facilitated her emigration across the Atlantic as an allegedly unhappy bride in 1929. As we pull away from the center of a social world, beyond family and village, the characteristics that determine who fits in each tree ring grow murkier. Where does someone from a different region of the country fit? Someone whose parents speak a different language? Someone whose family believes in different prophets?

This chapter begins our exploration of similarity and difference by looking at how both the grounds of possibility for mixed marriage and sect as a category have taken shape over time.

Historicizing Circles of Similarity

We don't know much about interreligious marriage in the region before the mid-twentieth century. We know that family status and wealth mattered and that marriages among the elite in Mount Lebanon regularly crossed religious lines. Intermarriage or conversion meant elite extended families were often mixed, with cousins of various degrees marrying across religion.[5] We can surmise that outside the elite, mixed marriage was noteworthy. In his memoirs from the early twentieth century, Jerusalem-based composer and writer Wasif Jawhariyyeh tells us that when a Muslim civil servant fell in love with a Roum Orthodox woman, "their story became a gossip topic for everyone" and their marriage was "a rare and strange thing to happen at the time."[6]

If I were to sketch a timeline based on my interviews and the scant available data,[7] we would see interreligious marriage increasing, but still rare, until the mid-twentieth century.[8] A brief acceleration gives us a peak on the graph from the late 1960s through the early 1980s; these are couples who met during the leftist and student activism of the era. A lull in the 1980s shows the impact of the civil war and the splintering of Lebanese University on marital possibilities. The gradual increase resumes at the war's end in the 1990s, accelerates at the turn of the twenty-first century, and spikes upward into this century's second decade.

Born in the 1930s, Layla was one of my oldest interviewees. She exuded strength and confidence in her own skin. Defying Lebanese gender norms, she wore her gray hair in a long braid and eschewed the bright lipstick marking many older women's lips. Her sneakers allowed her to traverse Beirut's treacherous sidewalks and streets to arrive safely at the café where we met.

Hailing from a Roum Orthodox village, Layla grew up in Ashrafieh, a Christian suburb of Beirut. Unusually educated for her time, she met Ibrahim during her university studies in the early 1960s. He was from a good family, making a decent living, and of a similar class background. But, Layla told me, "it was a double sword. He was both Muslim and Palestinian." She paused, watching my face. "Does it ring a bell? For a closed Ashrafieh society?"

I smiled in coconspiracy, and replied, "Yes. I can't really imagine."

"It was a big rocket," Layla laughed. "Not for my parents as much as for their neighbors and acquaintances."

Layla and Ibrahim quickly fell in love. She appreciated his easy-going and kind nature; he appreciated her intelligence. A year later, Ibrahim proposed. "My parents liked him as a person," Layla explained. "But when I told them we were in love and thinking of getting married, I can't say it was easy for them. It wasn't as horrible as it was for others. But it wasn't easy to accept."

Layla's mother, who was entrenched in neighborhood social networks, struggled with the match. All would be well when Layla left for work in the morning, and then when she returned home for lunch, her mother would express hesitations about Ibrahim. Layla would ask, "Has anyone visited you today?" The answer was always, "Yes, so and so came over and said he will divorce you," or, "So-and-so came over and said it won't last a month."

"It was the neighbors," Layla explained, "those women who have nothing to do but make themselves beautiful and put on their jewelry and gossip. To them, this was a phenomenon from outer space. Ashrafieh is a very closed society." In contrast, Layla traces her family's more open-minded perspective to their origins in the Koura region in the North. "We are not Ashrafieh, we just lived there. Our mentality is Koura. The people of Koura are open-minded and educated." She paused. "We were surrounded by people of greater wealth. Maybe that made them more closed and conservative? I don't know."

Despite the pressure, Layla's parents gave the couple their blessing. Her father had asked around about Ibrahim and heard streams of praise about his character and career prospects from friends and relatives who knew him. He was from an established intellectual family—and both families were linked to the same elite Ras Beirut academic institutions. Her brother supported the match. And her mother was comforted by the fact that Layla could marry without changing her religion.

Layla and Ibrahim married soon after. At the eleventh hour, just before their *katab kitab*, the Muslim marriage contract, her mother mounted a final protest, objecting dramatically and pretending to faint. Layla teared up, but stood firm, and gave her mother an ultimatum: "If you are *that* opposed to Ibrahim, I won't marry him. But I will move to the US, and I will never marry anyone else." Her mom pulled herself together for the ceremony, which was followed by an informal church blessing and a party to celebrate.

———————

The most common interreligious combination before 1990 was Christian women and Muslim men. Some of my interviewees who married in the 1950s and '60s were working-class or lower-middle-class Maronite women who eloped as teenagers with young Muslim men of similar class background. Others were like Layla and Ibrahim, Orthodox Christian or Catholic women in their twenties marrying Sunni Muslim men a few years older—both from educated, professional or elite urban families with similar social circles. The ease with which such couples can legally marry in a *katab kitab* that doesn't require anyone to convert has facilitated this combination over the years.

Christian-Muslim couples connected to longstanding Lebanese émigré communities in West Africa were also able to marry relatively easily. Race and national identity were more important in calculating similarity than religion. A Roum Orthodox woman from northern Lebanon who had lived primarily in West Africa told me her story. While at university in Europe, she fell in love with another Lebanese student, a Shi'i man who had grown up in Beirut. Her parents readily gave the couple their blessing. They liked the young man and his leftist sensibility, and they were comfortable in mixed spaces; their West African Lebanese community was religiously integrated. The young man's parents were also pleased; there were multiple mixed marriages in their family already.

Mixed marriages in other combinations didn't increase much until the civil war ended in 1990.[9] There is one moment of exception. Many couples married between the late 1970s and early 1980s, couples that met and fell in love in the '60s and '70s, before the civil war began. To meet someone from a different religion, one must be in mixed spaces. By the 1960s, urbanization had created the conditions for social mixing, connecting people from around the country in Beirut. These conditions of possibility were further nurtured by the public Lebanese University, established in Greater Beirut in 1951. For the first time, the country had an institution of higher education that served as an integrating force, a centrifuge tumbling young people of all sects and regions and classes together. By the 1960s, attending the university wasn't just about taking classes or eating lunch together. It was also about sharing political hopes, working for social justice, and coming together to challenge sectarian divisions.

Many mixed couples, of all combinations, who met at Lebanese University credited its classrooms and political spaces. "Everyone was dating mixed," one person shared. "No one married someone of their same religion, except for one couple. That's what the '70s was like for us."

"Our generation didn't have a problem with mixed marriage," said another. "That was part of our liberation. Many of my comrades from Lebanese University had mixed marriages. It was a culture of refusal. . . . We leaned to the left, we were Marxist, so we exited from the trap of sectarianism."

This "culture of refusal" extended beyond the campus. A Sunni woman and a Maronite man met at a Communist Party meeting in Beirut and married in Cyprus ten months later, informing their families afterward. Another mixed couple got married because their parents didn't approve of their premarital cohabitation. A Druze woman and a Shi'i man fell in love as teenagers at a leftist youth group, then married a decade later with their parents' blessing. With only two exceptions, mixed marriages at this time were accepted by families, usually because the couple had learned their leftist politics at home. Shared political outlook brought a potential spouse into a more similar social circle, closer to center. The two exceptions are both cases where the couples' parents didn't share their leftist commitments. Those couples saw only political similarity; their families saw only religious difference.

Had the civil war not erected its barriers, it's likely the increase in mixed marriage that began in the 1960s would have continued. Beginning in 1975, the war spanned a decade and a half and, at various points, involved over twenty-five Lebanese militias, Palestinian liberation fighters, invasions by Israel and Syria, and troops or intelligence agents from those countries plus the United States, France, Italy, Iran, Iraq, Libya, and probably elsewhere. The extraordinary ecosystem of possibility nurtured by Lebanese University was decimated in 1980, five years into the war, when the university fractured into multiple branch campuses around the country. Most specialties now had both a primary branch plus a secondary one in a Christian area. This disassembly ensured that the university's promise of mixed social worlds in Beirut could no longer be met.[10]

Lebanese University was never put back together again, even after the war ended. It still provides public education, but on over fifteen separate campuses embedded in local milieus. Existing universities that provide integrated spaces are private and expensive. Students from a variety of regional and sectarian—but not class—backgrounds attend elite institutions like the American University of Beirut (AUB), Lebanese American University, and Université Saint-Joseph. But Lebanese youth from lower-class backgrounds have lost the opportunity to develop mixed social worlds through a university experience.

The same conditions of possibility—spaces of interaction and shared politics—led to the post–civil war increase in mixed marriage. The "Golden '90s" was an era of rebuilding and optimism. As Lebanese stitched their country back together, NGOs held programs connecting youth from different communities to one another, and high schools that had splintered into multiple campuses during the war reunified. Young people ventured out together, whether to organize or party. A generation came of age with the combination of peace and the internet, meeting in web cafés, the rare spaces outside their homes and schools where they could mingle. Lebanese who lived through the war were more cautious about mixed encounters than those whose families had fled, raising them in diaspora. Many who returned to Lebanon in time for high school or college were missing information about social divisions and sectarianism. These sheltered returnees were both open to mixed relationships and confused by the consequences. Some of my interviewees who married between 1990 and 2009 scorned boundaries while others were oblivious to them. Some of their stories are uneventful; others described years of intense arguments, waiting a decade for a blessing, or dramatic elopement.

By 2010, mixed marriage seemed easier. Instead of the elopements or subdued weddings of the '90s and early 2000s, couples threw galas to celebrate their union. A critical mass of mixed couples normalized the idea in Beirut circles and among youth educated at the city's elite institutions. NGOs were now a major employer for Lebanese, connecting people to other parts of Lebanon, to foreign funders and consultants, and to staff drawn from across the country.[11] And as in the 1970s, some of these twenty-first-century mixed marriages grew from the cluster of left-leaning political movements that culminated in the October 2019 uprising. Once again, not only did these movements bring people together physically, but they also cultivated shared ideas—against political sectarianism and corruption, for public services, environmental protections, and civil marriage laws—that downplayed sectarian difference. These stories also ranged from the uneventful to the dramatic, but the pendulum had shifted to the former. Few people eloped or waited a decade, and they were usually either Druze, a community relatively new to the mixed marriage scene, or Maronite women who wanted to marry Shi'i men.

No matter when they married, mixed couples agree that they found someone with whom they have a lot in common to share their life. For some, the conviction that they had found someone "just like them" helped them fight for the relationship. "Of course we had chemistry," one woman told me, "but it was also a set of principles that brought us together. Our core values are exactly the same. It was like, 'This person has all the things that I want plus there's chemistry, so let's *fight* for it.'" She's talking about fighting people who told them they were too different to marry because of sect.

Making Sect

Sect didn't always matter in Lebanon the way it does today. Faith communities were certainly important, but maintaining their boundaries was primarily the domain of religious clerics. During the Ottoman Empire, each religious group went to their clerics for personal status matters, until 1917, when the Ottoman Family Law established personal status rules for all Muslims with separate statutes for Christians and Jews.[12] But, as historian Elise Semerdjian explains, people weren't readily identifiable by religion.[13] Byzantine Christians had converted to Islam. Intermarriage had muddled extended families. Immigration into the empire had changed the social mix. And in the empire's waning days, pragmatic conversion between Islam and Christianity, in both directions, intensified.[14] It was easy to tell an elite from a nonelite because sumptuary laws regulated clothing, but religious difference wasn't as clear. Semerdjian describes how clerics, Christian and Muslim, panicked in the eighteenth century when they saw religious boundaries blurring and tried to regulate women's social interactions to enforce separation between religious groups. This tells us that enough people were interacting across religious boundaries in their everyday lives to alarm religious leaders. It wasn't until nineteenth-century political changes in the Ottoman Empire that sect gained power and, as Ussama Makdisi writes, ". . . a culture of sectarianism developed in the sense that all sectors of society, public and private, recognized . . . the beginning of a new age . . . defined by the raw intrusion of sectarian consciousness into modern life."[15]

At the end of World War I, the French mandate created the borders of contemporary Lebanon. From 1920 until Lebanese independence in 1943, mandate authorities and the Lebanese elite working with them embedded sect into Lebanon's institutions. They delineated eighteen official sects and laid the groundwork for the political-sectarian government system. An effort to place marriage under civil jurisdiction failed and personal status law defaulted to the Ottoman system.[16] A 1938 decree allowed non-Muslim Lebanese and mixed couples to marry civilly outside the country, and in 1951, the new Lebanese state passed a law to regulate the registration of marriages, including those civil ones. In the modern Lebanese state, citizens are born into a sect and must follow the laws of their personal status category for marriage, divorce, child custody, and inheritance. To marry someone in another category, one person may have to convert, or the couple must marry abroad.

In the decades since Lebanon's independence, political elites and leaders have used sect to divide and regulate citizens. Sectarianism is not only embedded into institutions and laws; it also influences how people think and act as they maneuver through these institutions and laws. It's a dialectical process—the more politicians use sectarian discourses and strategies to bolster their power and separate Lebanese into mini-constituencies loyal to them, the more people work with—instead of against—those sectarian categories and processes. Writing about South Africa, anthropologist Donald L. Donham provides this lucid explanation of why social categories like sect are so thorny:

The first methodological challenge involves the peculiar complexity with which identity terms are socially mobilized. At base is the issue of how an individual views him- or herself: "I am Zulu," "I am black," "I am Jewish." But no individual unilaterally determined these terms. Others label him or her as well: "Yes, she is Zulu," "He's not really black," "She's not an observant Jew." How any one person ultimately views him- or herself is the result of a dialectical, always social, not just individual, process. Moreover, organs of society, like the state, also classify persons, and such classifications, given their institutional power, carry a weight of their own."[17]

In Lebanon, sect has become an invented affinity with deep ramifications. Long before sectarianism was the word we use, the fourteenth-century scholar Ibn Khaldun formulated the concept of *'asabiyya*, which translates loosely to "group solidarity," "social cohesiveness," or "esprit de corps." He used *'asabiyya* to describe social cohesion within larger societies, the force that holds people together in a political structure. The political-sectarian system in Lebanon has allowed elites to splinter this group solidarity into subgroups beholden to them for resources and representation. In this context, sect became the most important category of social difference.

Discrimination as Expulsion

Knowing that sect is a human-made category doesn't dilute its impact on people's lives.[18] Black feminist scholars, like anthropologist Faye Harrison, have long made this argument about race and racism.[19] For many Lebanese, sect *feels* real. John L. Jackson Jr. helps us understand why: "Classifications by race, class, gender, ethnicity, and nationality [and sect!] are all . . . shortcuts, templates we use in lieu of absolute interpersonal transparency. We employ them to get at the truth of the world . . . which is why it is so much more *comforting* to think about these categories as natural occurrences and not man-made conventions."[20]

The comfort of imagining human-made groups as natural helps us to understand discrimination. Stuart Hall classically explained racism as "a structure of discourse and representation that tries to expel the

Other symbolically."[21] Ghassan Hage links these ideas about comfort and expelling the other. He uses the word "domestication" to describe how racists try to keep their "home" a comfortable space by eliminating anyone who doesn't fit. Racists protect their comfort by defining anyone different as utterly different and then trying to exclude them from their home, which can be their family or community or nation.[22] Defining others as utterly different depends on the idea that social categories are natural, so one can say, "There is essentially *nothing* about them that is like us."

Hage's conceptualization of a domestic space applies doubly in Lebanon; it explains both racism and sectarianism. The domestic space—the family or home—that many Lebanese try to protect by barring people of a different sect from the family tree is simultaneously a Lebanese nationalist space created by excluding non-Lebanese. We see this most vividly with the migrant domestic workers who may physically live in a tiny room in an apartment or house but are racially excluded from the home. In fact, their residence may be predicated on that racial exclusion—the laws that bring migrant workers into Lebanese households place them in a separate, racial category that denies them basic rights and ensures that the boundaries of the Lebanese family will not be breached.[23] The idea that a Lebanese man could marry a migrant domestic worker is outside the realm of possibility, speaking to racism's power.

Kinship brings out the worst discrimination because adding someone different to your family through marriage changes the categories of family members in future generations. In a survey of over 27,000 Lebanese from around the country, the Lebanese Center for Policy Studies found that while most respondents were "very" or "somewhat" comfortable having neighbors, work supervisors, or business partners from a different sect, when asked about marriage, most responded that they were "not too comfortable" or "not comfortable at all."[24] Even though the survey question asked about sect, we don't know whether respondents were imagining interreligious marriage (like Muslim-Christian) or intersectarian marriage (like Maronite–Roum Orthodox). The impulse to naturalize sect to bar it from one's home is related to ideas about heredity. People act as though mixed marriage will bring something into a family that will then be biologically inherited.

What about Heritability?

While race and sect are both socially constructed categories, human-made conventions, they don't have the same relationship to the idea of being "natural" for two reasons. The first is that sect doesn't usually rely on people categorizing bodies based on phenotype or ideas about biology. Some Lebanese claim they can "tell" another person's sect based on dress, regional accent, mannerisms, or even skin color, eye color, or appearance. None of this necessarily holds. Many of these cues conflate sect with class or region: clothing cut and color, makeup application, facial hair fashion, hair style and dye, accent, how someone walks and talks. Others rely on claims about physiognomic differences: "Shi'a are darker." "Christians are blond." "Maronites have rougher features." "Roum Orthodox look more Arab." "Druze have big eyes." Others link sect to nationality, insisting that Shi'i Lebanese are "really Iranians" and therefore look different—a statement revealing political fears about growing Shi'i power in the country and efforts to write them out of the Lebanese nation-state.

The simple fact is that you can't tell someone's sect—unless they express it through their clothing or jewelry—just by looking at them. Many Lebanese, especially in secular circles, have no idea what sect a classmate or acquaintance or even a friend is. Some begin every conversation with a new acquaintance with an ordered line of questioning: It begins with, "What's your name?" If that doesn't place a person, "Where are you from?" follows, open code for "What sect are you?"—a request to identify yourself in Lebanon's sectarian geography. If the answer remains elusive, an intrepid inquisitor might even ask in frustration, "*Tayyib inti shu?*" (Okay then, what *are* you?)

The second reason sect and race have different relationships to ideas about the "natural" is that a person can convert easily between most sectarian categories in Lebanon. People convert to solve problems. If you want to get divorced but your sect doesn't allow it, you convert to a different one. But despite the commonplace understanding of conversion as pragmatic, many Lebanese still treat sect as if it were a natural category one can never shake off. Assumptions about heredity appear in mismatches between official sect, belief, and social perception. I know a young Sunni man whose father had converted from Druze to Sunni Islam to facilitate his marriage to a Sunni woman. The young man fell in love with a Druze woman, a distant relative. Her family blocked their marriage because they viewed him as Sunni, due to his father's pragmatic conversion. Yet other people still refer to that same young man as Druze, despite the fact that his official sect is Sunni. Such discrepancies are common. A young Christian woman told me that her family regularly warns her not to date a young man, who is, unbeknownst to them, already her boyfriend. The young man and his mother converted from Druze to Christianity years ago out of conviction and attend church regularly. But, she explained to me, "according to my parents he will always remain Druze, as if religion is in our DNA." A man from a large Shi'i family in the South not only converted to Christianity but also became a priest. Twenty-five years later, people still refer to him as "the Muslim."

—————

Of all the Lebanese sects, Druze and Armenians most readily collapse into assumptions of heritability. These are also the sects everyone assumes are most vehemently opposed to mixed marriage. This makes sense. The more you believe that membership in your group is inherited, the more likely you are to defend its boundaries to keep others out.

An offshoot of the Isma'ili sect of Islam, the Druze "call" to religion appeared at the turn of the eleventh century and closed a scant thirty years later.[25] No one new could become Druze, and existing Druze souls would be reincarnated into future Druze bodies. Every Druze today has the soul of an original convert to the sect.[26] Some people believe that you "relinquish" your membership if you marry a non-Druze.[27] Beliefs differ as to whether mixed marriage corrupts the original Druze soul or is evidence that the soul is already corrupted. Both views agree on the consequence: an eternal sentence as a nonbeliever, a condemned soul. Mixed marriage may also jeopardize future generations. Some people believe only "pure" Druze inherit a Druze soul. Others believe that as long as the father is Druze, the child might be "impure" but count as Druze—reincarnation here lines up with the state's patriarchal inheritance rules for sect. Druze who believe in reincarnation generally don't marry non-Druze. Druze in mixed marriages generally don't believe that religion is hereditary.

Dana is an example of the latter. Born and raised in her parents' Druze village, she met Hasan, a Shi'i man, at the Lebanese University campus near his village in the Bekaa Valley. Dana knew her parents would never allow her to marry him. "My dad used to say to me, 'You can do whatever you like, and marry whoever you want, he just has to be Druze,'" she explained. "He would say, 'You're so lucky to be Druze. You should thank God every day that you are Druze." As her graduation approached, suitors began to visit, forcing Dana's hand. "I decided I would either marry Hasan or no one at all! I can't let anyone else touch me! I still feel that, I'm still in love! So I decided to run away with him. We chose a date and a time, and it was so weird because I wasn't stressed out, and I never regretted it."

Dana was twenty-two when she eloped. Thirty years later, she hasn't seen her parents since that day, though she speaks with them on the phone once in a while. Her siblings resumed contact with her, and their children all know one another. She knows of only one other woman from her village who has married a non-Druze.

Most Druze in mixed marriages don't come from families or villages—like Dana's—where belief in inherited Druze souls motivates opposition.[28] Druze regularly explained to me that there are "two types" of Druze in Lebanon: open-minded and closed-minded, linked imperfectly to Beirut versus the village.[29] To a certain extent, this paralleled Druze who knew little about their religion versus believers.[30]

Noha used her own family to illustrate the difference for me. Raised in a Druze village, she moved to Beirut for university and stayed. Noha chose not to tell her parents she was dating a Sunni man until they decided to marry. Her father supported her choice. Her mother sobbed about what the extended family and village would say. When her boyfriend proposed, her father accepted, but her mother, and most of her maternal relatives, refused to attend the engagement gathering and the wedding. A year later, when their first child was born, Noha's mother finally spoke to her again. Each of Noha's parents comes from a different "type" of Druze family. Her father's side was connected to non-Druze and urban areas and included mixed marriages. Her mother's side had no mixed marriages and included religious elders. "My mom was super Druze," Noha said. "My dad was like, 'Okay, you were born Druze, but you can choose what you want to be.'"

———

Similar ideas about heredity motivate Armenian opposition to mixed marriage. Unlike other churches in Lebanon, the Armenian Orthodox Church doesn't allow Muslim or Druze men to convert, be baptized, and then marry an Armenian woman. The church views being Armenian as a matter of blood; no amount of genuine conviction can change one's heritage. By canon law, women who marry Muslims are cast out for eternity and cannot be buried with church rites.[31] I met Armenian women who wanted a church wedding but turned to civil marriage in frustration with the church's intransigence. The church doesn't prevent non-Armenian women from converting, but like Druze parents, Armenian parents do their best to stop their sons' mixed marriages.

Sevan, an Armenian Orthodox woman, met her Sunni husband at a North American university. When they first began dating, Sevan told him the relationship wouldn't lead to marriage. I asked her why. "Because I didn't want to go through it all with my parents," she replied. "I told him it wasn't about *him*; it was about the principle of marrying outside the cult." When Sevan changed her mind and told her parents about the relationship, as expected, they protested. A decade later, she obtained her parents' blessing by using their anti-Black racism. She told them she would either marry her Lebanese Sunni boyfriend or "a Black friend who is also Muslim." Her ploy worked. "We waited a long time," Sevan told me. "That was dreadful, but then it was all okay."

Sevan explained her parents' opposition to me. "First and foremost, it was because he was non-Armenian. Religion may have also been an issue." After thinking aloud for a while, she circled back, "Actually, I think anyone who didn't speak Armenian would be treated the same way as [my husband] was treated. I don't think the main thing is religion. Because my cousin got married to a [white] American woman. She was Christian, and they *still* resisted. My other cousin married a [white] Canadian, also Christian, and they had the same problems. Another cousin also. The common denominator is being non-Armenian. It's the *odar* concept."

Odar is an Armenian word used for strangers, meaning non-Armenians. It's not a polite word. More polite are *Arap* ("Arab" as an ethnic marker), or *deghatsi*, which, translated literally, means "belonging to this place" or "from this land"—Armenian Lebanese naming non-Armenian Lebanese "native" or "indigenous" to Lebanon, and marking themselves as other.

It's worth remembering that these Armenians are Lebanese, with Lebanese citizenship, divided into three sects by the state: Armenian Orthodox, Armenian Catholics, and Protestants (a category that includes all Lebanese

Protestants and Evangelicals, not only Armenians). Many identify as both Lebanese and Armenian. While language and religion may identify someone as Armenian in diaspora, Armenian Lebanese place especial emphasis on language and are renowned for their "pure" language skills, the product of an intentional educational project in Lebanon.[32] These identity markers ignore, or at best are disturbed by, Armenian-identified people who don't speak Armenian, aren't Christian, or don't "look" Armenian, like Ethiopian Armenians. Armenians who oppose marriage with non-Armenians are holding on to the idea that being Armenian can only be inherited biologically. They discount the possibility of Armenian identity persevering in forms that can be taught—like language—or that children of mixed parents might still identify as Armenian. Whereas Druze focus on souls that can be corrupted, Armenians focus on blood that can be diluted.

––––––––

Druze and Armenian fears of dilution—whether of souls or blood—can be read as minority fears.[33] Druze likely make up around 5 percent of Lebanon's population, and Armenians slightly less. People believe mixed marriages contribute to the dwindling of their communities in the world, a belief that hinges on the idea that Druze and Armenian identities are heritable solely biologically. Those who are politically minded also worry that mixed marriage lowers their sect's numbers and therefore political clout and resources within Lebanon's sectarian system. All Christian sects are also minorities in Lebanon, and opposition to mixed marriage is fomented by political discourse highlighting fears about their dwindling numbers in both the country and the region. However, as soon as we factor in gender, the disappearing minority fear falls apart as an explanation for why people oppose mixed marriage. Sure, if a Druze or Christian woman marries outside her sect, numbers will be lost. But if numbers matter, it should be acceptable for Druze or Christian men to marry outside their sect, as the couple's children will count as their father does. This logic is why many Druze support civil marriage; it allows Druze men to marry non-Druze women while remaining Druze.

Yet fears of disappearance aren't always rational. An Armenian woman's uncle walked into her family home as she was dressing for her wedding to a non-Armenian, said, "There should be music!" and popped a tape into the cassette player. The chords of a lamentation dirge, a genocide mourning song, filled the house. Most Armenian Lebanese are the descendants of survivors of the Armenian genocide. As the Ottoman Empire came apart at the seams during World War I, the Young Turk government orchestrated the massacre and deportation of Armenians from what is today Turkey. Estimates suggest that from 1915 to 1916, over one million Armenians were murdered or died while being marched through the desert or starving in concentration camps.[34] Many survivors ended up in Lebanon. Toward the end of World War I, the French tried to repatriate Armenians from Cilicia, now in southwest Turkey, but that project failed, and those Armenians, including my maternal ancestors, were also settled in Lebanon.

This history is echoed in the lamentation dirge this woman's uncle played as she donned her bridal gown. The Armenian genocide looms large in Armenian memory, epigenetic anxieties, and family narratives. Some view mixed marriage as continuing the loss of Armenian language and legacy that began with the genocide. Opposing mixed marriage becomes part of an imperative to fight the erasure of Armenians from the planet. Each renewed moment of existential crisis—like the recent Azerbaijani attacks on Artsakh (Nagorno-Karabagh) and Armenia—adds to that resolve. Even Armenian parents who don't ascribe to biological ideas about identity worry that mixed marriage will lead to the loss of teachable identity markers in the next generation. Their worry reminds us that sect is learned and that, despite beliefs about its heritability, it is an unstable category.

Sects Moving Together, Sects Moving Apart

Observing sectarian categories as their meanings change over time also reveals their instability. History shows us how these categories were born of power struggles between religious authorities vying for control and influence over populations. Christian sects grew from arguments about matters like the nature of salvation and church authority; Muslim sects grew from a dispute over leadership of the community after the Prophet Muhammad's death. In both cases, prayer, ritual, calendars, and clerical authority evolved along multiple distinct lines. There have been conflicts over theology or ritual practice, long periods of coexistence, and violence that has nothing to do with religious differences. Other factors, like territory and political power, shape conflicts even as political leaders use sectarian rhetoric to instigate or inflame the fight. The European religious wars following the Protestant Reformation reordered boundaries and sovereignty. Conflicts between the Ottoman and Safavid Empires intensified as their borders solidified. The Iran-Iraq war was related to control of territory, populations, and natural resources. The Troubles in Northern Ireland were about self-determination and the form the polity should take.

Lebanon's sectarian government system has extended those power struggles to political appointments, electoral politics, and resource distribution. Marriage is a lens into the effect of these divisions on personal lives. As political alliances have shifted in recent decades, intersectarian Christian couples have seen the boundary between their sects erode while intersectarian Muslim couples have seen it deepen.

――――――

I met Layla, whose story I share above, through a friend married to one of her nephews, but by the end of our conversation, I realized I knew who she was from a different set of connections. Growing up, I had heard the one sentence version of her brother's story whenever my father mentioned his classmate: "You know, when Milhem and Teresa got married her father chased him down the street with a gun." As Layla and I laughed at how the small Lebanese world had struck again, she filled in the gaps in the story of her brother's Orthodox-Maronite romance.

Layla had introduced the couple. Teresa's parents were abroad at the time, and when they returned, Milhem and his parents visited them, bringing chocolate and gifts. They reciprocated the visit, but didn't bring Teresa with them, signaling that they didn't acknowledge the relationship. No one was surprised when Teresa's father rejected Milhem's marriage proposal, insisting that his daughter had to marry a Maronite in a Maronite Church. Layla tried to mediate, and when her efforts failed, she told the couple that elopement was their only option.

One morning Teresa left home at her usual time, wearing at least six layers of clothing. She stopped at Layla's house to shed clothes into a suitcase, then went to Layla's mother-in-law's house in the suburbs. Teresa's siblings each went about their lives that day wearing layers of her clothing under their own, adding them to the suitcase at Layla's place. That evening, Milhem and the suitcase joined Teresa at Layla's mother-in-law's home.

They wrote Teresa's father a letter explaining that she wasn't returning that night—signaling her decision to elope—and had a messenger deliver it. When he read the letter, Teresa's father began screaming and breaking things. He got his gun and ran around Ras Beirut looking for Teresa, or perhaps Milhem. He never found them, safe in the suburb. The next day, the couple married. Once it was a done deal, Teresa's father stopped protesting. But he never spoke to his daughter again.

This story has always puzzled me. Roum Orthodox and Maronite are both Christian sects, so shouldn't they be compatible? Sure, people made snide comments and jokes all the time, revealing deep prejudices on both sides. Someone visiting a Maronite village asks, "How many churches are there?" "Three Roum Orthodox and four Christian." I've heard this one in reverse too. It reminds me of a campus tour at Pepperdine University. "We're a Christian university," said the guide, "but we accept Catholics too." A Roum Orthodox man teases his mom, saying, "You should be happy I brought home a Shi'i bride instead of a Maronite." An elderly man in a friend's village was called so-and-so Maroun his entire life. When he died, the announcement listed a different last name. Apparently, people had named him Maroun because he was the only Maronite in that Roum Orthodox village.

Still, a Maronite–Roum Orthodox mixed marriage didn't seem like something worth grabbing your gun over. Teresa's father may have been especially stubborn, prone to anger and a staunch believer in Maronite supremacy. But he wasn't the only parent before the 1980s opposed to such a marriage, simply the most dramatic. Maronite women who married into my father's Roum Orthodox village have felt deep bias against them, in their mothers-in-law's jibes or terrible jokes told in their presence. The art of Lebanese *talteesh*, "hitting words," throwing snide verbal darts, has long been used to snipe at them, pull them into a spotlight of difference, just as it has for Roum Orthodox married into Maronite villages. An expert at *talteesh* can push all your buttons, scraping at scabs, with a chuckling audience. Learning to let it slide, to laugh along, to throw a few darts of your own, is also a Lebanese art. But *talteesh* does more than interpersonal damage; it etches over the lines dividing categories, deepening their grooves.

Teresa's father and others may have imagined Christian sects as inherently different from one another, but the categories rely on historically created rifts. For Lebanon's two largest Christian sects, ideological and party divisions fall along imperfect sectarian lines. Maronites have long been associated with right-wing political parties like the Kata'ib (Phalanges) and Lebanese Forces and with Christian-supremacist ideologies; Roum Orthodox are associated with the left-leaning Syrian Social Nationalist Party and calls for unifying Lebanon with Syria (and its large Roum Orthodox population).

By the early 2000s, demographic changes and civil war political machinations had muddied these associations. Political differences among parties associated with sects persist but carry less weight in the interpersonal realm than do fears that Christians are dwindling. This century, while Maronite–Roum Orthodox couples may still prompt snide comments, most people no longer consider their marriages "mixed."

———

Change in the opposite direction is taking place for Sunni-Shi'a Muslim marriages. In earlier eras, because people tended to marry within their village or region, these marriages were less common. By the latter decades of the twentieth century, they were fairly routine. Sectarian difference didn't go unremarked on, but it wasn't a huge problem. Sunni *talteesh* poked at assumptions that Shi'a were rural and poor: "Do they know how to use forks and knives?" Parental hesitations were based on status and regional differences and faded quickly. Small frictions around how to do the *katab kitab*—Which shaykh? Which location?—were readily resolved. Most couples married without prolonged drama.

Rasha and Jad were an exception. A Sunni from Tripoli, Rasha met Jad, a Shi'a from the Bekaa Valley, at an elite Beirut university in the 1990s. As Muslims raised in secular homes, it never occurred to them that their parents would object to their marriage. When Rasha told her parents that Jad was "the one," they deflected, saying they were too young to marry and should establish careers first. The summer after graduation, as potential suitors appeared, Rasha announced that she would only marry Jad but didn't want to marry without her parents' blessing. Arguments filled the household. Rasha's father asked her to end the relationship, and she refused.

"Fine," her father said. "Marry him, but it will be *without* our blessing. We will do everything properly to keep up appearances, but you will know that you are doing this against our will and are no longer our daughter."

"I will not marry anyone then," Rasha replied. "I have years until I am thirty, and we aren't in a hurry. When you are ready to accept my choice for a groom, let me know." Rasha and her father stopped speaking to one another. The couple went on with their lives and waited.

A year later, Rasha's father agreed to meet Jad and realized that he was educated enough to fit into their world. He also realized Rasha wasn't going to change her mind; the couple had been together for six years.

Planning the engagement was complicated. In Rasha's family, couples exchanged rings when they got engaged but didn't have the *katab kitab* until the wedding. In Jad's family, the *katab kitab* marked the engagement, allowing the couple to get to know one another privately, with the expectation that they wouldn't consummate the marriage until after the wedding. Both families reacted to this difference. Rasha's parents thought it reflected Shi'i backward conservatism; Jad's parents believed it revealed Sunni immorality.

Rasha and Jad solved the problem pragmatically. They had found jobs outside Lebanon and wanted to emigrate. The sooner they did the *katab kitab*, the sooner they could complete the necessary paperwork as a married couple. Rasha's father accepted this logic as long as the shaykh was Sunni. The couple agreed and quickly married. They left Lebanon a couple months later and, despite their promises to do so, never held a wedding, to avoid family hassles.

Rasha's parents viewed Shi'i Muslims as lower status than Sunnis. Her mother was so adamant that Jad was beneath them that she didn't tell anyone Rasha had married. Her aunts found out when they sent a potential groom to visit two years later, forcing her mom to reveal the marriage.

Years later, Rasha continues to manage her family's ignorance. Her mother once called her in-laws to wish them a "Happy Ashura." A time of mourning, not celebration, Ashura is the commemoration of the martyrdom of a key figure in Shi'i Islam at the hands of a Sunni leader. Laughing at the end of our interview, Rasha told me, "I was like, *Mom*, please don't do that again!"

When I met Rasha, the first thing she said to me was, "We got married twenty years ago. If it were today, there is no way I could have fucking pulled it off!" She may well be right.

In the early 2000s, changing regional political conditions shook Sunni-Shi'a relations and relationships. US rhetoric and actions positioning Iran as archenemy and Saudi Arabia as friend nurtured the divide. Kali Rubaii shows us how the US invasion and occupation of Iraq divided the Iraqi population by sect so that "sect became a social fact" for the first time.[35] She explains that despite a history of oppression of certain groups in Iraq, it wasn't until the US instituted its policies that sect came to matter in deeply internalized ways for people there. As these regional politics bled across borders, they took Lebanese form.

In Lebanon, the assassination of Prime Minister Rafiq Hariri in 2005 was the quake that divided Sunni and Shi'a.[36] The country coalesced into two sides, each with a sect-based political party at its core: the Sunni Mustaqbal and the Shi'i Hizbullah. When Hizbullah's militia defended Lebanon during the July 2006 Israeli war on Lebanon, Mustaqbal's leadership accused it of provoking the attack.[37] The drama that followed included cabinet resignations, protests, media campaigns, and, in 2008, a brief armed standoff in the heart of the capital. Hizbullah was a key participant in government for the first time, flexing new power that challenged traditional Sunni political leadership. And anti-Shi'a sentiment grew.

Sunni-Shi'a couples who had married in the twentieth century told me how, after 2005, it was like their family members suddenly remembered sectarian difference. Fierce arguments that were unimaginable before now dominated gatherings, *talteesh* clouded dinners, and couples thought twice about mixing their families. A Sunni woman was asked not to bring her Shi'i husband or children to visit her family anymore. Shi'i women described Sunni friends announcing that they would never allow their children to marry a Shi'a.

During this time period, Zeina and Muhammad met at the same university where Rasha and Jad had connected decades prior. "I didn't consider dating him," Zeina, who is Sunni, told me. "I knew how my family would see him, I knew that no way, *no way*, would they allow it." Despite her reluctance, the couple soon fell in love. It took Zeina four years to tell her parents.

"I took my time to get to know him secretly first, because I knew I was going into a fight," she explained. "I had to be convinced he was the person I wanted. When I knew it was worth it, and I had decided, I told them."

Her parents were angry. "Who is this? Where did you *find* him? Where is he *from*? Why didn't you tell us about him before?" They couldn't fathom their daughter marrying someone they didn't already know or at least someone from a known "good family." Zeina was financially independent and nearly thirty, but the pressure escalated: "You're not our daughter if you marry him." "You are betraying your family if you marry him." Her siblings joined in: "What are you doing to our parents?" "Our father is old; you will make him ill."

This emotional pressure weighed on Zeina, but she persisted and finally convinced her parents to meet Muhammad before judging him. Her father remained unconvinced, but her mom liked him and saw that Zeina was happy. She worked behind the scenes to support Zeina's choice. Eventually, Zeina gave her parents an ultimatum: "I'm done arguing. I will either marry who I want or no one at all." Her parents agreed to meet Muhammad's Shi'i family. Over tea and sweets, they learned that his family had spent time in the city, valued education, and had an open-minded perspective. Muhammad's parents effectively broke the stereotypes that Zeina's parents had about village Shi'a. Zeina's father set two conditions for his blessing. He asked the couple to wait another year to allow the families to get to know one another. And he asked Muhammad to sell his apartment in a primarily Shi'i suburb of Beirut and promise that the couple would live in a "neutral" neighborhood. Despite the major hassles this created, Muhammad agreed. The couple married a year later.

These two Sunni-Shi'a stories may seem similar, but they show the two Muslim sects moving further apart as social worlds parallel political shifts. Rasha and Jad's experience was exceptionally difficult for the 1990s; Zeina and Muhammad's story was easy for the post-2005 era. Zeina's father's stipulation about where the couple could live stems from political worries born in the twenty-first century. Muhammad had to prove that he wasn't embedded in Shi'i political parties, or areas of the city associated with them, in order to marry his daughter. Rasha was surprised by her father's opposition, while over a decade later, Zeina anticipated it. Between the moment Rasha and Jad fell in love and the moment Zeina and Muhammad did, the groove between Sunni and Shiʻa had deepened. People coming of age at these different historical moments learned different ideas about sect and how it mattered to their lives.

Learning Sect

Everyone has to learn how to read the rings of their social worlds. As part of that process, Lebanese learn about sect. My interviewees raised during the civil war or by especially sectarian parents felt like sect had always been there, part of the air they breathed. Others usually learned about it at around age eight or nine—when Muslims begin to pray and fast and Christians have First Communion. A Sunni might see a Maronite classmate buying a communion dress or be invited to the party. A Roum Orthodox might see a Shiʻi friend fasting during Ramadan. This seems to be the age when classmates begin asking questions about identity, questions many of my interviewees didn't know how to answer. Teachers at nonsecular schools sorted students into the appropriate classroom for religious study. "World religions" units in secular school curricula prompted students to sort themselves into categories. Political events triggered questions. When Prime Minister Hariri was assassinated, many children came home from school asking whether they were Sunni or Shiʻa. Being bullied woke some up to sect. When he was nine, during the war, a man recalled, classmates in his mixed Druze-Christian village beat him up in retaliation for a kidnapping. That's how he learned he was Druze.

Revelations about sect could come even later. One Druze woman remembered being fifteen when she asked her parents why some of her classmates were fasting. Another was twelve when friends asked, "How do you cross yourself? With how many fingers?" She went home and asked her mom, who explained that she was Shiʻa and they didn't do that. Alumni of the elite International College remembered the moment when students from the middle school in a Christian town joined them in Ras Beirut for high school. That was when many of those students met a Muslim for the first time and when Ras Beirut residents of all sects first encountered Christians who wore crosses and spoke with a different accent.

People raised in segregated towns in Lebanon sometimes didn't learn about sect until university. "It was the shock of my life to learn that there were all these sects," one told me. Another admitted that she didn't know there were non-Christian Lebanese until she went to college. Those raised in diaspora who returned with their families after the war also learned about sect late. Schools in the UAE, Kuwait, or Saudi Arabia had divided them into Christians and Muslims but didn't prepare them for sect's importance. Muslims raised in North America knew only that they were Muslim, often because they had been taught to avoid pork. The exceptions were those raised in isolationist Maronite or Orthodox church communities in the US or Australia.

The alleged differences between people, differences they could neither see nor decipher, frustrated many diaspora returnees. "Everyone was speaking a language I couldn't understand," one explained. There was a steep learning curve about social cues that linked names, sects, neighborhoods, and sometimes dress and accent. "I didn't even know that someone named Philippe would probably be Christian," a woman told me, laughing at her naivete as a college student. Others were stunned when classmates told them who to vote for in campus elections based on their sect.

I don't have the data to assess whether people in mixed marriages are more likely to learn about sect at a later age than those who marry within their group, but some of my interviewees believe that is the case. As one put it, "I think that if I grew up in a different context, a different school, a different area of Lebanon, I wouldn't have been who I am or been with who I am with. Perhaps I would have been a sectarian person, a person who is very bounded within the social boundaries of the Lebanese sectarian society." Others expressed appreciation for how carefully their parents had protected them from sectarian language and identifications or for the exposure they had to diversity growing up.

Whether or not this led to their mixed marriages, how people learn to read and navigate social difference is part of how sectarianism is perpetuated or diluted in Lebanese society. That people have to learn about it at all reminds us that it's all made up. By the time they wanted to marry, some people expected their parents' objections. Others were blindsided by the sudden importance of sect for their parents when it came to marriage, because they believed they were living the values they had been taught by ignoring sect as a factor in their love lives.

———

Sect is both meaningful and meaningless. It carries weight for people's lives but is an empty box that people fill with a variety of connotations and assumptions. Over time, both weight and meaning change, showing us how people make and remake sect as a category of difference that matters.

Because sect is the most available and acceptable way of talking about social difference in Lebanon, sectarian language permeates parental efforts to control their children's marriages. Each parent who says, "You can't marry them because they are X sect" reinforces sectarianism. For some parents, these statements reflect their feelings about the importance of sect as a source of belonging, but for quite a few, sect is simply the easiest way to express their expectations and objections. It's the language everyone in Lebanon uses, after all, as a shorthand explanation for why someone or some group is a problem. But people have to add meaning to sect, filling it with content that proves how different the other sect is from them. When all the people involved are Lebanese, that takes work. Each time a parent panics when their child wants to marry across sectarian lines, they do some of that work, filling that empty box with certain characteristics, with content and value. Family responses to mixed marriage fill sectarian categories with meaning one phrase or snide comment or tasteless joke at a time, one refusal to bless a match at a time. In the Lebanese Ouroboros, sectarianism feeds itself.

Two

Who Will You Marry?

Ibtisam's maternal grandparents eloped in the early twentieth century. Sitting in the breakfast nook of her Beirut apartment, the aromatic tea and cake before us lit by the late morning sun streaming in the window, Ibtisam shared the story with me and her daughter, Hiba.

"This was back in the Ottoman days," she began. "My grandfather used to hide weapons at my grandmother's parents' house." Her opening, in tones redolent of "Once upon a time" or "There was and there was not," cued us in to the family myth that would follow.

Hiba interrupted to ask what year it was, and Ibtisam shook her head at this request for precision. "It was during the Ottomans," she repeated. "Before World War I. He was young." Why was he hiding weapons? Perhaps he was affiliated with a clandestine Arab nationalist group organizing against the Ottoman Empire before the war. Or perhaps he was linked to a movement seeking regional autonomy as the empire crumbled.

"One time, when he was hiding weapons, he saw a beautiful girl sewing. He didn't know that the woman who hid his weapons had a daughter.

He asked her, "Who's that?"

"My daughter." (Let's call her Faiza).

"I want to marry her."

"I cannot give her to you in marriage," Faiza's mother replied.

Despite being too young to marry, not yet a teenager, Faiza sensed the young man's admiration. Today we would likely call it a crush, but in Ibtisam's tale, Faiza loved him: "She saw him whenever he came over, and they were in love. She loved him very much. Still, her mother refused."

"Let me marry your daughter."

"Never! I can't give her to you in marriage because her cousin wants to marry her."

Hiba and I now understood that Faiza's mother was stuck—even if she wanted to allow her daughter to marry this man, she couldn't break an engagement agreement within the family. Ibtisam leaned in, her conspiratorial tone bringing us into her confidence as she explained how the young man solved this problem.

"Once, Faiza was walking in the street with her mother. My grandfather put a gun to her mother's back. The gun was only for show. He said, 'Give me your daughter, leave her with me and go.'

He took Faiza to the shaykh and they had a *katab kitab*. Then he took her home to her mother and waited for her to grow up. And then he married her."

To our twenty-first-century ears, this sounds like a crime: a young man kidnapping a preteen at gunpoint. But Ibtisam's tale was one of romance, young love prevailing over arranged marriage. She is clear that Faiza was happy to elope with the youth. His gun allowed Faiza's mother to save face and tacitly consent to the match without being blamed for breaking her word. She had no choice in the matter. After all, there was a gun to her back. After the ceremony, Faiza returned to her parents' home to "grow up," indicating that the marriage was not consummated until she was an appropriate age. The *katab kitab* served as a public engagement, preventing Faiza from marrying anyone else, ensuring that the couple would end up together. And indeed, they lived happily ever after.

This story is unusual, likely honed over decades as family lore. No matter how the details may have shifted, it tells us that love was lauded as a reason to marry against family will much earlier in Lebanese history than is often imagined.

A few decades later, in the late 1920s, Faiza's daughter (Ibtisam's mother) had a traditional marriage arranged by her Sunni family. "When my dad married my mom, they didn't know each other, and she was covered. Afterward, he found her beautiful. They lived with his parents. Each son and his bride had their own room."

Hiba and I were rapt, but Ibtisam paused to top up my tea before continuing.

"My father used to tell mom at night, 'Let's go out.' They jumped out the window! He brought her evening dresses, and she wore an *abaya* over them and covered her face until they reached the road. They went with his friends to the coffee shop. Imagine!

Once, someone saw them and told my grandmother. Teta went crazy: 'You went out at night with your husband?!' But he always took her to dinner with his friends secretly."

This opening up of society, seen in her parents' boundary pushing, created space for Ibtisam to choose an appropriate spouse—of the same class, sect, and neighborhood. She fell in love with her husband at school. Hiba knew this story and nodded along, smiling at the image of her parents flirting, her mom on the balcony like Juliet.

Ibtisam smiled too, as she shared this memory. "I stood on the balcony waiting for him to pass by. And when we went to school, he would follow me. Little by little, things developed. We were so young, it was early. We stayed in love from afar until the last year of school. Then his family spoke to mine, and we got engaged."

Both Ibtisam and Hiba see this trajectory of social change as the ground that enabled Hiba's later choice to marry someone of another religion, in a civil ceremony, for love.

Love and Connectivity

One of the stories we tell ourselves about how the world has changed is a story of love conquering all. We imagine that Romeo and Juliet's love is contemporary in its passion but historical in its calamitous outcome. Many people assume arranged marriage is in the past or elsewhere in the world. My Lebanese interviewees share this view, believing that romantic love and individual choice go hand in hand and discounting how other forms of love may shape their actions.[1] Possibilities galore lie between meeting your spouse at your wedding and choosing whom to marry, possibilities that reflect both family dynamics and different understandings of love. This chapter explores those possibilities, looking at marital choice within families, across generations and gender, and at the double standards that raise the stakes of marrying for love for women.

Scholars agree with my interviewees that marriage has shifted toward love, or "companionate" forms, the result of globalizing ideas about love and the value of personal emotions, plus local economic and social changes.[2] "Companionate marriage" conjures images of couples as friends and lovers, individuals who choose one another, marriages where the couple takes precedence over broader family obligations, and social worlds where people marry for fulfillment and not necessarily to reproduce. Most relationships fall somewhere in between. Even in US communities that valorize romance, couples must manage extended family pressures, whether deciding where to live or how to spend holidays.

In the Middle East, the ideal of companionate marriage emerges, unevenly, in the early twentieth century.[3] Today, this ideal coexists with broader kinship obligations.[4] In one Turkish village, families arrange long engagements hoping that couples will fall in love.[5] Young Egyptian Muslim men see love as one concern alongside family and social networks when deciding whom to marry.[6] Some young Jordanian women view compatibility between families as necessary for a good marriage, and both accept and chafe at family involvement in decisions.[7]

Love can be a point of intergenerational contention. A Lebanese Druze woman who protested her son's mixed marriage used her own story to say that love shouldn't be prioritized. Unlike Ibtisam, she grew to love her husband after they married. "It wasn't like we met and fell in love. He saw me at home because he was my brother's friend." She rejected his first proposal. "Then I thought to myself, Why not? He's a good person. He's handsome. He's well educated." After one date, the young man and his father proposed to her father. They married three months later. She was twenty-one. "It wasn't a love story," she said. "It was different then."

Companionate marriage is linked to ideas about where the boundaries of a person lie.[8] Are we individuals with definitive boundaries, like the outer bark and space between aspen trunks after they emerge from the soil? Or are we like an aspen grove understood as a single organism, roots connected, edges porous, desires and identities never quite distinct from our families? Eschewing these extremes, feminist anthropologist

Suad Joseph instead uses the term "connectivity" to describe how intimate relationships knit people together.[9] Rather than an aspen—where many trunks aboveground are a single clonal organism underneath—we are a grove of Aleppo pines or Lebanese cedars, the roots of separate trees of the same species entwined, sharing nutrients, talking through electromagnetic pulses and mycorrhizal networks, protecting one another, stronger in communion. Ways of being a self change from place to place and era to era. Multiple modes can coexist within a cultural context or even within a person at different life stages. Believing in individual choice doesn't mean that your parents' approval is trivial. Some people express connection as a debt—"Our parents did so much for us"—to be repaid by trying their best to craft a life that meets expectations.

My interviewees were tangled in this system as they tried to make choices within it. When writing about family relationships in Lebanon, Joseph modified connectivity as patriarchal to emphasize that relations are planted in soil where power difference privileges males and elders. She explains, "Those who occupy the masculinized and aged positions are culturally entitled to direct intimate others as parts of themselves, to expect service and compliance from significant others as expressions of familial love and loyalty, and to receive affirmations and deferential respect as rights due those acting on behalf of the familial good."[10] When the ideal of love marriage runs into patriarchal connectivity, entangled roots limit paths or even strangle, trapping people in untenable situations.

Patriarchal connectivity explains why people break up with someone they love or avoid falling in love with the wrong person. It explains why elopement is a last resort, why couples wait years for a blessing, and why, sometimes, parents surprise their children and support their choice, as Hiba's did.

———————

Ibtisam's daughter Hiba told the story of her marriage to a Maronite man, Charles. "I knew he was the one immediately," Hiba told me, "even though I was only twenty-two, and marriage wasn't on my mind ... I told Charles I come from an open-minded family. But I also told him there's a possibility my parents won't accept it. From day one, I said, 'If I feel my parents are 1 percent against this, I won't fight them.'"

She paused. "Maybe I said that because I knew they wouldn't go against my will. But I also never thought a person could sustain happiness if they were unhappily separated from their parents. No matter how much you're in love."

Hiba's parents knew Charles as one of her friends, but Ibtisam sensed he might be special. When Hiba confirmed it, Ibtisam was supportive and kept the information to herself for several years before urging Hiba to either try to marry or break up. I asked Ibtisam why she had nudged the couple. She explained that she wanted Hiba to be happy and living in uncertainty was unacceptable.

Hiba asked her mom to break the news to her father. Ibtisam was direct: "Your daughter loves a guy, and he loves her back, but he's Christian."

"Why are *you* telling me? Let Hiba talk to me," her husband replied. He surprised Ibtisam, saying, "Didn't you fall in love? We fell in love, so why not Hiba?"

So, Hiba went to talk to him. "Dad, I decided to get married."

"Okay, good," her father replied. "Who do you want to marry?"

"I want to tell you, but there might be a problem. You might have a problem with him."

"Just tell me."

"Charles and I decided to get married."

"Yes, and where's the problem?"

"He's Maronite."

"You're the one starting with the problem! This is the problem! Instead of you starting by telling me how much he loves you, how well he's going to take care of you! This [sect] is a problem on paper, it's the easiest problem to solve. Tell me that he loves you, he'll care for you, you love him, where you'll live."

Relating this conversation to me years later, Hiba laughed: "He almost asked me, 'Where's the fridge going to be? Where's the closet?' For dad, the question was, 'Is he going to give you a good life?' So I told him, 'I'm twenty-six, I've been with him for some time now, and I think he's the right person.' And they already loved Charles. They knew him. And I think everything about his CV worked to my advantage, you know?"

Hiba and Charles' story was among the least eventful I heard during my research. Hiba attributed this ease to the open environment of

Ras Beirut where both families lived, but the area's multisectarian harmony wasn't always powerful enough to overcome difference. Hiba's personality and relationship with her parents played a role. She and Ibtisam are close and exude the same warmth in how they treat others. Spending time with them in Beirut was an oasis of calm amid the city's intensity.

Hiba married in the late 1990s. The only other mixed marriage in the extended family, according to Ibtisam, was an elopement in the 1930s. The family lore Ibtisam shared shows how marriage has changed for Sunni Beiruti women over generations, a history that places Hiba's marriage at the end of a shift toward love.

Opening the Door

Lebanon today contains the full spectrum of marriage ideals and practices. Generational change doesn't have a standardized timeline. The Druze woman who said hers wasn't a love story married in 1983; Ibtisam's love marriage was a couple decades earlier. Changes in love's definition also don't have a standardized timeline. Ibtisam narrates her grandmother's elopement as love—though it reads to us as a preteen crush. Her own story shows love as glances and passed notes, a far cry from Hiba's multiyear dating relationship with Charles.

Location matters. Companionate marriage is far more common in Beirut than, say, Arsal, a rural region near the Syrian border where even in the early 2000s, youth seeking love matches confronted elders' preferences for family-orchestrated marriages.[11] The degree to which extended family members are involved in one another's lives also matters. Are they an aspen grove or a pine forest? Parents who seek specific sorts of spouses for their children choreograph encounters. An annual *mawlid* at the posh Phoenicia Hotel becomes a debutante display where mothers introduce daughters as eligible brides in Beirut Sunni society. An invitation to accompany mom on a morning coffee visit to a friend's house is an invitation to meet women with eligible sons or nephews. Networks of connection grow from new technologies. Alongside the annual Druze convention in North America, a venue for diaspora youth to meet partners, there is a Druze-only dating app.

Generational change overall flows toward the "choice" end of the spectrum but remains tangled with social worlds.[12] Many Lebanese live with their parents until marriage. While age brings independence, they rarely meet spouses without introductions. Nearly half of my interviewees across generations met their spouses through friends, cousins, or siblings. Others met at university or work, as volunteers or activists. A few were high school sweethearts, childhood neighbors, or schoolmates. Only eight couples met as strangers at a café, pub, beach, or, in one case, online. Marriage in each family drifts toward choice at a pace shaped by class, location, education, religious or political inclinations, and the strength of relational knots connecting members. The most accurate predictor of responses to mixed marriage is how many relatives have already broken the rules.

———

Rima and Majid were the first in their families to marry across sect. They "opened the door" for others, including their daughter Line. Line met Walid at work, dated him for three years, had a civil marriage abroad in 2017, and threw a gala in Lebanon afterward. Their parents supported them from the start, as if this match were typical.

Line is considered Druze like her father, but her mother is from a Beirut Sunni family. She believes her parents' struggle to marry in the mid-1980s explains their support. I visited them to hear their story.

"My family calls me the pioneer!" Rima declared. The proud tilt of her head would have seemed defiant in a younger woman recounting recent family battles.

"Welcome," Majid added, his arm around Rima. "Now help us remember!" A migrant domestic worker brought us coffee and biscuits as they bantered in English and Arabic, recalling their romance and struggles, Rima smiling and Majid laughing in a gravelly voice.

A mutual friend introduced them when they were in their late twenties. Rima knew it was a setup. "Our friend invited us to dinner. But I didn't want to go."

"Why not?" I asked.

"Because I knew the guy he wanted me to meet wasn't Sunni. It would be different than meeting someone by accident if I did it on purpose. But our friend was like, 'Just come anyway, not necessarily to meet him.' So I went."

Majid was clueless. "I probably wouldn't have gone if I knew he was introducing us," he laughed. "I wasn't thinking about marriage. It was the last thing on my mind. I was used to being independent."

"So I went," Rima continued, "and I thought, Oh, he's quite handsome. Then I turned away, I said to myself, What do you want with this? And I tried to focus on something else. But . . ."

"From the first time I saw her, I knew I fell for her!"

Majid introduced Rima to his mother after their first date. His late father had objected to Majid's Christian ex-girlfriend and disowned relatives over a mixed marriage. Majid told us that he hoped his father would have accepted Rima, because by then he was older and financially independent. Still, it took his mother a few years to adapt to the idea. By the time Majid was in his thirties, her desire to see him married with children overpowered her desire for a Druze daughter-in-law.

Rima waited two years to tell her parents about Majid. When she was ready, Majid went to ask her father for her hand in marriage. He had a drink to quell his nerves and parked sideways in front of the house. The men spoke for four hours. Majid could only recall the part of their conversation when Rima's father had asked him, "If you had a sister who wanted to marry outside your sect, would you accept?" He had replied that he would see what the groom was like and then decide. Her father had said, "I have a family whose opinion I must also ask, then I will let you know."

The couple left the situation to time. "We never thought about marrying against our parents' wishes," Majid explained. "We agreed that if her father didn't accept, then that's it for us."

Over a year later, Rima's father had not replied to Majid's proposal. When another—appropriately Sunni—suitor asked for Rima's hand, she gave her parents an ultimatum. "I won't marry in such a traditional way, I can't! I will only marry the way I want; I am independent, I won't marry just to get married."

After Rima's outburst, fate—and her brother—intervened. Speaking over one another, the couple told me what had happened.

"I opened my door and heard the phone ringing. It was her brother. Imagine if the key had stuck and door hadn't opened quickly. It wouldn't have happened!"

"My brother called Majid and said, 'You have half an hour to come and propose, because we are all pressuring my dad right now to accept you."

"I had only thirty minutes!"

"Poor thing, he didn't know how was going to gather his family that fast."

Majid managed to collect his family on that Sunday morning and rush to Rima's house. This time, her father accepted his proposal. The couple insisted on a civil marriage in Cyprus so Majid wouldn't have to convert. Because it was during the war, the family held a small party on the island before returning to Beirut.

Rima and Majid were the first in their families to break the marriage rules. Many people described the first mixed marriage in a family as "opening the door." When Rima and Majid opened the door, not only did their daughter Line walk through it, but so did several nephews and nieces on both sides. Interviewees explained undramatic stories by pointing to the person who opened the door or listing their relatives in mixed marriages. Parents were sometimes counseled to avoid earlier mistakes in the family: "Don't do what Aunt So-and-So did to her child. They haven't spoken since."

The first person always has it the hardest. Families are marked by the moment someone marries outside sanctioned circles. That moment destabilizes the walls between similar and different just enough for another family member to weaken them further. Then another. And another. Degrees of acceptable similarity shift as new categories of people are knitted into kin. Someone marries outside their village. Outside their region. Outside their sect. Outside their religion. In some families, this collective force builds until the walls grow porous and crumble. Longtime mixed families are diverse. Shiʻi families linked to West Africa or to Communist villages in the South have long intermarried with Christians. Druze and Maronite families on the mountain and Sunni and Roum Orthodox families in Beirut have also intermarried, provided status was similar.

Line and Walid feel lucky that their parents get along. They go out to dinner without the couple, and their mothers shopped together for dresses for the wedding. Walid attributes his parents' acceptance to his sister Caren's marriage to a Sunni man several years earlier. Unaware of the details, he told me, "My parents didn't even react badly to *that* one."

———

Caren tells a different story. When she and Muhammad, who goes by Mo, got together, her mom disapproved but agreed to meet him. When Mo came to dinner, Caren's parents liked him, but that wasn't enough. Her conservative father didn't object, but her mother kept making what Caren described as "cliched, very stereotypical judgments." Caren stood firm: "I didn't give them an option. I'm like, 'This is the guy I like and at the end of the day I'm going to make the decision.' Every time mom gave me an argument, I always had an answer."

"You know your kids will be Muslim."

"Mom, do you think if I'm marrying a Muslim, I mind that my kids will be Muslim? I don't believe it's something bad."

"He can marry three other women."

"Christian men can basically just have affairs." And so on.

Caren's mother feared that she would suffer social consequences for her daughter's choice. Her fears were warranted. Her siblings and in-laws scolded her; one refused to attend the wedding or congratulate Caren. Her colleagues at a predominantly Christian workplace disparaged mixed marriage. But when Caren and Mo eventually got engaged, her mom acquiesced, and most relatives attended the destination wedding.

Caren knows her mixed marriage made her brother's easier: "I opened a door, you know, I paved the way for Walid and Line." At the same time, she thinks her mother was more open to Walid's marriage "because she felt like he was bringing Line into the family, in this traditional conservative mentality, while she's losing me to Muslims." It's also possible that had Walid married first, their mother would have protested, fearing he would open the door for Caren.

Parents understand the consequences of allowing the door to open. A Druze mother who battled against her son's Christian fiancée explained that she had to do so to prevent her other children from thinking they could marry non-Druze. "I will not set an example for my other children!" she exclaimed. "They were waiting to see what I would say, waiting to see if they could do the same thing!" Aunts and uncles—fearing that their children would follow—sometimes shunned nephews or nieces. A few didn't tell their children about a cousin's marriage, hoping the door would stay out of sight.

Fearing contagion, one uncle forbade his children from speaking with their cousin when she married outside her sect. "It won't be me influencing his kids!" she exclaimed. "There is an internet nowadays, so people are not waiting for other people to influence them. I mean, come on, seriously? Your children are living in an era where there are no borders anymore. So it's not gonna be someone from another sect, it's gonna be someone from another nationality!" Laughing, she concluded, "So prepare yourself for that!"

Fears of contagion are well founded. Ten of my interviewees opened the door for siblings' mixed marriages; many more opened it for cousins. They are called "revolutionaries," "pioneers," or "bad influences" by family elders. In one social circle, mixed marriage is called the "[so-and-so] effect" after the woman who opened the door. As people in mixed marriages bend or break rules to create their families, they provide one ingredient for broader social change.

The stories we have seen thus far—Hiba and Charles, Walid and Line, even Caren and Mo—fall on the "easy" side of the spectrum. Most stories I heard—some 80 percent—included greater conflict, from intense discussions to fierce decade-long battles. Their resolutions ranged from family harmony to ongoing disownment. Open doors don't always lead to a smooth path.

———

Jana's father is Catholic, and her mother is Sunni. Khaled is Sunni. When Jana and Khaled dated during university, their parents assumed the relationship wouldn't last because they were young. When they maintained their romance transnationally for years, their parents assumed it would buckle under the pressures of distance. When they endured, both families interfered.

Khaled's mother expected him to marry from within their Sunni Beirut social circle. Jana's Sunni mother was from Beirut, but not of the same status. So Khaled's mother began introducing him to potential brides.

If open doors always led to paved roads, Jana's mixed parents would have embraced Khaled. Instead, they forbade her from visiting Khaled abroad. "That is when I boycotted my parents," Jana said. "I went only to work. I didn't go out. I didn't see them. I didn't see anyone." She took a deep breath. "It wasn't only about them. I missed Khaled. I cried every day."

Seeing her tears, her father allowed her to join a group of friends going to visit Khaled. He also opened up to her, finally explaining his concerns about the match. Jana recalled their conversation with deep empathy for her parents' perspective: "My parents knew that he was a good guy, from a decent family, educated, the whole nine yards. They didn't have a problem with Khaled. They were trying to protect me because they suffered in their marriage because of my grandparents. They wanted to spare me the misery of going through what they went through."

To this day, Jana's parents haven't shared their full story with their children. Jana learned snippets from relatives and gleaned bits from her own observations. She knows they fell in love in the mid-1960s and that all hell broke loose. Her Christian paternal grandparents fought the match, apparently even with a suicide attempt. Or perhaps it was Jana's father who considered suicide. The story is murky. "And then they eloped. But how did they elope? We don't know," Jana said. "No one talks about it." When her parents returned and announced they were married, people in her father's village made racist comments about her mom, like, "Where is her tail?"

"If you talk to my mother," Jana mused, knowing well that her mother would never talk about those days, "she will say it's still there, in her heart and mind, how they treated her." Even when her mom converted to Christianity for pragmatic reasons, her father's parents didn't accept her. Jana remembers her mom waiting outside the house when they visited those grandparents and arguments about her father's inability to stand up for his wife. Time eventually eroded the rifts. The civil war forced everyone to seek shelter together. When her paternal grandmother grew ill, Jana's mother cared for her. She has heard rumblings about a private reconciliation between the two.

Jana's father told her that despite their experience and worries, they would accept her choice if things worked out. The couple persisted, and both advanced in their careers. Jana visited Khaled's mother regularly, trying to win her over. When those efforts failed, the couple—who had grown into a thoughtful, assertive, mutual confidence—announced they would get engaged with or without approval. Khaled's parents conceded.

An open door can jam when the couple who opened it, like Jana's parents, were scarred in the process. Parents who faced backlash wanted to protect their children from similar pain. Doors can also stick when parents hold on to expectations that at least one of their children will marry appropriately. Some fight a second child who wants to break the rules even harder than the first. Doors that appear open may be illusory. Many Lebanese families include men married to European Christian women, who receive citizenship and are integrated into the family's sectarian affiliation. These marriages don't necessarily open doors for people who want to marry *Lebanese* Christians. Bound by sectarian categories, Lebanese women are not "neutral." Their families are assumed to have a stake in the identities of any future grandchildren. Nor do they provide the ethnic mobility and whitening—status on a global stage—that European women bring to the fold. And doors may open differently for men than for women.

If a person chooses their spouse without family involvement, they have to decide how and when to tell their parents. These decisions can also change a story's course. Upending expectations around social rituals can make matters worse, adding another broken social norm into the mix and slamming an open door shut.

Introductions, Engagements, and Missteps

Donna and Amer met in the United Arab Emirates. "I didn't tell my parents at first," Donna told me, "because I suspected they might object." We spoke almost entirely in English during our Skype interview, reflecting our Lebanese diaspora upbringings. Two years later, the couple was still together. "We woke up one day and realized like, 'Wow, I don't think I can live without you.'"

Donna still didn't tell her Roum Orthodox parents, but she didn't hide it either: "I always brought Amer up. You know, 'Amer got me this. He did this. He did that. Amer picked me up. He wouldn't let me take a taxi. Look, Mom, what a good guy he is, he drove me home.' I made him look really, really good. I never for one second let them think I was making a bad decision."

Two years, they both had stable jobs, and it was time. When Donna told her mom, she replied that she had known for years and that she should talk to her father. Her father agreed to meet Amer, so he came to dinner one evening. "My father asked Amer 101 questions, basically. And they loved him, thank god." But when Amer left, Donna's parents said they were surprised she had allowed herself to fall in love with a Muslim because she knew they were "off-limits." "But we lived in Muslim areas all my life," Donna replied. "We have always been surrounded by Muslims. Your friends are Muslims. You raised me among Muslims. You never told me to differentiate based on religion."

For a few months, her parents pointed out Amer's differences, fixating on small details, down to their alma maters. They kept asking, "How will you live your lifestyle?" as though Amer would suddenly turn religious and force Donna to change somehow. Donna continued to rebut, "But you didn't raise me to see Muslims as different." Recounting these conversations, she described her parents' objections as "differences of background," though I heard class as a key factor. Amer is from a much larger family. His mother doesn't have a university degree and never worked outside the home. His parents haven't traveled the world as much. Eventually, Donna asserted that she wanted to get engaged, and her parents acquiesced.

Donna thinks that the couple's strategy—keeping their relationship an open secret for years and delaying the moment her parents met Amer— backfired. Because they didn't already know him, they couldn't see their similarities and how much sense they made as a couple.

———

Introducing a partner to one's parents is rarely easy, even under good circumstances. A lot rides on the conversation. My interviewees chose different tactics, reflecting personalities, family relationships, communication styles, ages, degrees of financial independence, and expectations about the situation. Most broke the news to their parents face to face. A few wrote letters. Some people enlisted help from supportive siblings or family members. Others tested the waters with hypotheticals or "a friend's situation." They couldn't always control the circumstances. Mothers found out by stalking their children on Facebook, or they sensed something was up and nudged, "Do you have anything you'd like to tell me?" One father found out from a neighbor.

Some people told their parents immediately because they always shared their news with them. Others told them early because they anticipated disapproval and wanted to prepare them or start laying out their arguments just in case this was "the one." Some allowed their partner to appear as part of their circle of friends so that by the time the relationship was announced, parents already knew their future child-in-law. Others hid their relationship until they were absolutely certain they wanted to marry. They needed to know the fight was worth it.

In some homes, a "don't ask, don't tell" atmosphere reigned. Parents didn't want to know about a relationship until it was serious. Until marriage was on the table, there was nothing to talk about. And some parents wanted everything done by the book. No matter the circumstances, the *how* of the conversation mattered, sometimes as much as the *what.*

———

Nadya and Marwan are both children of mixed marriages. Her father is Druze, and her mother is Sunni with a Shi'i mother. His father is Shi'a, and his mother Catholic. The couple met as student activists but didn't date until five years later, when their paths crossed at a party in Beirut. Nadya told me, "Because my parents are mixed and his parents are mixed, I didn't have to think about the other person's identity, I was very sure there wouldn't be any problems with it. He just started to come over to our house, and I started to go over to their house, and he met my parents, and I met his parents." Two years later, the couple invited both families out to dinner and made an announcement.

"We want to tell you something. We want to get engaged today!" Nadya and Marwan exchanged the rings they had brought with them. To their surprise, there was no outbreak of joy or congratulations.

"Why didn't you tell us before?"

"No one gets engaged like this!"

"It shouldn't be a surprise like this!"

"Where is your respect for tradition?"

"We would have helped you with an engagement party!"

A few months after their failed effort to surprise their parents, Nadya and Marwan flew to Cyprus on their own and married. They threw a party for their friends when they returned and then attended their first family event as a married couple. No one knew they had married, so everyone began asking, "Why weren't we invited to the wedding?" In the face of this social pressure, Marwan's father hosted a dinner to finally celebrate the marriage.

———

Many Lebanese families believe there is a correct way to mark an engagement. Of course, there are many "right ways." Traditions vary by class, region, sect, education, religiosity, family, and whim. Most agree that a "traditional" engagement begins with the groom's visit, along with his parents or relatives, to the bride's parents. During this visit, called the *tleebeh*, from the Arabic root for "request," the groom or his father should formally ask the bride's father for her hand in marriage. Speeches are made, sweets shared, congratulations given, rings often exchanged, and two Lebanese families begin suturing themselves together.

Every interviewee who had a *tleebeh* had already obtained their parents' blessings or acceptance beforehand. Couples facing protracted or vehement opposition gave their parents ultimatums or eloped. The *tleebeh* is the ritual that marks an engagement as publicly acknowledged and accepted. If the path to acceptance left wounds, the *tleebeh* might initiate a healing process. At one *tleebeh*, the groom's father announced that the couple was clearly going to marry with or without permission, so they might as well all bless the union and do things properly. At other *tleebeh*s, parents debated wedding details or voiced concerns about how future grandchildren would be raised.

Nadya and Marwan had no idea their families expected a *tleebeh*. They had miscalculated the importance of tradition and assumed that their mixed backgrounds immunized them against Lebanese social norms. Other interviewees wanted to skip the fuss or avoid highlighting differences of tradition between families. Donna's family didn't usually do things like *tleebeh*s; Amer's did. Her parents wanted to impress his family by doing everything right.

"During the *tleebeh*," Donna remembered, "Amer's father gave mine the speech, 'We're here to take your daughter, we want to ask for your daughter's hand, blah, blah, blah.'" Her father didn't reply to Amer's father as tradition dictated. Instead, he turned to Donna. "I'm going to divert this question to my daughter and ask her," he said. "Out of all the people in the world, why did you choose Amer?" Put on the spot, Donna gave the longest impromptu speech of her life, using all the arguments she had been making for months. Amer was sweating through his suit. Afterward, he explained why he was nervous: "I thought my dad was going to be offended that your dad didn't respond, only you did. But then when I got home, I learned that they really respected that he gave you the chance to answer and didn't speak on your behalf."

Generational shifts toward love marriages are also generational shifts away from traditional rituals. When neither the bride nor groom knows how to do things "properly," miscommunication arises. The wrong number of people might show up. The timing might be off. The person who was not supposed to offer sweets might do so. Some Lebanese think the groom's family brings baklava while the bride's family provides other refreshments—a bride's family offering baklava means they are eager to lose their daughter. Other families believe the bride's family provides all refreshments on this occasion, as the groom's family will host the wedding. Some families expect an exchange of gifts or rings. In some Shiʻi families, the *katab kitab* takes place at the engagement, though the couple isn't considered married until after the wedding.

Whatever their ritual preferences, patriarchal connectivity means that most Lebanese families believe a bride's father must give his permission for a marriage, even if she is a financially independent adult. Properly speaking, the groom doesn't propose to the bride; his family proposes to hers. The insult to a woman's family if she marries without permission is greater than the insult would be to a man's family. Social change toward love marriage hasn't negated this double standard.

Double Standards

Ghada asked to meet me in a neighborhood where she neither lives nor works and insisted we sit on the café's secluded patio in case someone she knew entered. Born and raised in Beirut in an elite Sunni family, her caution about privacy hid a warmth and willingness to tell her story. Ghada and Pierre were elementary school classmates who began dating in high school. Around graduation, Ghada's mother figured it out. Furious that Ghada was dating, and worse, dating a Maronite, she told Ghada's father. He was livid.

"Everything went haywire," Ghada remembered. "My father went crazy. He kept saying, 'How could *my* daughter possibly marry a Christian? How could you do this to me? What will people say?'" Reputation at stake, Ghada's parents forbade her from going out on her own, monitoring her movements. They sent her abroad to stay with relatives for a time. A male relative threatened Pierre, sending militia men to find him on campus.

Facing this onslaught, Ghada lied to her parents and hid the relationship as it continued long-distance after graduation. She half-heartedly met the potential grooms her family presented but believed she was destined to be with Pierre. When they were twenty-three, Ghada and Pierre found new jobs in the same country. Ghada left home at the usual time one morning, but instead of going to work, she met Pierre at the airport. They flew to Cyprus, married, and took another flight that afternoon to their new home.

Ghada asked an aunt who was married to a non-Muslim to break the news to her parents. Her mother and female relatives accepted the marriage. Her father and his brothers urged Ghada to return to Lebanon, saying they could work something out. But her aunt warned her this was just another tactic to separate the couple. When Ghada didn't return, her father requested a *katab kitab* in addition to their civil marriage. When Ghada said no, her father stopped calling. A year later, when the couple visited Lebanon, Ghada's father asked to meet Pierre's family.

This time, Pierre's parents threw up a barrier. They refused to meet, saying Pierre was too young and shouldn't have married a Muslim.

"I didn't expect that to happen," Ghada told me, "because we always said, 'I'll handle my side; you handle yours.' So that was a big punch in the face, and the shit thing is that my parents were about to accept the marriage, but now his father didn't want to accept it."

Despite this new hurdle, Ghada's parents met Pierre and began reconciliation. Meanwhile, her father-in-law started arguing that Ghada, who had been married to his son for a year at this point, was an unacceptable bride. It wasn't just "She isn't Christian," but also, "She doesn't know how to cook," "She doesn't know how to take care of you."

Ghada interprets her father-in-law's belated opposition as denial: "He thought his son was just having a fling. He thought he was playing around, that it would eventually end." His denial persisted for years. Once, when Ghada and Pierre were staying with her in-laws, they entered the living room from their bedroom and her father-in-law introduced her to the guests seated there as though they were unmarried, insulting her virtue. Ghada was hurt and offended by such attempts to deny her place in the family.

It took grandchildren to break the denial. By the time Ghada and I spoke, years later, she had a close relationship with her father-in-law. He's even admitted he was wrong for treating her that way. Pierre's relationship with Ghada's parents has also grown warm. But the respective in-laws have yet to meet, two decades later.

―――――

More than religious difference instigated Ghada's parents' rage and Pierre's father's denial. Her father's reputation concerns centered on controlling her sexuality; even dating was out of the question. His father's denial also hinged on her sexuality; he didn't acknowledge her as a daughter-in-law until she became the mother of his grandchildren. Women's sexual activity outside heterosexual marriage and reproduction was inconceivable. Daughters are supposed to preserve sexual activity for marriage, and sons are supposed to date widely, with the understanding that those girlfriends will never be appropriate brides. Patriarchy means that parents of daughters can't say to themselves, "She's just having fun with him" the way parents of a son can. For these reasons plus exorbitant housing costs, most Lebanese couples don't live together before marriage, unless they live outside the country.

Sonia was an exception. Trying to dilute opposition to her non-Druze boyfriend, Sonia told her mom they were living together, banking on premarital sex being worse than the wrong husband. "You do the big shock first, and then you do the little one," she explained. "And then you can say, 'It's a good thing I got married, right?'"

Her mom didn't take the news well. "She went crazy," Sonia remembered. "She texted me one evening saying, 'Are you happy now? I'm in the hospital. You're gonna kill me.'"

Then Sonia's brother texted her. "Don't look at mom's message. She's not in the hospital. She's at home crying, but she's fine."

"The faked heart attack tactic," I commented.

"Yes! A common tactic among mothers!" Her mother then tried the silent treatment for a few months.

Sonia and Ali were together for a decade before they married. She told her parents, "I'm getting married in Cyprus in a month. I've made your travel arrangements, and I hope you'll attend. It's your choice." Time had done its work; they attended her wedding.

During that decade, two of Sonia's three siblings had fallen in love with Muslims. Her sister opted to elope rather than endure endless arguments. Her brother converted and married in a *katab kitab* that their mother did not attend. And when we spoke, Sonia's mother was upset about her youngest child's Muslim partner, her last chance at a Druze child-in-law fading. She accused Sonia of being a bad influence. Sonia replied, "No, I actually succeeded where society failed."

Sonia's mother objected to both daughters and sons marrying outside their sect. Patriarchy isn't a reliable predictor of how a family will respond to mixed marriage. For example, Muslim personal status law forbids women from marrying non-Muslims, but not all families abide by that rule.

———

Tarek and Maya fell in love in college. Her mother knew, but Maya didn't tell her father. Growing up, they had regularly argued about the rule requiring Muslim women to marry Muslims. She described what she called her dad's "prevention strategy" to me:

"You can't marry someone who isn't Muslim," her father would begin.

"I can't marry someone like who?" Maya would retort. "Can I marry so-and-so?"

"Of course, he's Muslim."

"But he is an atheist, so what is the prerequisite? Does he just need to be Muslim on the identity card even if it has no meaning to him?"

"Yes, he's Muslim. He'll return to his religion later."

"There's no guarantee he'll return to his religion. What are you talking about? The identity card? Not the person's characteristics? Besides, if you wanted me to marry a Muslim, you should have sent me to a religious school, not [elite secular institution]."

After graduation, Maya told her father she wanted to marry Tarek. He replied, "No way, over my dead body."

"I'm marrying Tarek with or without you. I'm simply informing you of my plans."

Her father dug in his heels for a few weeks. His mother—a pious Sunni elder—changed his mind. "My grandma knew I wasn't the kind of girl to bring just anyone home and say I want to marry them," Maya explained.

"She knew me and knew I must really like him, and then she met him and liked him, so she told my dad she didn't care that he wasn't Muslim. She said, 'As long as they love each other and he's a good person, I don't give a shit about anything else because she could marry someone Muslim and be miserable for the rest of her life.'" Hearing this assessment from his mother melted Maya's father's opposition.

A Pew Poll conducted between 2008 and 2012 found that 30 percent of Lebanese Muslims said they would be comfortable marrying their son to a Christian, while only 21 percent would be comfortable marrying their daughter to one.[13] Given that the first combination is permissible and the second prohibited, this isn't a significant difference. Just as parents imagine the right groom for their daughters, they imagine the ideal bride for their sons.

Like grooms, brides should also come from a "good family," but until the later twentieth century, while education was appreciated, employment was irrelevant. Brides must embody femininity, have a warm smile and a polite demeanor, and navigate competing ideals for women. Some parents look for tastefully applied makeup, highlighted and straightened hair, form-fitting clothing, and heels. Others want modesty, looser clothing, and less makeup. One woman told me that after years of comments about her appearance, she eventually realized that her Maronite mother-in-law's objections to her had less to do with sectarian difference than with her natural curly brown hair and refusal to wear heels and makeup.

Brides must also be potential good mothers. Children of a mixed couple are raised by a mother from a different sect. For some parents, this difference is insurmountable. A Christian woman who fought to marry a Muslim was incredulous that her brother and his Muslim girlfriend thought they wouldn't face problems because she had "opened the door." As she suspected, when her brother mentioned marriage, their mother objected, arguing that a Muslim bride was worse than a Muslim groom. Many parents of all sects agreed, opposing son's mixed marriages because "whatever it says on paper, the mother raises the children. They will be like her."

Still, in most sects, it was easier, though not always *easy*, for a man to marry outside his sect than for a woman. This pattern fell apart for Druze. Druze parents protested their sons' mixed marriages as intensely and regularly as they did those of their daughters. Three Druze brides eloped. Three Druze grooms eloped. Druze women who fight their families to marry may think that their brothers won't have similar problems, but plenty of them do.

The Druze Exception That Proves the Rule

After Maya's father finally gave his blessing, Tarek's Druze family entered the fray. "As long as he was just dating, in their minds, it was fine," Maya mused. "He is a man, you know? He is enjoying himself. This old mentality. They were happy actually that he had a girlfriend. But when it became serious, they completely refused it."

Tarek's parents had never lived in their mountain village but were terrified about what family in that village would say about them. His mother called him several times a week in tears, begging him to leave Maya. She called Maya too, saying things like: "He's not rich, what are you after him for?" "He's my only son, and you're taking him from me." She threatened that they would never be happy.

The couple tried reasoning with his mother. They enlisted help from supportive relatives. Finally, they eloped and married outside Lebanon. Full reconciliation with Tarek's family didn't happen until Maya became pregnant. Soon after that child, the first of several, was born, the relationship grew warm.

"Now, it's love. It's all love!" Maya exclaimed. Tarek opened the door for his sister. It only took a few weeks for his parents to give her and her Muslim fiancé their blessing. And this time, "They went to the wedding! His sister married a Muslim, and they *went to the wedding*!" Maya exclaimed. "I tell you, our marriage created so much change for our families. It's unbelievable."

As for Tarek's parents' fears about what people would say, in the end it was fine. Only one great-uncle objected. Most people ignored the situation or kept their opinions out of earshot.

––––––––

When I first heard this story and others where a Druze man faced intense opposition to his choice of spouse, I thought it might reflect gender equity in Druze antagonism to mixed marriage—it turns out it's more complicated. While Druze parents do oppose mixed marriage for their sons and daughters to similar degrees, far fewer Druze daughters try to marry someone of a different sect in the first place. Patriarchal pressures prevented them from dating or made them hesitate before breaking the rules. This may be changing, as our 2018 data shows more Druze women in mixed marriages than Druze men. I also found that where a Druze person lives—village versus Beirut versus in diaspora—affects mixed marriage for women more than men. Women living in villages are under closer scrutiny than those in urban areas and less likely to meet non-Druze men. Urban Druze women, especially if highly educated, often feel like they have escaped the village sexism and bemoan the fates of cousins who haven't. But once a mixed couple moves toward marriage, gender differences in pressure fade.

Double Standards, Again

As Lebanese choose their spouses, they navigate generational and gendered social pressures. I interviewed both women and men whose families fought their choices. Though some men were disowned, faced intense battles, or eloped, adding it all up, choice remains more difficult for women. We shouldn't be surprised. Fictional and nonfictional heroines alike are the ones who usually fight for love. Think of *My Big Fat Greek Wedding. Guess Who's Coming to Dinner. Crazy Rich Asians. Fiddler on the Roof. Meet the Parents. Downton Abbey.* Even *Lord of the Rings*, where Arwen must give up immortality to be with Aragorn. And in real life, when Charles and Diana were allowed to choose whom to love, her storyline is the one with a heartbreaking end.

One way to measure generational change in the relative power women have to choose a spouse is by looking at the average age of marriage. In Lebanon, this was twenty-four in 1970, an increase from earlier decades, and thirty by the twenty-first century.[14] In the stories I gathered, the bride's age affected the degree of parental involvement or opposition. Age is also linked to financial independence. It's easier to refute your family's wishes if you can live without their support. Younger women are less likely to feel capable of challenging authority and less willing to risk damage to family relations.[15] Women who eloped after turning thirty told me it would have been unthinkable for them to do so at a younger age.

"I was one of those girls who wouldn't marry anyone for love against their parents' will," one explained. "That idea is unimaginable, literally. I wasn't an individual." Another spoke pragmatically: "No matter how much you know and love the person, if you don't have your family standing with you, then you are weak. If you get upset, you have nowhere to go. I'm not talking about divorce, just a fight or problem. You need your support system."

The combination of age and gender—the elements that make up patriarchal connectivity—is one reason parents oppose mixed marriage. Serene, a Druze woman, told me, "If you love someone and you tell your parents, it is like you blew up a volcano!"

Serene met Zayn at Lebanese University. Aside from his Shi'i sect, they had much in common: both lived through multiple displacements, disruptions, and traumas during the civil war. She was in her midtwenties when they decided to marry. When she told her parents, they wouldn't let her leave the house for two weeks. They raged and threatened her. Mediation efforts by siblings and relatives failed. "If you leave our home, don't return," was their final word.

It was midnight. A sympathetic uncle took Serene to his house. The next day, she went to Zayn's house. They couldn't afford to travel for a civil marriage, and Serene didn't have a passport, so they went to a shaykh's office for a *katab kitab*. Because she was Druze, Serene had to convert, but she didn't care. Zayn's family welcomed the couple. His mother understood what Serene had given up to be with Zayn. Serene's grandmother, aunts, uncles, and siblings all visited her the next day, but her parents didn't communicate with her for nearly a year. She wasn't surprised because she had never heard of a woman from her village marrying an outsider. "There weren't even normal love relationships, unless a girl loved someone secretly," she told me. "Marriages all happened the traditional way. He comes to propose at her parents' house, and they agree. And if they refuse, maybe she will cry if she wants to marry him, and then they agree. But she is always obedient."

Like Serene, several interviewees interpreted their parents' obstinance as a rejection of the idea that a daughter could decide whom to marry or fall in love outside a traditional family-sanctioned romance. "This whole thing, *all of it*, is all about women deciding for themselves," one woman told me. "You don't get to decide who you marry as a woman. I think people just have a problem with the idea of women leading their own lives." For her, the problem wasn't about *whom* a woman married, but about the act of making the decision itself.

At the same time, women in mixed marriages aren't upending patriarchal connectivity; they still choose heterosexual marriage, which keeps them within this relational system of entangled roots. They find a path through the tangles, breaking some rules, asserting greater control over their lives, and perhaps most importantly, *feeling* like they exerted their will because they had to fight their families to marry. In their stories, they prioritized romantic love and individual choice and viewed their marriages as love's victory over social norms.

When a couple is mixed, it is impossible to ignore the possibility that they married against family will. Mixed marriage shines a light on efforts to abandon, or at least dilute, family involvement in marital decisions. For couples who get a blessing, those family complications have just begun.

Three

How Will You Marry?

A bride and her future mother-in-law ordered wedding invitations together. As they inspected the final product, which were exactly what they had ordered, the groom's mother frowned. "We need to add *Bismillah al-rahman al-rahim* at the top," she instructed the printer.

This request contradicted the couple's explicit wish to have a secular wedding. The bride suggested they consult the groom, who was traveling, before making any changes. The groom's mother agreed. During the two days it took to confirm that the groom did not want to add the opening line of the Qur'an, his mother returned to the print shop and ordered new invitations with the verse. So be it, the bride thought to herself when she found out. What's done is done. Let's move on to the next thing.

That evening, she handed her father a stack of invitations to send to their side of the guest list. He frowned. "How am I going to distribute them with this written on top?" He imagined the faces of family and friends in his conservative Christian village when they saw the cards. "Please return to the print shop. Make our own invitations without the verse."

The bride wanted to please all the parents, so she complied. She left the print shop confident the problem was solved, unaware that the printer would call her future mother-in-law before placing the new order.

A few days later, the groom's father scolded the bride. "You can't do this! If your father has an issue with the invitations, he should talk to me. End of story!" He forbade her from interfering with the invitations.

She relayed the message to her father. "Please speak with my father-in-law directly and solve this problem." The men spoke. The bride has no idea what they said. In the end, her father accepted the cards with the verse. "Don't worry about it," he told her. "We will distribute them as they are. It's done." By this time, the bride no longer cared what the invitations looked like or even who was invited. She just wanted to get married.

————

Under the best of circumstances, wedding planning is stressful. While in the US, brides take center stage in a wedding industry that has spawned multiple reality shows, in Lebanon, the groom's family traditionally hosts the wedding. For mixed couples, lingering hesitations their families had about the match often erupted as conflicts over wedding details. Should invitations appear "Christian" or "Muslim?" What type of paper? What color? What font? Arguments about venue reflected the politicization of space in Lebanon, plus different ideas about how far guests should have to drive and whether weddings should be outdoors or in banquet halls. Alcohol was a conundrum. One couple returned from Cyprus to the surprise that their parents—all of whom drank—had decided their wedding celebration would be dry so pious Muslim relatives would attend. Another couple canceled their wedding after planning had begun because they couldn't manage different expectations around alcohol.

Several women I interviewed—and more of their mothers—harbored dreams of a bride walking down the aisle in a fluffy white dress, accompanied by her father, a princess wedding fantasy globalized by Disney. But where is that aisle outside a European Christian imagination of a wedding? Muslim *katab kitab* ceremonies are contract signings, usually attended by close family members and few guests. Most people join the celebration at the reception venue. Other traditions stemming from European customs include forbidding the groom from seeing the bride before the wedding and throwing the bride's bouquet and garter.

Some couples wanted the whole shebang, especially the *zaffeh*—the couple's grand entrance to the reception, often accompanied by professional drummers and dancers. Others wanted none of it. One woman vented, "Oh my god! We went through so many discussions where our families were like, 'This isn't the right way! You don't want a big wedding?' No! I *don't* want a big wedding! This is all shit. Come on, like in Lebanon you have to pay like fifty thousand dollars just to get married! I'd rather buy a house! It doesn't make any sense!"

Before the economic collapse, Lebanese weddings were extravagant. Parents fantasized about inviting friends to a gala. Trends came and went. Fireworks. Towering cakes. Fire dancers. Butterflies. Elite destination weddings in Thailand, the Seychelles, the Alps. Guest lists in the hundreds fulfilled demands of reciprocity and ensured that social and economic capital circulated. Banks gave huge wedding loans. To save money, couples with large families might levy a civil marriage into a smaller wedding abroad. Others "eloped" with their parents' knowledge. In those cases, the economic cost of throwing an appropriate wedding outweighed the social cost of telling people their child married without them. In other situations, the risks of dropping social obligations were greater than those of an inappropriate spouse, and disapproving parents threw a party to save face.

In the end, most mixed couples who married with a blessing—however long it took to get—had a public celebration. Weddings preserved dignity and smoothed social tensions. They provided evidence that parents weren't upset or ashamed of their children (even if they were). They reintegrated a family into society, however imagined their temporary banishment may have been. In the wake of family conflict, weddings were social bravado.

But first, a mixed couple had to figure out *how* to marry.

How Will You Get Married?

Jana's father asked the question a few months into her engagement to Khaled. "How will you get married?" Would they do a *katab kitab*? Or fly to Cyprus for a civil marriage? Would Jana convert? How would she protect her rights? What if they divorced? What if she became a widow? Most parents shared such concerns but rarely expressed them so clearly. Because Jana's parents were a mixed couple, they drew on experience to try to protect their daughter. Their questions were left hanging until the last minute.

Jana and Khaled walked a tightrope trying to please everyone. They wanted a civil marriage but were overwhelmed with the logistics of obtaining family registration documents and figuring out the paperwork. Her parents wanted a civil marriage; his wanted a *katab kitab*. Then her father changed his mind and decided a *katab kitab* would better preserve her rights as a wife and mother. It was all just too much.

"In the end," Jana recalled, "I told Khaled, 'You know what? I don't care as long as I can do the *katab kitab* and stay Christian.' And that's how we decided." Khaled knows this made things easier but remains unhappy about it. "I gave in," he told me. "Fuck it. But I would have been prouder if we had a civil marriage."

As the wedding approached, conflicts flared over the dress, the invitations, even the food. Then a final hurdle: Jana's father insisted on discussing every detail of the *katab kitab* contract with Khaled and his father, especially the two-part payment the groom provides the bride. When she learned about these negotiations, Jana put her foot down. She argued with her father about his interference, left the house, and refused to speak with him until the ceremony.

Looking back, Jana described the *katab kitab* as "a disaster no one talks about." The couple wanted to go to the shaykh's office with two friends as witnesses, but their parents overruled them and planned a small ceremony at Khaled's parents' home. The marriage contract disputes were settled that morning, but Jana was still angry. Her mother-in-law was also unhappy; she wanted a larger event with family and friends.

"There was no joy in the house," Jana remembered. "People asked me, 'Where are your parents? Where is your mother? Where are your sisters? None of them will stand by you?' And my father came but we didn't speak." The shaykh proceeded despite the tension. "And that was it. We got married." At the party two days later, the in-laws didn't speak much. "But we were happy!" Jana exclaimed. "We don't talk about those days. We don't mention them."

Jana and Khaled regret caving in to their parents' wishes and having a *katab kitab*. In 2002, they were the first in their social circle to marry across religious lines. A few years later, civil marriages in Cyprus were the norm.

Personal Status Obstacles

Lebanese inherit both citizenship and sect from their father; Lebanese women can pass neither on to their children. In addition to an identification number (like the US Social Security number), every citizen has a paternal family number listed on their registration document (*ikhraj al-qayd*), alongside their sect-based personal status legal category, marital status, and place of registration (which determines where they vote). When a woman marries, her registration and family number move to her husband's paternal family file.[1]

You can't just decide to get married in Lebanon, complete the paperwork, and have a nondenominational civil marriage. Unless you can afford to fly elsewhere, gamble on being able to register an online marriage,[2] or risk legal limbo by deleting sect from your identity documents,[3] you must marry via one of fifteen personal status laws that differ by sect and sex.[4] This means that a religious cleric must marry you, that someone might have to convert, and that matters like minimum age and prerequisites differ. For example, Muslim authorities require blood tests for genetic diseases like thalassemia; Christian authorities require baptism certificates. There are also different personal status court systems and procedures for divorce, child custody, and inheritance, compounding the problems Lebanese women face.[5] It's so complicated that one guide to marriage is seventy-six pages long, replete with "if this, then this" options.[6]

Most clergy insist couples marry according to the male partner's law. Ideally, the bride converts so that she and her future children will be the same sect. Quite a few parents also tell their daughters to "follow their husband." A few women, like Loubna, agreed. In her mid-thirties, she converted from Sunni Islam to Orthodox Christianity, with her family's blessing, to marry in church. Her age and financial independence, plus her acquiescence to patriarchal norms, smoothed her path. It made sense to both families that she would follow her husband. "Society, in the end, is patriarchal," Loubna told me. "You have to follow the man's religion. It's just easier."

Conversion isn't always easy and can be expensive. One Maronite couple paid four thousand dollars to convert to another sect so that they could divorce. Conversion can also jeopardize inheritance. A Muslim woman convinced her Christian fiancé's mother to drop the topic of conversion by saying, "If I convert, I'll lose my inheritance, but I will, if you want, as long as you give me the amount I'll lose." That ended the conversation.

Clerics don't approve of pragmatic conversions, though they know most conversions in Lebanon are about solving personal status problems and not a change of faith.[7] While it's easy to convert to Islam, the Christian sects' rules vary and the bishop in power shapes their implementation.[8] Clergy may deviate from their diocese. And despite official denials, some clerics accept financial persuasion to facilitate a marriage. Catholic clergy (including Maronites) will marry parishioners to a non-Christian (or non-Catholic partner or non-Catholic male partner—depending on whom you ask) if the couple signs a document promising to baptize their children and raise them Catholic. The Armenian Orthodox sect refuses to allow non-Christian men to convert and marry Armenian Orthodox women under any circumstances. Other Orthodox sects officially require six to twelve months of religious study, weekly mass attendance, and an examination of one's faith and knowledge before conversion and baptism. "Go get married civilly," one Roum Orthodox priest suggested to my research assistant. "It will be easier for you." And many did.

———

Nada's Roum Orthodox mother had her heart set on a church wedding. Nada's fiancé didn't mind as long as he didn't have to convert, because then he would lose his inheritance. The couple decided to register a civil marriage and have an unregistered church ceremony to make Nada's mom happy. Religious authorities in Lebanon thwarted their plans. No Roum Orthodox priest would marry them without the groom's conversion. Hearing that Protestants might be more open-minded, they consulted a minister. He agreed to marry them if the groom signed a document promising to baptize their children. The couple refused. They were about to ask a Maronite priest when Nada's father objected: "I've never in my life been in a Maronite church, why should I go to one now?" Civil marriage alone had to suffice.

A Christian woman tried to marry her non-Christian Lebanese fiancé in a church in Europe. She was instructed to obtain a document from her parish priest in Lebanon attesting that he had announced her impending marriage on three consecutive Sundays. She gave up and had a civil marriage instead.

A poor Armenian Orthodox woman told me she wanted to marry her boyfriend, a Sunni Syrian laborer who worked with her brother, in church. Her family supported the match, and her boyfriend was willing to convert. The priest wouldn't baptize him or marry them, so, out of options because Cyprus was unaffordable, they had a *katab kitab* instead. When we spoke, they were fighting with church authorities who refused to baptize their children.

———

Faced with this legal morass, most interviewees (79 percent) married in civil ceremonies outside Lebanon. For some, it was a matter of convenience, the less complicated option for those who could afford it. Travel agencies facilitated arrangements and guided couples through registration paperwork, a process involving the Lebanese Ministries of Foreign Affairs and Interior, the Lebanese embassy in the country of marriage, and notary offices in the places of origin of both the bride and groom.

For others, civil marriage was a matter of principle. "I would have had a civil marriage even if I married someone of the same religion," several people told me. One elaborated, "Neither one of us cared whether we converted, but why *should* someone convert? What would be the point? We don't believe any of it anyway." Several people had joined a Facebook group advocating for civil marriage, Tazawajna madani . . . w a'balkun, that formed when, during parliamentary consideration of a civil marriage law in 2013, Lebanon's grand mufti threatened to excommunicate the law's supporters.[9] "Within four hours," one of the founders reported, "we had thirty thousand followers."

People also chose civil marriage believing it would better ensure their rights. In theory, they're correct. Lebanese law holds that couples who register civil marriages conducted abroad with the Lebanese state follow the civil law of wherever they married for future matters.[10] That means disputes should be handled in a Lebanese civil court. In practice, none of the legal options solve the problem of women's rights in child custody and inheritance. Civil marriages where both people are Shi'a, Sunni, or Druze aren't recognized by those personal status courts, so one partner can turn to sect-based law during disputes even if the couple married abroad.[11] For all couples, unless the civil law where they married includes provisions about custody, it reverts to Lebanese personal status courts. In a mixed marriage, if a woman doesn't convert, she can't easily pass assets on to her children as inheritance or retain custody in a divorce.

Some couples consult lawyers or other mixed couples before marrying to understand these murky legal grounds. One person complained, "Every time we talk to our friends, we discover a new thing we haven't done yet. We don't really know the laws. We don't know how they'll apply because we hear a million things but don't know the truth." Another person panicked when I asked her whether she and her husband had planned their legal futures. "To be honest, we know nothing about this," she said. "We have a big gap in our knowledge. I'm afraid that God forbid something will happen and we won't be ready for it."

She wasn't alone. People often avoid thinking about nightmare future scenarios. "When you get married, you aren't thinking about anything else," another person said. "You aren't thinking about divorce. You aren't thinking about death. No one wants to think about death when they are planning their wedding! We just wanted to be together!" My question prompted her to put "Call a lawyer" on her to-do list. Others have had that item on their lists for over a decade. Even lawyers or activists in the civil marriage movement spent months working out legal details. "We all go to Cyprus and do this thing we believe in," one told me. "We have civil marriages, thinking civil is civil, you know? But there is a step that's missing, because there is no law here that fulfills the affairs of people who marry civilly outside consistently."

In addition to pragmatics and principles, mixed couples must contend with parents' opinions about how they should marry. For many Druze parents, civil marriage was preferable to their child converting. For some Christian and Muslim parents, civil marriage was as much or more of a problem than mixed marriage. One father tried to convince a couple to marry in Lebanon because "he just didn't understand the idea that someone should have to pay for a visa and a ticket and a hotel, and travel to a whole other country just to get married." Even if there were an easy, affordable way to have a civil marriage in Lebanon, many families haven't accepted the concept.

The Troubles with Civil Marriage

A Sunni woman had been in love with a Maronite man for years. Their relationship survived the stresses of international long distance. They chose civil marriage so no one would have to convert. Their parents concurred. Wedding planning went smoothly. A few weeks before the event, the bride's parents changed their minds and declared they would only accept the marriage if the couple also had a *katab kitab*. The groom would have to convert. The groom's parents responded that if the couple had a *katab kitab*, they also had to hold a church wedding. The bride would need to be baptized. Years of long distance couldn't break this couple up. Parental pressure did. They ended their engagement, both feeling the other person didn't fight hard enough for them, didn't love them enough to convert for their sake.

I don't know why this bride's parents changed their minds. Perhaps it was social pressure. Perhaps it was religious conviction that marrying without God didn't count. The groom's parents seem to have reacted to their stipulation. Fair is fair. A balance of impossible concessions, multiple back-and-forth conversions. Despite regular headlines about civil marriage in recent decades, a robust movement supporting it, and multiple bills debated by parliament, many Lebanese still don't understand what civil marriage entails. They remain convinced it is invalid, that these couples are living in sin, committing adultery. Religious clerics of all stripes foment these ideas to control personal status matters and keep the income adjudicating such matters generates.

Catholic and Orthodox Christian sects formally teach that civil marriage is adultery. Priests may refuse Communion and confession to people married civilly. In the past, some sects wouldn't baptize their children, though that has changed. Protestant sects accept civil marriage, because for them, unlike baptism and the Eucharist, marriage isn't a sacrament. It is a covenant, a blessed contract between spouses. One might expect that this idea of marriage as contract would make civil marriage palatable for Muslim clerics, but they concur that it leaves a couple unmarried and therefore adulterous. The Sunni grand mufti issued a fatwa against it, and the Higher Shia Islamic Council opposes legalizing it. Even the most progressive Shi'i interpretive school in Lebanon (that of the late Sayyid Muhammad Hussein Fadlallah) hedges on civil marriage. Fadlallah stated that civil marriage is acceptable for Muslim men marrying Muslim, Christian, or Jewish women *if* the conditions for annulling the marriage comply with divorce in Islam. In other words, civil marriage is permissible but civil divorce is not. And while Druze often choose civil marriage to avoid conversion, Druze clerics may excommunicate them, refusing to conduct burial prayers for both the person who broke the rules and their parents, in what amounts to spiritual blackmail.

————

Other than not knowing anyone in common when they met, Najib and Mira told a typical story. He grew up in a Druze mountain town. She was raised in a Beirut suburb, in a Sunni leftist family. Najib liked to catch up on work after hours in a coffeeshop in Mira's neighborhood. After seeing her there a few times, he worked up the courage to strike up a conversation. They began looking forward to running into one another and chatting. Eventually, Najib worked up another burst of courage and asked Mira out. Until she corrected him, he thought she was Christian, misreading clues from her name and accent. Mira, however, had immediately placed Najib's Druze mountain accent. She hesitated, remembering stories about Druze men who broke up with non-Druze girlfriends before marriage. But she liked Najib enough to date him anyway. A year and a half later, he worked up a third bout of courage and proposed, in that same coffeeshop. Mira accepted.

Their families knew it was coming. Najib prepared his parents early. "I won't back off from this relationship," he informed them. "We might break up tomorrow over a fight over the remote control, but we might not, and this might progress. I am committed to Mira, and the fact that she isn't Druze won't stop me." His mother spent the rest of that day in tears. Mira's mother also cried when Mira told her about Najib. Both fathers were more amenable, assuming class parity between the families and provided the wedding was a suitably grand affair.

Najib orchestrated a meeting between the parents to show them how similar they were to one another. It worked. Reassured about shared status, class, and lifestyle, everyone blessed the engagement and asked what came next. "When will you marry?" "How will you marry?" "We don't want you to convert to Islam." "You need to convert to Islam." Mira and Najib agreed to each handle their own parents to avoid drama.

Najib's efforts to convince his parents that he should convert failed. "Druze" to him was just a word Lebanese wrote on ID cards, but his parents couldn't wrap their heads around the idea. Other mixed marriages in their family were civil ones. Mira's efforts to convince her parents that civil marriage is a contract just like a *katab kitab* also failed.

After a year of negotiations, the couple needed to move things along. Najib had accepted a job in the Arab Gulf, and Mira wanted to join him. They married in Cyprus with a few friends and promised Mira's parents they would have an unregistered *katab kitab* afterward. And they threw a suitably grand party in their new country of residence for their families.

Several years later, they still hadn't done the *katab kitab*. To be fair, they tried. Mira's mother wanted it to happen in Lebanon; for her, this is a moment of social importance. But the shaykh she asked to do the ceremony insisted on registering the marriage. When she then explained the groom was Druze, he refused to marry them altogether and told her the marriage was doomed. Disheartened, she gave up.

————

Some parents feared both God and society. Jamil's Maronite parents were always polite to Randa, his Sunni fiancée, but complained to him privately. "This is going to cause problems in society. All these Maronite girls, and you couldn't find one of them instead?" In keeping with assumptions that a bride follows the groom's sect, they didn't ask, "How will you marry?" but rather, "Which church will you marry in?" When Jamil explained they were having a civil marriage, his mother exclaimed, "Why would you do that? It's so bland and devoid of any meaning!" Unable to envision the couple's atheism as an alternative to Christianity, she thought this meant her son was becoming Muslim, until Randa told her, "We're not being Muslim by not being Christian."

Other parents supported civil marriage in theory but wanted to avoid social outcry. Surveys regularly find that most Lebanese oppose a broad civil marriage law.[12] Relatives, friends, neighbors, acquaintances, and colleagues often asked couples or their parents, "Is it really a real marriage?" I heard about morning coffee gatherings where one guest scolded another, suggesting her child was going to hell because of their civil marriage. Several fathers worried about losing face among friends and colleagues if they permitted a civil marriage.

Friendships ended over weddings. In one case, when two Muslims got engaged, their mothers, who moved in the same social circles, disagreed. One wanted a civil marriage, the other a *katab kitab*. After months of argument, the couple flew to a country where they both hold a second citizenship and had a civil marriage that they didn't register in Lebanon. They returned and had a *katab kitab* they did register. A decade later, their mothers' friendship remains broken, and the couple is legally married under two different laws in two different countries.

They weren't the only couple to elope because of pressure against civil marriage. Dina didn't want to elope. She knew her Sunni family wouldn't accept John, her Roum Orthodox boyfriend, but he was perfect for her and from a similar high-status Beirut social circle, so she dated him hoping things would somehow work out. An artist who loves curating her vast rooftop garden, her whimsical ceramics interspersed among vegetables and bright blooms, Dina is always hopeful. Throughout her twenties, she ignored suitable Sunni grooms. When John proposed, Dina tried to tell her father. "It was impossible," she told me. "He objected, a lot, and the atmosphere in the house became unbearable. He told me I couldn't even marry outside my sect, let alone a Christian. He refused to meet John." Thinking for a moment, she explained, "He *had* to refuse to meet him, because if he met him, he was afraid he'd like him."

Dina's father's objection centered on the idea that because civil marriage was unacceptable in Lebanese law and society, the only possibility was a *katab kitab*. Yet he didn't he want John to convert, saying he couldn't respect him if he converted on paper to marry. Nor did John want to convert; he believed in civil marriage as a principle.

As months went by, Dina's hopeful outlook waned. "I thought about eloping then, but I couldn't. I didn't want to lose my parents and cause them pain." So she broke up with John. It was the worst six months in her memory. "Eventually I couldn't do it anymore. I missed him so much." She left her parents a letter and flew to Cyprus with John. After they married, they took an extended honeymoon, traveling around the world waiting for their families to calm down. When they returned, everyone in Dina's family greeted them except her father.

John repaired their relationship. Three months later, on Dina's thirtieth birthday, he visited his father-in-law at work. "It's Dina's birthday," John said. "And the nicest thing I can get her would be for us to all be a family."

To his surprise, Dina's father replied, "Of course, what do you want to do?" John returned the question to him, and her father suggested he bring Dina to their house for a surprise dinner. That evening, John blindfolded Dina and drove her around in circles before they arrived at her parents' house. Thrilled when her blindfold was removed, they had a pleasant, almost normal, birthday dinner.

In some families, two doors need to be opened, one leading to mixed marriage and another to civil marriage. When couples couldn't convince parents that a civil marriage was sufficient, they sometimes added a symbolic religious ceremony. Whether church ritual, *katab kitab*, or Druze blessings (in two cases), this compromise could appease religious or social anxieties.

Symbolic Ceremonies

To be fair to everyone, Hiba and Charles married three times. They found a shaykh willing to do a *katab kitab* without requiring Charles's conversion or registering the Muslim marriage. They found a priest willing to do a church ceremony without requiring Hiba's conversion or registering the Christian marriage. Then they flew to Cyprus and registered the civil marriage they had there with the Lebanese state. Marrying in triplicate proved a panacea for any dissent in their parents' social worlds. Each side told their people what they needed to hear: that the couple had married twice, according to their religion plus civilly. They left out the detail that the other family had also had their religious moment.

Years later, Hiba speaks openly about having all three ceremonies. Initially, when she told people, "I did all three, all three!" she was met with disbelief. "That's impossible, this one cancels that one, and that one cancels this one," was a common response. Yet as the numbers of mixed couples around them increase, Hiba and Charles have become a model for how to merge traditions. Their parents spend all the holidays with them as a mixed family. Their children are officially Maronite like their father but haven't been baptized. Hiba and Charles teach them both faiths and tell them they can choose when they turn eighteen.

Twenty couples had a religious ceremony in addition to a registered civil one. Like Hiba and Charles, two more couples had "all three." Most did so for their parents' sake. A few wanted divine sanction of their marriage, ducking into a mosque or church for a *katab kitab* or blessing while in Cyprus. Outside Lebanon, documentation for religious marriages was given to the couple, so they could rip it up or file it away. Inside Lebanon, it was complicated.

Religious clerics insist there is no such thing as "symbolic" marriage; marriage must be recorded within their sect's personal status court. This can cause problems if one person tries to revert to personal status law over the civil law of wherever they married. Technically, if the civil marriage is registered, it should take precedence in divorce, but this isn't always the case. For example, if a couple registers their Cyprus civil marriage with the state and also has a Catholic wedding in Lebanon, the latter will be registered with the diocese. If the couple later divorces according to Cypriot law, the church won't accept that divorce, making remarriage in a church impossible.

There clearly are clerics who will marry couples without having them sign paperwork or without registering it. I tried asking several priests and shaykhs if they would do so, and they all said no. My research assistant tried too. More refusals, even denials that it was possible. Clerics who marry couples without registering it are violating the law. But my interviews suggest that if you know the right person, or have the right connections, or pay the right amount, it can happen. One priest told a bride to pretend to sign paperwork without uncapping the pen. Couples found shaykhs willing to marry Muslim women to non-Muslims with only the groom's oral conversion. Some Christian and Muslim clerics gave marriage documents to the couple rather than registering them. These ceremonies were for God, not the state, and sometimes, for society. Very few of my interviewees registered religious marriages instead of civil ones.

"Choosing" the Religious Option

After spending a year convincing her Roum Orthodox father to accept her engagement to Ayman, a Sunni man, Suzanne spent another year navigating debates about how they should marry. She and Ayman didn't want to fight for a specific method—their priority was to marry with everyone's blessing. But Suzanne's father kept changing his mind about which type of marriage was better.

"One week it was civil marriage," Suzanne recalled. "Then the next week he woke up and said, 'Okay, since you agreed to marry a Sunni, you might as well have a *katab kitab*.'" He then decided that she should convert, telling Suzanne, "You follow the man. If you agree to marry a Muslim, you become Muslim, and you shouldn't have a problem with that because at the end of the day, your kids will be Muslim."

Suzanne didn't respond, but thought to herself, This is literally irrelevant. You want me to become Muslim, fine. You want me to become Buddhist, Hindu, whatever. I really don't give a damn. I just want to get married.

Ayman's father added to the confusion when, a few days before the ceremony, he approached her. "I gave the *'esmeh* to my wife decades ago, and my son will give it to you as well."

She had no idea what he was talking about, so she thanked him and reported to her parents. "Ammo said that Ayman would give me the *'esmeh*."

"What does that mean?" her dad asked.

"I don't know, I just said thank you and moved on."

Suzanne's father asked around and learned the *'esmeh* was the right to divorce.

Then Suzanne told Ayman, "You know your dad said you're gonna give me the *'esmeh*."

"What does that mean?" he replied, equally puzzled.

"It means I have the right to divorce you." She started laughing.

"Does it mean I'll lose my right to divorce you?" He was also laughing.

"I don't know, I think we both have the right to divorce each other now."

Sharing this conversation, Suzanne started laughing again. "It was a big joke," she told me. "No one understood what was going on. We just wanted to be done with it!"

The couple married at Ayman's parents' home with a few witnesses. Suzanne decided not to convert. Ayman's father arranged the ceremony with a shaykh he knew and debriefed him beforehand. "He told the shaykh that I am Christian and to cut back on unnecessary talk and tone it down. Basically, he told him, 'You have five minutes, get it over and done with.'" Honoring this request, the shaykh married them in ten minutes, her father-in-law thanked him, and Suzanne and Ayman were finally married.

———

Religious marriage was atypical among my interviewees. Eight Christian men married Muslim women in church; five of those women converted. All but one were working class and married during or just after the civil war. Eleven Muslim men married Christian women in *katab kitab*s without the bride's conversion. Five non-Muslim women (Christian or Druze) converted for *katab kitab*s—two out of conviction and the others because they thought they were protecting their rights. Three non-Muslim men converted to marry Muslim women via *katab kitab*.

Some of these couples chose religious marriage out of conviction. Most felt they had no other choice. During the war, it was difficult to leave Lebanon. One couple took a military helicopter. Another went by ship. Then and now, many Lebanese can't afford to marry abroad; even Cyprus is far more expensive than a small local wedding. Plus, not everyone has a passport. Some couples didn't want to wait for visas. Some found the bureaucracy too daunting to navigate.

People who married in Lebanon chose the religious option that seemed easiest, often a *katab kitab*. Unless the bride was Druze, she didn't have to convert. If the groom had to convert, it could happen quickly. And some believed it was the best legal option in a context where civil marriage doesn't clarify postmarital matters—an idea based on misinformation that paints a rosier-than-warranted picture of Lebanon's personal status laws.

Regardless, when parents *believed* religious marriage would give their daughter more rights, it was difficult to change their minds. The key appeal of a *katab kitab* was that stipulations can be added to the marriage contract—like the *'esmeh*, which grants a wife the right to request a divorce and removes a husband's right to unilateral divorce. *Katab kitab* ceremonies could be awkward when one father was unfamiliar with ritual details. "I remember, my dad went to the sharia court as if he was going to Mars. It was so weird for him," one person told me. They could also be occasions for laughter for couples unfamiliar with the process. Many Muslims, like Suzanne's fiancé, are as clueless about the rules as their non-Muslim partners.

———

Suzanne and Ayman have similar life trajectories as war-generation Lebanese who moved frequently. They met in middle school and began dating years later, while studying and working outside Lebanon. Suzanne believes living abroad was key: "If we hadn't nurtured our relationship abroad, there is no way it would have happened. We were lucky to have that space and liberty to develop a relationship that we believed in, before fighting with our parents." After several years, the couple made two big decisions: to get married and to return to Lebanon.

Ayman's family fussed but came around quickly. Suzanne's parents had a CV in mind for their future son-in-law. Not merely a good profession, but a specific one (doctor or engineer); not only Christian, but a specific sect (Roum Orthodox); not only Roum, but from a particular region (where they were from); plus an appropriate number of years older than her and able to provide well. Suzanne jokes that Ayman didn't hit a single mark on this CV. Relatives and her parents' friends took up a running commentary: "Do you really know what you're doing, *habibti*?" "This will be very difficult." "You're asking for trouble."

Mustering her own troops, Suzanne recruited an older sibling to praise Ayman to their father. Her mother switched sides, more worried that Suzanne would remain single or leave the country again than about mixed marriage. She played a typical maternal "filtering" role, channeling information selectively between her daughter and husband. Support from other family members helped. "I think my dad needed to hear from other people that it's okay, because he was venturing into new waters," Suzanne mused. "He didn't know how people would react. He was under more direct peer pressure than I was, so he had to sort of justify things."

All told, it took a year to convince her father to bless the engagement plus another year to navigate the details of the process. The couple celebrated their twenty-fifth wedding anniversary in 2022 and have brought their three children up to be, in Suzanne's words, "secular, to enjoy both worlds!"

———

To marry someone who doesn't have the ideal CV, a person must be ready for the fight. Some couples must also fight for a civil marriage. A few, like Suzanne, simply wanted to get married and cared little about the details. She sees the contradictions in how she was raised. On the one hand, she was encouraged to be educated and independent, to travel for education and work abroad. On the other, she was expected to listen to her brothers, help men in her family, and marry "well." Her father's insistence on a *katab kitab* was both an assumption that she would follow her husband's tradition and an effort to ensure her rights in a legal system where personal status laws codify gender inequality. This fundamental inequality between male and female citizens affects marriage choices, fights over mixed marriage, and capacities to fight for love in the first place.

Confronted with personal status law, family dynamics, and social norms, most Lebanese women pragmatically refuse to marry, or even date, someone of a different religion, to avoid problems.[13] Recent polls confirm their hesitations.[14] Recall the image of a cedar grove, roots entangled underground. Patriarchal connectivity is not a simple formula of top-down authority. Its power knits those roots together tightly. Entangled roots may form nooses that chafe and stifle—whether through guilt over failing to meet expectations or violent efforts to strangle or amputate anyone who tries to pull in a different direction. The power of family relationships, for better and worse, explains why so many women suppress their feelings and break their own hearts. It also explains why some wait over a decade to marry and others elope.

Four

Which Ultimatum, Elopement or Time?

Lama met Ahmad when she was sixteen. She was thirty-one when they married. Raised in what she described as "a pure Christian environment," Lama's Catholic family included multiple priests. She lived in a mostly Christian city, attended a strict Catholic school, and was in a Christian scout troop. On a high school field trip with another Catholic school, a young male student sat next to her on the bus and introduced himself. His name and accent told Lama he was Muslim. That meant he was off limits, even though they had a great time hanging out that weekend.

"I knew," she told me. "*Khalas*, no way, no way! That's how I was raised. My parents never said Muslims were off-limits. But you just *know*. It didn't even cross my mind to try. That was it, Ahmad is Muslim." Her hand traced a large X in the air as she verbalized it, "X! Even though I liked him and felt that he liked me a lot. But no way, no way, it couldn't work!"

The next time Lama saw Ahmad was during the national baccalaureate exams at the end of high school. Ahmad was dating someone else at the time, but when they said hello, Lama remembered the magic she felt on that weekend over a year before.

Several years later, Ahmad reached out. They were at universities in different countries, and he again had a girlfriend, but they struck up a phone friendship. "We talked for hours," Lama remembered. "Hours. But we didn't dare think it was more. We were just friends." Her thoughts occupied with Ahmad, Lama began to wonder if she was wrong.

Another year passed. Lama and Ahmad now lived as expats in the same city. They ran into one another at a café and made plans to meet again. After a few coffee dates, Lama wanted clarity. "When we're talking on the phone," she told Ahmad, "you make me feel like you want us to be together, but when I see you, you're dating someone else. You need to decide to be with me or not." When Ahmad said nothing to reassure her, she did her best to forget him.

Four years later, Lama was in a taxi heading to the airport when her phone rang. "I didn't call," Ahmad said, "but I'm always thinking about you. I don't know why we didn't see each other."

"It's too late," Lama replied, steeling her heart. "I'm moving back to Lebanon. It's always too late with you!"

This time, only a few months passed before Ahmad called again. He was in Lebanon and wanted to see her. Lama agreed to meet for coffee. As they talked, she learned about Ahmad's perspective on their relationship. While she felt like he popped in and out of her life, hurting her each time, he had been afraid she would break his heart because she wasn't ready to fight her parents for him. This revelation upset Lama, and she decided, yet again, to move on.

She tried dating a Christian. Her parents were outraged that he was of a lower social status and class background than her elite family. The relationship succumbed a year later to parental pressure and her inability to stop thinking about Ahmad.

As though he had a radar tuned to Lama's relationship status, Ahmad called immediately. "Please stop calling me. Please don't reenter my life," she pleaded, "I can't bear it."

"I never look back, but with you, I'm always rethinking everything," Ahmad replied. "We met at the wrong time, but I want to try again." He had also just ended a relationship because he couldn't stop thinking about Lama. "Please, give me this chance," he pleaded. "We've both changed. Let's try."

Lama remembers the exact date in 2014 when they reconnected. It was four years before she and I spoke, and they've been together since. "We put our hands together, and we said, 'Whatever happens, we will be together.'"

Taking advantage of her parents' relief that she had ended her last relationship, Lama told them about Ahmad. Her mom asked for his family name.
It was a respectable one. When her mom mentioned that she knew one of Ahmad's cousins, who had married a Christian, Lama breathed a premature sigh
of relief. But their mild response meant they thought Ahmad was a temporary
rebound. When her parents realized they had underestimated the relationship, their tone changed. They forbade Lama from visiting Ahmad abroad.
They pressured her to end it. They accused her of destroying the family. No
one stood by her, not even her siblings.

In her first act of open rebellion, Lama visited Ahmad anyway. When
she returned, she announced that she was one hundred percent certain she
wanted to marry him but wouldn't do so without permission. Their objections simmered in the background.

Ahmad proposed during their third year together, first to Lama, then to
her parents. They spoke openly for hours. He described his life and family.
Her parents shared their concerns—from wanting to baptize their grandchildren to fearing Ahmad's family would prevent Lama from attending
dinner parties with alcohol. They had seen Lama grow into a confident
woman and understood that her mind was made up. Ahmad struck them as
a responsible and caring adult who would be good for their daughter. They
gave the couple their blessing.

Until marriage was on the table, Ahmad's parents had stayed out of it.
Now his mother expressed fears that Lama was too independent and would
pull Ahmad further from their conservative milieu. The first visit between
families was nerve-racking. Lama's parents had never hosted Muslim guests
before. All went well enough, though it was clear the families wouldn't in-
tegrate smoothly.

As the formal engagement party approached, both sides pressured the
couple to change their minds. Lama got so fed up that she suggested flying
to Cyprus. Ahmad said no, insisting they would marry with their families.
The couple stood their ground as a united front, through engagement, civil
ceremony in Cyprus, and huge wedding back in Lebanon.

Today, Lama and Ahmad are loved by their in-laws, and their parents
are developing a relationship despite having "not a single thing in common."
Lama looks back with pride: "Our wedding was a message to guests from
both sides. It was a message to our families. It told everyone you can get to

know people from a different religion and they're amazing, that you should be open-minded. Is there anything better than diversity?"

————

Many of the stories in this book are stories of love against all odds, where people have crafted lives despite the forces working against them, their relationships strengthened in the face of opposition in what psychologists call the "Romeo and Juliet effect."[1] Most mixed couples break up when their relationship grows serious. A woman who broke her own heart by leaving a man she was in love with told me she never told her parents about him because she didn't want to see the looks on their faces. A man left his partner of seven years when his family threatened to disinherit him. Other couples broach marriage then crumble under the weight of disapproval. More than conflict avoidance, the desire to avoid problems is also a desire to avoid injuring one's parents.

By the time most mixed couples decide to marry, they have assessed their family situations and come to one of three, sometimes overlapping, conclusions: They won't have a difficult time convincing their parents. They are committed to one another and ready for anything. They are madly in love and proceeding blindly. Most who make it to this point believe their families are open-minded, are in denial about what lies ahead, or are ready to eschew social norms. It takes time. Over and over, I heard, "There's no reason to do this unless you're in love and you know you'll do anything to be together. You have to really want it. You have to really be in love and ready to fight."

Whether or not they see themselves this way, my interviewees are the brave ones, the rebels, the principled ones, the planners. Some were willing to give up their parents, severing roots if that's what it took. Many wouldn't cross that line, unable to bear the idea of causing pain. They played the long game, waiting to confirm their decision or ready for battle. Some couples broke up for periods of time. I heard about valiant efforts to meet a suitable partner, doing their best to stay apart before accepting love was fated, and years of on-again, off-again drama until someone set an ultimatum. Some women waited to turn thirty. Some hoped the fight would fizzle out. The stories in this chapter are among the most dramatic, yet they typify the kinds of struggles people faced and the strategies they used to be together.

Waiting Parents Out

"My parents are both Christian, but my mom is Maronite and my father is Syriac, a minority Christian branch. Here the story begins." Born and raised in a Christian town in the Bekaa Valley, Liliane moved to Beirut for university and stayed for work. In her midtwenties, she met Nidal, a Shiʻi colleague.

"We were together for years as very close friends, even more than close friends," Liliane told me, trying to explain their relationship that was not quite a Relationship. "We were committed to each other without having a clear definition to it. The truth is, you don't dare define it. You are in a kind of denial; you don't want to say it aloud." Her voice was soft but clear as she chose her words. "Usually if there was someone in my life, my parents would know, but with Nidal, my parents didn't know anything. I had other priorities. I was thinking about my career. And so was he." Still, Liliane saw Nidal every day for years.

When she approached thirty, she decided to tell her father and to leave the not-quite-relationship if he reacted badly. "My father was shocked," she remembered. "I didn't expect his reaction to be so extreme. He is open-minded. He is educated and educated us as well. He believes people are independent, that you choose for yourself. So I didn't expect my independence to be blocked when I choose my partner. All my life, I made decisions for myself, everything was up to me, except in this area. In this area, it was impossible that I was thinking this way. He was disappointed with my choice and judgment. He couldn't believe I was considering Nidal as a partner."

I asked Liliane how she responded to her father's disappointment. "I told him he didn't know Nidal, that he was a good guy and we had been close friends for years. My father fell silent. He is not a talkative man. He looked shocked and said, 'Baba, have you gone crazy? Or is something wrong with you?'"

Liliane's father grew depressed and stopped taking his medications. "Imagine the pressure I was under. My mother asked, 'What have you done? Your dad is going to die because of you.' I told her everything, and I was firm. I said they didn't have the right to behave that way." But Liliane didn't want to risk her father's health. "I didn't push it. I have a lot of respect for Baba. You know, there was a moment where I knew something was broken, and I couldn't repair it. So I stopped there."

She called Nidal the next day. "This is the last time I'll speak with you," she said. "And I won't answer your calls." Then she went to his house and said to his face, "This is the last time you'll see me. I will never answer your calls or see you, because if I do, I'll return to you. We can't be together because of religion."

It was Nidal's turn to be shocked. He didn't believe her.

When I asked her why she took this path, Liliane explained, "Because I couldn't live under two forces: an internal force that drove me to be with the person I loved and another force, which was my strong respect for my father. I didn't want anything to upset him. So I made a very hard decision."

Nidal asked Liliane, "Have you lost your mind? Is something wrong with you? What's this about religious difference? Do you, yourself, believe it's a problem?"

"No, I don't." She explained the situation with her parents.

"Have your parents ever met me?" Nidal asked, shocked and angry. "How in the world did you make this decision? Have you ever seen me do anything religious? Have you ever noticed any difference between us? This is nonsense! Ask me to become anything you want. I don't care."

But Liliane was implacable, and they broke up.

Nidal wasn't done. He visited Liliane's parents without telling her, just showing up at their door. They invited him in, and he told them Liliane had broken up with him, but he wanted them to meet him. Liliane's brother called her and told her Nidal was at their house. Her legs started shaking.

Liliane's parents explained that it was impossible for them to marry. Confident that Liliane would never elope, her father said that in the end, it was her decision. Nidal was mistakenly reassured, assuming that meant she would agree to marry him. "My dad said that because he knew I wouldn't do it without his blessing," Liliane explained.

For nearly a year, she dated Christians. Nidal texted her every day: "Even if you marry, I will love you." Or, "You're making a mistake."

In retrospect, Liliane reflected, "You know, sometimes there's a person you have a bond with, not just emotional but spiritual. I knew it was wrong to leave him, but I couldn't fight my family. My parents are very fragile and polite. They wouldn't be able to fight my aunts and uncles, nor the church near our house, nor the bishop who controls the community. I couldn't put them in that situation." She almost quit her job to avoid

Nidal, but instead transferred to an office outside Lebanon. That move was the turning point.

Nidal said he would travel to spend every weekend with her. A close friend counseled her to choose Nidal, assuring her things would be okay. And her parents realized how much Nidal meant to her. When she visited six months later, Liliane told her father, "Baba, you are my life. I make all my decisions for your sake. I will never marry unless you are okay with it. You know I've tried to forget Nidal, but I can't. Do you care for my happiness? *This* is my happiness. *This* is my choice."

Her father replied, "We respect Nidal. It is your choice. But please get married in a way that will not upset us or the family, because we have to live in our society."

Liliane was stunned and thrilled. She understood her father's request to mean that Nidal should convert. Nidal didn't mind, but when he contacted the bishop to start the conversion process, the bishop summoned Liliane's father to scold him. "Your daughter should marry a man from our sect! Your daughter is doing something very wrong! If she dies, we will not pray for her soul in the church!"

When Liliane found out, she confronted the bishop. Recalling their conversation, she told me, "The bishop said these things, unacceptable things that had nothing to do with reality or facts, things about the Prophet Muhammad, things a person cannot accept hearing. My entire objective was to neutralize him and show him that I am not someone you can speak with like this, to show him that Nidal and I are highly educated and we didn't make a rash decision. I reminded him that his duty as bishop is to facilitate our marriage, not obstruct it. I achieved my aim, but I made another decision on the spot. I decided not to let Nidal convert."

When Liliane told her dad she no longer wanted Nidal to convert, he agreed. He was also offended by the bishop's anti-Muslim rhetoric and thought Nidal's conversion would compromise the equality and integrity of their marriage.

A few months later, Liliane was about to turn off her phone as the couple's flight to Cyprus readied for takeoff when her father called. "I am so sorry we gave you a hard time," he said. "We made a mistake, and we hope you will forgive us." "You're the ones who need to forgive me," she replied.

Over a decade after their relationship began, Liliane, now in their mid-thirties, married Nidal in a civil ceremony. Her parents chose to stay home to keep up appearances as a buffer against social criticism. Extended family was split between people who wished they had been invited to the wedding and people upset about it. Liliane's father told everyone to mind their own business and threw the couple a party upon their return. "Immediately, everything was over because my parents have good hearts," Liliane concluded. "They love us unconditionally."

———

Time can be a tactic, a form of ultimatum presented to parents. A woman approaching—or better yet, past—thirty, can more easily convince parents to accept her choice by threatening to remain a spinster. Parents worry that she will be lonely or unfulfilled, miss out on happiness, or lose the ability to have children. One woman called it her "expiration date." Unstated is another worry: as a daughter ages, she is more likely to have sex outside heterosexual marriage.

For Ani and her sister Anjali, Armenians who both married non-Armenian Christians, age made all the difference. For years, their parents saw them coming and going with their non-Armenian boyfriends without comment. "It was a taboo in our house," Ani told me. "Sometimes, when I got home and went to bed, my mom would come and stand at the foot of my bed for hours, just crying, crying, without saying anything to me."

As Ani approached thirty, her father noted her upcoming birthday and that she was still unmarried. She asked him to meet her boyfriend, and said that if he withheld his blessing, she wouldn't marry him, but she also wouldn't marry anyone else. Her father agreed to the meeting, so Ani brought her boyfriend home for a visit. After the two men chatted for an hour and her father had asked all the usual questions, Ani and her mother found them on the balcony playing backgammon. Apparently, they had found enough in common to become kin. Ani's father gave her his blessing and told her sister to bring her boyfriend over. Ani knows her parents faced social pressure from relatives and friends. The sisters still avoid mixing their extended family with their in-laws.

Waiting parents out doesn't always work. One Druze woman waited until she was forty-six to marry the man she loved. He still asked her father for her hand in marriage. Her father still rejected him. They married in Cyprus without her family. As of this writing several years later, her parents are still shunning her. In lieu of waiting, some women use elopement as a threat. "I said to my mom," one explained to me, "'Do you want to be like those people, the ones whose daughter runs away and now they don't speak to her? I am telling you this is who I want to marry. I am telling you so we can do this with dignity, with honor. I don't *want* to run away to marry him, but you need to give me permission to marry, or else I will.'"

Some make good on that threat.

Elopement

Fadwa was fourteen when she eloped with her brother's friend, a nineteen-year-old Shiʻi Muslim. Her Maronite parents asked the authorities to retrieve their underage daughter from the groom's parents' home. When the police knocked on the door, Fadwa refused to return, saying it was her decision and that a shaykh had already married them. Had she accused the groom of kidnapping her, he would have been jailed. But she made her wishes clear, and the police left the couple alone. Almost half a century later, Fadwa thinks she married too young and wishes she had finished school first. She and her husband were madly in love—and still are—but, she said, "Love can't pay for food, for electricity, for anything. I had a difficult life. Any problems I have had in life are not about different religions, they are about money."

Fadwa miscalculated her parents' response to her elopement. She knew they would be angry but imagined a reconciliation a year or two later, when she had a child. It took a decade. Her family told people Fadwa had passed away instead of admitting the truth. Her father shaved his mustache, embodying the dishonor his daughter's actions had brought upon him. He visited her twice to beg her to return. Fadwa was moved by the intensity of his reaction—his missing mustache symbolized the family's wound—but she remained with her husband.

By the time her parents spoke with her again, she had three children. When we spoke in 2019, Fadwa looked back on her life of arduous labor with contentment. She takes great pride in her seven children and twenty-five grandchildren and is grateful they developed relationships with her parents before they passed away. "It was love. I don't regret anything. Even though we are old now, we still love each other. My husband loves and adores me. He can't be alone without me for five minutes. He can't sleep if I'm not beside him. We really love each other."

———

At its core, an elopement is a marriage without parental blessing or permission—usually, from the bride's parents. The stories I heard included twenty-three elopements, less than 20 percent of the total. Six couples married without the permission of either family. One man eloped without his parents' blessing; the bride's were in cahoots. The remaining sixteen elopements followed the traditional gendering of the word "elope" in Arabic, though they bore little resemblance to its connotations. The Arabic word for "elopement," *khatifeh*, literally means kidnapping.[2] When used as a verb, it is usually conjugated masculine to say, "He kidnapped her." A woman whose Druze husband eloped with her collapsed into laughter as she flipped the word around, saying, "*I* kidnapped *him*!" Elopement conjures scenes of a rider on horseback sweeping an unsuspecting woman off her feet and taking her to his village to wed. "Taking" a woman from her parent's home and keeping her overnight forces her hand because everyone assumes her virginity is in jeopardy. The couple must marry quickly lest she be "ruined." Mediators from the groom's family are usually involved in the process of reconciliation. Sometimes compensation is paid to the bride's family. Often the birth of a grandchild sweeps the remnants of history behind a new generation.

While this might seem exotic, there is a similar elopement narrative in English-language romance. Here it's usually class that divides the bride and groom. The heiress or daughter of an earl runs off with the chauffeur or a servant. Family members give chase and try to retrieve the young woman, again before she is "ruined." The longer she spends outside the home, the less likely her chances of returning with virtue intact. The pressure then shifts from trying to retrieve her to ensuring the man she has run off with "does the right thing" and marries her. Marriage partially reinstates her reputation and that of her family. Over time, and with the birth of children, she may be reembraced, usually forfeiting title and wealth. More contemporary American and English ideas about elopement highlight the romance of a couple marrying on their own, but families may still be upset to be excluded from the big day.[3]

One woman told me she hated the word *khatifeh* because it made it sound like she had no say in the matter. Despite its connotation of kidnapping, the reality is that brides have always been in on elopement. Earlier in the twentieth century, a young couple may have flirted through notes and glances for months before planning their escape together. I once spent a memorable evening with a fierce older woman who regaled me with tales of her teenage love for a neighbor boy in her village. She looked up periodically, as she diced tomatoes and chain-smoked Marlboros, to emphasize the intensity of their feelings. They never spoke, expressing their love for years through pauses under balconies, fervent glances, and love letters passed through cousins or left in a delivery basket. When she was sixteen, her parents found one of their letters. A month later, she was married to a distant cousin, living miles away from her love. Describing him to me in her seventies, sitting at a kitchen table in a country far from her natal village, her eyes held an emotion that had never quite left her. Had her parents not discovered their romance, this couple may well have eloped.

Most of my interviewees spent years arguing with their parents before eloping. Some then married with a willing shaykh or priest, cementing their relationship before God. Others flew to Cyprus to wed, informing parents afterward. And a few coordinated elopement with emigration, linking their newlywed life to new employment abroad while avoiding the immediate social fallout. Some of them said they had gone *"khatifeh,"* while others just said, "I left my parents' house" when they reached that point in the story, the meaning understood.

————

Nayla and Usama are second cousins who have known each other their entire lives. They grew up in working-class families in the same mixed village in the South. Their grandmothers are sisters and were both Shi'i Muslim until Nayla's grandmother converted to Christianity to marry a Christian neighbor. Nayla and Usama fell for each other when she was nineteen and he was twenty-eight.

They kept their romance a secret for three years before a neighbor told her father. He was irate. It didn't matter that his mother had raised him with both religious traditions. Nayla was shocked by her father's response. She tried to change his mind for a year before Usama informally broached marriage with him. Her father's refusal was absolute.

"So I left my parents' house," Nayla told me. One afternoon, she drove away with Usama, declaring their elopement. They stopped at the village shaykh's office for a *katab kitab*, then moved into the home they had rented in a nearby town.

Over the next several months, members of Usama's family, including mutual relatives, visited Nayla's father to discuss reconciliation. Her mother and siblings visited her in secret. They all thought it was a great match. It took nine months for her father to come around. A decade later, their relationships are normal. No one brings up the elopement. And Nayla remains baffled by her father's reaction.

Many people shared dramatic elopement stories with me:

"Maybe seventy or eighty years ago, my mom's cousin eloped on horseback with a Christian and her parents disowned her."

"I know a couple whose brother smuggled them out of Lebanon through the Damascus airport so her parents wouldn't find out."

"Forty years ago, a Maronite woman and a Druze guy from the same village ran off together, and the bride's father wandered around the area for a week with a double-barreled shotgun yelling, 'Give me back my daughter!'"

People telling me these stories often thought elopement after the 1990s was passé for urbanized Lebanese. They imagined it as village melodrama or a relic of an earlier era, an imagination quite far from the experiences of some of my interviewees.

When Dalia and Hashem met at work, she avoided his flirtations. "I tried so hard to avoid this drama, but I couldn't," she told me. "I had to follow my heart, follow the love." It took over a year for Hashem to convince Dalia to date him, and another two before they were ready to face their families. Hashem wasn't worried about his side; the door was already open. Dalia would be the first to marry outside the Maronite sect and anticipated a struggle. They were both right. Hashem's parents made a short-lived, pro forma effort to ask him to marry a Druze. But Dalia's parents and siblings wouldn't even consider the possibility. Facing this opposition, Dalia agreed to end the relationship but continued seeing Hashem secretly. A year later, as the civil war ended, she left a letter on the kitchen table for her parents, flew to Cyprus with Hashem, and got married. When they returned, the couple moved into an apartment together. Two weeks later, Dalia's sister or-chestrated a quick reconciliation.

Dalia understood what she was doing as eloping. Some couples who married without permission didn't think about it in those terms, while their parents did. Generational differences in expectations of the role family plays in marital choice show cracks in patriarchal connectivity. Elopement is a compound problem. A person is marrying someone their parents don't want them to marry. On top of that, the couple has broken all the social rules about *how* a Lebanese couple is supposed to get married.[4] Technically, my husband and I eloped, though we didn't understand that we were doing so. We lived in the US, and one day, we went to a courthouse and got married. We had our own reasons for the timing. Our parents knew we were together and wanted to marry, but we hadn't asked for anyone's permission. I learned we had eloped when my mom said, "What am I supposed to tell people? That my daughter eloped?"

My parents wanted a wedding. Other parents view elopement as a useful strategy to avoid one. Whether or not a couple is mixed, they might elope with a nod from their family. That way, parents can avoid the cost of a wedding without losing face. Some parents even bless the upcoming nup-tials privately but decline to attend the wedding to show their community that they opposed a mixed marriage while maintaining relations with the couple. A few fathers who were under intense family pressure to prevent a mixed marriage even suggested this idea. "Just go elope and spare us this drama!"

Fleeing Violence

Physical violence was rare in the stories my interviewees told me, playing a role in only a scant handful, usually as threats or warnings. In 2013, a Sunni man was beaten and castrated by his Druze bride's relatives; that story cir-culated in Lebanese media all summer. Castration is a form of gendered vi-olence, targeting a male victim. I heard a few stories of threats against male partners. While men are the targets, such violence is a response to the per-ceived violation of the bride's virtue. I heard very few stories of threats made against women in mixed relationships, though stories also circulate in the Lebanese media from time to time. Tanya was the exception.

Tanya and Samir fled Lebanon in the wake of her father's violence and are seeking asylum in the United States. A young Maronite woman with a warm, bubbly personality and indefatigable spirit, Tanya grew up during the civil war in a Christian suburb of Beirut. After graduating from Lebanese University, she met Samir at a pub with mutual friends. Almost a decade her senior, Samir hailed from a Druze mountain town. It was love at first sight, and within a matter of months, they were inseparable.

"We clicked from the first moment," Tanya told me. We sat on the balcony of a café in the US, a few months after she and Samir had moved here. "I believe in fate. There was something about him. My heart kept..." Words inadequate, she made a fluttering sound that matched a set of rapid hand gestures. "I think it was meant to be."

Tanya kept Samir a secret from her parents for years. "I knew they would react badly—they are super conservative—but I didn't anticipate the extent of it." She made eye contact with me and paused after each word. "Super. Extremely. Conservative."

As Tanya approached thirty, the couple decided it was time to marry. Tanya tried introducing Samir to her mom in a group of friends, but her mom ignored him. Tanya's siblings had already expressed disapproval. "You're going to kill your father," they said. "You're going to create problems at home."

Then Tanya's father saw the couple in her car. When she got home that evening, he was waiting. "He hit me, yelling and cursing, and then he threatened that if he ever sees me with Samir again, he will shoot both of us."

She moved in with a relative for a few weeks, hoping her father would calm down after his initial shock. When she returned home, she was careful never to be seen with Samir. But her mother didn't let it drop.

"I want to talk to you," her mom said one evening. She closed the door and asked Tanya to sit facing her.

"Who is this Samir?"

"He is my friend," Tanya replied, cautious.

"What does 'friend' mean? Does he want to marry you?"

"He is my friend. He hasn't come to propose, has he?"

"Your dad is threatening to divorce me."

Tanya reminded her mother that this was her father's usual method of proclaiming his unhappiness with a situation, but the conversation upset her. She called Samir and asked him to meet her at a coffee shop. An hour later, as they sat in a back corner sipping their coffee and chai lattes, Tanya's phone rang. It was an uncle on her father's side who had never called before. He insisted on seeing her, so she told him where she was and sent Samir away so they wouldn't be caught together.

When her uncle walked in, he sat down and asked, "Who is this Samir person?" without a greeting.

"He's my friend."

"Who is this friend? Is there more than that? Does he want to marry you?"

"He hasn't proposed, so how can I marry him?"

"I don't want my brother upset because of you."

Her uncle's questioning persisted, and she continued to deny that she and Samir were anything more than friends. Their voices rose, drawing attention from other café patrons. He finally stormed out, after having the last word, a death threat: "If we wanted, the flies would never find either of you."

Over the next two years, arguments with her family escalated. Tanya's mother begged her to end the relationship. Her dad threatened to shoot Samir. Her siblings used emotional manipulation. "Your mom is sick, she is stressed, you should leave him," said one. "You will kill your mother, she is going blind, her blood pressure is too high," said another.

During this time, the couple met once a week, far from Beirut. They trusted no one and began making plans to emigrate, saving up from their meager salaries. When they could afford airfare, they traveled on tourist visas to the US. Friends picked them up at the airport and helped them marry at a courthouse.

"I bought my wedding on the internet the night before," Tanya told me, laughing. "The documents, the dress, the cake. We ordered a white cake with cream and a ribbon with three sugar flowers. Samir bought champagne, and we rented a car. A few friends came, and we got married."

That evening, Tanya sent her parents and siblings a long text message.

"My dear family, I wish the situation was different, that you would all be with me and I would be talking with you directly. That we would have found a solution because you are my family and I love you a lot. Thank you for taking care of me, you taught me to be a kind and smart person, and to know what's best for me. Today, I made a big decision. Samir and

I got married, and I didn't want to wait to tell you. Samir is a decent man with good values, and I can see him as a loving and generous father with our future kids. He has rare traits I don't see in other men. I will be in safe hands with him. I hope someday we can talk again without any sorrow, and I hope you can see the situation from my shoes . . . I want you all to be in my life and my kid's lives in the future. I hope your hearts will soften and be open to a reconciliation soon . . . I apologize for the situation, but I don't apologize for marrying Samir. Dad, Mom, [sibling], [sibling], [sibling], you are a basic part of me. Please understand me. I don't want to be apart from you."

Her mother replied, "You are a liar. It's as if we didn't raise you. Don't think we will ever forgive you. This is the last time I talk to you, don't even try."

Her father replied, "Liar, dog, unfaithful one, I disown you until Judgment Day. May God send you far away, you are dead to me. It's as if you never came into this world. I wish you had never breathed air in this world. You are disloyal. And a person who comes into good people's homes without their permission [a reference to Samir 'stealing' her in the elopement] is a bad person who doesn't know good morals. I wish you bad luck in your life, and whenever anything bad happens to you, just remember that your dad is livid with you. You ruined our life because of a whim, you and this low bastard who doesn't have any roots. Remember that until the end of your lives. He deserves even worse words, but I'm not used to saying bad words even toward bad guys like him. Don't even try one day to come to our pure house. I don't know you anymore."

Her siblings warned her not to let their dad find out if she ever visited Lebanon.

The next day, Tanya and Samir found a lawyer and filed asylum papers.

After the wedding night text exchange, Tanya's father went to his village and mourned his daughter as though she had died. He accused his wife and children of helping her elope and forbade them from communicating with her. Tanya continued to text them regularly, and eventually her mother and sister began to respond. Neither knows the other is speaking with her again. Both fear her father.

Their extended families learned of the elopement via social media. Many cousins and relatives congratulated them on Facebook, but Tanya doesn't trust them. "You never know. They might congratulate you and say something behind your back," she said. The first time we met, less than a year after her elopement, Tanya shared these texts and posts with me. She was hopeful that someday, the situation would improve. "We have a plan, but not for a few years. And from now until then, my father can't know where I am."

The couple was waiting for the right time for some of Samir's supportive relatives to approach Tanya's father for a formal reconciliation (*solha*). They hoped a grandchild would help. Tanya joked that since her parents already had granddaughters, she would have to have a boy, the first grandson, to bring extra joy and facilitate her dad's forgiveness.

And indeed, a year and a half later, the couple had their first child, a son. When he was three years old, Tanya was still waiting for her father to cool down. She talks with her mom in secret, sending her photos and videos of her child. One of her sisters has emigrated to Canada, and Tanya hopes to see her soon.

———

Tanya and Samir made it to safety and received asylum in the US. I don't know whether her father and uncle would have acted on their threats. Family femicide, what sensationalist reporting calls "honor crimes," are less common than such reporting suggests. One study estimates that the rate of family femicide in Lebanon is one murder per month, about 1 in 500,000 women per year.[5] For comparison, a recent study estimates that one-third of women murdered in the US are killed by their spouses or intimate partners, at a rate of approximately 1 in 100,000 women per year.[6] Domestic violence and femicide are problems around the world that take different shape in different contexts, including in Lebanon.[7] While physical violence was rarely part of the stories I heard, it may well play a role in stories where mixed relationships don't make it to marriage.

As I listened to recordings of especially dramatic interviews again and again, and reread their transcriptions, I searched for clues that predicted how a family would respond or explain why some stories resolved with fewer tears and shorter estrangements than others. Clearly factors like whether the door had been opened, age and financial independence, and how deeply patriarchal expectations were rooted in a family structure mattered. But they didn't make enough of a pattern to be predictive. We have to factor in personalities and relationships with parents.

Tanya's father was the most extreme parent I heard about. Over the years, Tanya has tried to understand him from a variety of angles, on her own and with her therapist. Psychologically, she tells me, he is an abuser who was raised by an abuser. Politically, she tells me, he is a Maronite from a village devastated by Maronite-Druze violence during the civil war. Socially, she tells me, he is a man whose career requires violence and who has a reputation as a "strong man." I can't share the specifics of his job, but I can share an analogy from another career path in close relationship to violence: domestic violence rates in the United States are significantly higher in military families. The few instances of violence or threats of violence in my data all involved men in the military, police or security services, or the armed wing of a political party, highlighting how security apparatuses reinforce patriarchal violence and abuse.

Waiting versus Elopement

Personalities—of the parents and the people who wanted to marry— mattered. Consider this story of two Druze cousins, Samar and Nisreen, who took divergent paths toward mixed marriage in the face of parental opposition.

Samar met Firas first, in high school in the early 1990s. They remained friends through college and afterward. When Firas wanted more, Samar hesitated, fearing damage to their friendship. Eventually, she saw him differently, and their relationship took an intimate turn. Samar was raised with strict rules. Dating was forbidden. Firas never called the landline, only her cell phone. He picked her up and dropped her off a couple blocks from their building. Samar knew her parents expected her to marry a Druze man. Her mom's response to an elementary school crush was "but remember, you will only marry a Druze." Always one to follow her own path, she dated Firas, a Shi'i Muslim, anyway.

While Samar and Firas were beginning a relationship, her cousin Nisreen met Khalil in an engineering class. She was one of the few female students in the program, and Khalil liked her down-to-earth vibe and ready laugh. Having mutual engineering friends, activist friends, even relatives who were friends meant that they spent a lot of time together in their Venn diagram social worlds. Just before graduation, they started dating casually. Nisreen was clear that she wasn't going to marry him. She wasn't sure she wanted to get married at all. Khalil understood that Nisreen's Druze parents were unlikely to accept him, a Sunni Muslim, as a son-in-law. Friends warned him, "Nothing will come of this." And, laughing, "We'll help you hide her in the mountains if you want to elope." Had his own parents given him a hard time, he might have taken these warnings seriously, but they were supportive, and he really liked Nisreen, so he decided to see what might happen.

Both Samar and Nisreen's parents knew their boyfriends as part of their circle of friends, and both mothers figured out that that there was more to it. Samar's mom told her to end her relationship with Firas. When Samar continued to include his name when she explained her evening plans, her mom would retort, "I know you're really just going to see Firas" and pressure her not to do so. The more obvious the relationship, the more open her parents' objections grew: "You know our situation; you know where we come from." "You need to understand our family circumstances." "We can't handle this." They tried matchmaking. They noted that while Firas wasn't a believer, his parents were. "Do you really want to marry into a religious Shi'i family? What if he bounces back and becomes like them?" Samar ignored them while never admitting that Firas was more than a friend.

Nisreen took a different approach. She is conflict averse, unlike Samar, who had always been the rebellious cousin, sharper-edged and mischievous. When Nisreen's mom saw her with Khalil at a concert one evening, she began to question her about their relationship. Nisreen deflected and acted like everything was normal. Khalil called the house like any friend would and picked her up at home when they went out.

Facing intense opposition from her parents, Samar decided the only way she could marry Firas was if they left Lebanon. She couldn't handle the emotional blackmail. So, Firas found a job in Canada and moved, and Samar made plans to join him. Firas placed a transatlantic call to Samar's father to ask for her hand: "We love each other and want to get married, and if you agree to discuss it, I'll fly to Beirut. I know you are Druze and I was born Shi'a, but neither Samar nor I are Druze or Shi'a. We went to a secular school and university. We belong to the same culture that is Ras Beirut and secular.

We'll live abroad, where the extended family won't see us." Her father refused: "Even if you go to the moon, everyone knows who my father is and who my grandfather is in the village."

One morning soon after, Samar left the house as though she were going to swim laps, a recent habit. She left her parents a note and boarded a flight. The couple, assisted by friends, had worked out logistics, like airline tickets and a fiancé visa. Before her plane landed in Montreal, Firas's phone was ringing nonstop. Samar's parents had informed his family. Firas' parents disapproved of elopement and were nervous about a Druze woman raising their grandchildren. Both sides tried to convince the couple to change their minds. Samar and Firas ended the pressure by getting married, making their elopement a done deal.

It took a year for Firas' parents to normalize relations with the eloped couple and for Samar's mother to embrace her during an emotional reunion in Beirut. "I don't endorse what you did, but you're my daughter, I miss you, I can't live without seeing you." Samar saw her mom and siblings on each visit to Lebanon, but her dad was intransigent. While he missed his daughter, he was under intense pressure from senior male relatives to refuse reconciliation.

Any fleeting thought of elopement Nisreen may have entertained vanished when she saw the effect of Samar's elopement on her aunt and uncle. She didn't want to lose her parents or Khalil. Plus, she was skeptical of marriage as a patriarchal institution. So, she waited and let the status quo stand.

Five years into their relationship, Khalil convinced Nisreen that marriage was their most pragmatic option given that they spent all their time together. He asked Nisreen's father when his parents could come for a visit. When her father laughed and tried to evade the question, Khalil interrupted him. "My parents want to meet you, do you want me to tell them, 'No, they can't come visit'?" Unable to refuse without being rude, Nisreen's father acquiesced. The timing, over a year after his niece's elopement, helped, and he appreciated that Khalil "entered through the door, not the window." Khalil instructed his parents not to discuss marriage during the visit, but just to go and meet Nisreen's parents. He initiated the traditional process toward engagement without explicit discussion of what was happening, which left no room for explicit objections.

Over the next several years, Nisreen and Khalil completed graduate degrees and built their careers in two different countries, maintaining their relationship long-distance. Nisreen's parents urged her to meet other people. She never argued but continued to date Khalil. They coordinated their visits to Lebanon and were a regular presence in both family homes.

Eight years after Samar eloped, she forced her father's hand by ringing their doorbell one afternoon. Her father teared up, speechless. She told him how she was doing and began to melt the ice between them. It took time. Samar stayed in touch, and everyone went on a family vacation together a few years later. This time, she had not only Firas, but also a toddler in tow, her parents' first grandchild. By the end of the vacation, it was as if nothing unusual had happened.

Relatives were a different matter. Samar's mother had been telling people for years that she was studying abroad. When Samar pointed out that had she been pursuing a PhD, she would have been long done, plus a toddler was difficult to hide, her mom started sharing the news selectively. Word spread through family networks. Relatives on the maternal side of the family accepted Samar's marriage. The paternal side did not, though Nisreen's father said little, well aware of his own daughter's inappropriate partner. Several paternal elders held Druze religious positions. As they passed away, social pressure lessened but never disappeared. To date, Samar's father hasn't announced her marriage in the village. Samar's and Firas's parents have never met, but their mutual opposition to the elopement ensured mutual respect. Living abroad, the couple doesn't have to bring their families together. Each has embraced their child's spouse and their grandchildren, and that's enough.

Meanwhile, Nisreen and Khalil arrived in their midthirties and survived eight years of long distance. It was obvious they would marry. Nisreen's parents had resigned themselves and wanted her to be happy. Privately, they treated Khalil as her fiancé. At dinner one evening, Khalil told them he was moving to the US to join Nisreen. The couple had already handled the legal logistics of his immigration. Nisreen's father said it was a good move and wished them the best. Marriage was assumed but never discussed. On future visits to Lebanon, the couple stayed together in their own Beirut apartment. Over time, Khalil began meeting Nisreen's extended family. He already knew Samar (and Firas) plus some open-minded cousins in Beirut. As with

Samar, Nisreen's mother's side welcomed them, and it remains unclear what her more conservative paternal relatives even know. Nisreen's father is embedded in the same village-family social and economic networks as Samar's father. Unwilling to risk damaging those networks, he has never introduced Khalil as kin. Since the marriage, their parents socialize occasionally and bond over their dismay that the couple remains childless.

––––––––

Samar, Firas, Nisreen, and Khalil grew up in the same neighborhood in Beirut during the city's golden 1990s, a bridge between the civil war and the political-sectarian tensions that emerged in 2005. They attended similar private elite secular schools and universities, had mixed friendship groups, and are all nonreligious, whether anti religion, atheist, areligious, or agnostic. From the same extended family on their fathers' side, the two women faced similar dynamics. To this day, each prefers the path she took. Samar regrets causing her parents pain but believes elopement was her only option. Nisreen defaulted to waiting. One forced her parents to confront her marriage, beginning her married life without them. The other delayed marriage for well over a decade until her chosen match was the only imaginable future. One sacrificed peace for time; the other time for peace. Both gave their parents ultimatums, and both have strong relationships with them today. As cousins, Samar's prying open the door and Nisreen's slow saunter through it have smoothed the path for future mixed marriages in the extended family. Personality, the minutiae of relationships, and the ideas their partners brought into the fold shaped each trajectory.

By the time I spoke with them, years had passed, and the cousins could look back with analytic eyes at their stories. Puzzled by the intensity of their secular Druze family opposition, I pushed our conversation deeper. Samar's father's comments highlighted worries about elders with key religious roles. Nisreen's father focused on the loss of social-economic networks. In this extended Druze family at the turn of the twenty-first century, powerful elders, entangled family finances, close relationships with relatives in the village, and norms of Druze endogamy combined into pressure so powerful that these Beirut-based parents could not fathom surviving it. Despite their gender, these fathers were caught in the generational power of patriarchal connectivity. For them, as for many parents, it was the fear of social consequences that motivated their refusal to accept a son-in-law from a different sect.

Parental objections to mixed marriage show us that the problem isn't always or only sect. Women making decisions about whom to marry is a factor. Idiosyncrasies clearly play a role. And perhaps the most powerful factor of all is status anxiety. Status anxiety provides the framework that holds the meanings people add to the category of sect.

Five

It's All about Status

Joulia described her journey from meeting Louay to marriage one afternoon as we sat in her cheerful Beirut office. Even recalling painful moments, she smiled, her animated gestures matched by the sunlight streaming through the swirling colors of our mugs of herbal tea.

After years of friendship that began at the American University of Beirut (AUB), romance blossomed in their late twenties. Joulia knew her Maronite parents would disapprove. They had crushed her siblings' relationships with non-Christians. "It was unthinkable," she said. "The whole family tree on my father's side is Christian. The whole family tree on my mom's side is Christian. Anytime it comes up, someone says, 'Eh, friends okay, but we don't marry them.' It's explicitly verbalized. 'We don't marry Muslims.' Their friends are all religions, but no one is married outside their religion." But like many interviewees, Joulia had always charted her own path and didn't care that Louay was officially Shi'a.

When her parents sensed the relationship, their resistance began: "Who is this? Why does he come over? We don't want to hear that you are more than friends! He's a nice guy, but nothing more! Do you understand? Nothing more!" Joulia denied everything, unwilling to fight until she knew Louay was worth it. A year later, she told them. "It got ugly for three years," she recalled. "You know the stages of grief? Shock, denial, bargaining, depression. There was no acceptance until the wedding. It was a nightmare."

Her parents tried everything. "You are going to give me a heart attack!" "This is not something we do!" "You'll be the end of me!" "It's either us or him." "You won't be our child anymore." The silent treatment. Matchmaking.

Joulia tried rational arguments. "We're both from Beirut." "We went to the same schools." "We know the same neighborhoods." "We have the same background." Nothing worked.

Her parents changed tactics. "What about the kids?"

"We share the same flexibility about religion. The kids will be like us."

"Why doesn't he convert?"

"Because it would be inauthentic and unfair to his parents."

"What about future problems?"

"We'll handle them."

Finally, her parents arrived at the crux of the matter: "What will people say about us?" Joulia's father's reputation was at stake, and he dug in his heels.

Two and a half years later, Joulia was fed up. She told her mom she was getting married that summer in Cyprus and hoped her parents would be there. "Either you lose a child, or you lose your narrow ideas. This is bullshit," she declared.

"Over my dead body," her mother replied.

Calling her bluff, Joulia started packing a suitcase. Her mother stopped her before she left the house. From that moment on, she was on board, even paying for Joulia's wedding dress.

But her father didn't budge. He avoided Louay's attempts to meet with him to propose. One day, Louay just knocked on the door. He sat in the living room, accepted a cup of coffee, and said, "You've been torturing Joulia for three years. It's enough! We're going to marry."

"Yes, but our family . . ." Joulia's father began.

"But she is *my* family."

The interruption snapped her father's fuse. The men began yelling at each other, in what seemed to be the final straw.

The couple married in Cyprus without his permission and threw a big wedding in Lebanon. Joulia's father hovered in the background. When they cut the cake, guests asked where he was. Someone fetched him and he accepted a plate from his daughter. "And suddenly, we were standing there, me, Louay, and my dad, eating cake and drinking champagne. I don't know what happened! I don't know what to say!" Joulia threw up her hands in laughter.

Joulia and I share a good guess as to what happened. Her father's panic about the social consequences of her marriage subsided when he saw his friends and family raising their glasses to toast the couple. His primary fear was that the marriage would jeopardize his status. When he realized he was secure, he accepted Louay. As this chapter shows, status anxiety is a potent catalyst for myriad parental tactics against mixed marriage, the most common catalyst across stories.

Elite Exceptions

Joulia's father is an urban professional whose reputation rests on the status he built for himself through his career. People outside society's upper crust who have earned their status through income or professional reputation are more likely to worry that their child's mixed marriage will damage their social worlds. The instability of the status earned in a single generation, or even two, tells us that status adheres to extended families over generations. Elite exceptions to mixed marriage rules highlight continuities of privilege.

Lebanon's political and economic elite have long intermarried. Druze political leader Walid Jumblatt and his son Taymour, prominent Orthodox newspaper editor and politician Ghassan Tueni, and many heirs to political power—including the son of Prime Minister Najib Mikati, the son of Maronite party leader Sleiman Frangieh, and Samy Gemayel, who is the son and nephew of two former presidents—have all married women of a different religion, though Gemayel's wife may have converted. I heard multiple versions of a joke where, when a shaykh tries to stop Jumblatt's wedding, Jumblatt retorts, "From the waist up is yours and from the waist down is mine."

It's harder for women. Tueni's granddaughter, parliament member Nayla Tueni, kept her civil marriage to a Shi'i media personality quiet until after she was elected in 2009. Lebanese American Rima Fakih, Miss USA 2009, converted from Shi'i Islam to Maronite Christianity to marry a wealthy Lebanese Canadian music producer. And in 2022, Jumblatt's daughter, Dalia, married Joey Al-Daher, the son of a powerful Maronite media mogul. Rumor has it Jumblatt asked the couple to postpone their engagement until after the 2022 parliamentary elections to avoid political blowback. Despite these gender differences, for elites, sectarian difference is often irrelevant provided status is maintained.

An elite woman whose mixed marriage was routine explained, "My family has been mixed forever, so none of this stuff matters to us." Another said my project was irrelevant because her family and other elite families "have always mixed easily with one another, like Europeans." Some of these families have been connected for generations in political and economic alliances forged through marriage, alliances that served their financial interests and helped them bleed the country into economic collapse. Others aren't part of the public-facing political elite but hold colossal intergenerational wealth in transnational family networks.

———

The first thing Fadi said to me, in English, was, "Let me give you a heads up. Our families aren't traditional, we're kind of *extra*."

From a cosmopolitan Druze family, Fadi spent his childhood abroad before returning to live between Ras Beirut and his parents' village. Soon after meeting Isabella at a party, he introduced her to his parents, saying she was "the one." When he took her to meet family elders, no one asked about her background. Isabella hails from a wealthy cosmopolitan Roum Orthodox family living across Europe and the Middle East. Fadi's family knew she was of similar social status. That was sufficient and in keeping with their marriage practices.

Isabella had a slightly harder time. When she told her father about Fadi, he frowned. "Is this necessary?" But he agreed to meet Fadi and his family and spent a few months investigating them through mutual social networks. Isabella promised to baptize their officially Druze children and allow them to choose a religion when they turned eighteen. As soon as her father's research reassured him of Fadi's status, he told Isabella to proceed. The couple had a civil ceremony in Cyprus and an extravaganza in Lebanon, replete with traditions but no religion.

Fadi and Isabella hail from elite families where both reputation and wealth are inherited. Gender difference required Isabella's father to verify

Fadi was an appropriate groom. Patriarchal norms hold that it is unacceptable for a woman to marry into a "lower" family; a man may marry "down" if the bride is young and attractive. As one mother, still smarting from her daughter's marriage, told me, "They gained a girl like my daughter for their family. *They* moved up."

———

Some parents link status to socioeconomic class. Like Americans, Lebanese often talk about class indirectly. Multiple mothers, patiently explaining to me why a daughter was about to make a terrible mistake, said, "There are certain *standards*," and then referred to "lifestyle" while naming expensive restaurants or beach clubs. To be fair, many upper-class or upper-middle-class women in mixed marriages shared this sentiment with their parents. "I don't care about religion," one said, "but obviously I wouldn't marry someone who's *that* different from me. It's not like my husband's parents are peasants or workers. They're educated. We have stuff in common."

Rawan, one of the most down-to-earth women I interviewed, is among the few who said she didn't care about class. She fell in love at eighteen with Richard, a new employee in her Sunni father's business. From a lower-class Roum Orthodox background, Richard never graduated from university. Rawan's parents griped about the relationship for eight years but didn't prevent her from seeing him. Her father liked the young man but expected her to marry a social equal. Richard's family accepted Rawan; the match afforded him class mobility and the door was already open. Richard wanted to elope, but Rawan opted to wait for her parents to worry that she would never marry. Her gamble paid off. As she approached thirty, they agreed to the match.

Other upper-middle-class or elite women I interviewed used status anxiety to their advantage. When pressured to end a mixed relationship, they dated people of the right sect but the wrong class. One went out with a trainer at her gym. Another with a car mechanic. Another with a line cook in a local restaurant. Their stunned parents quickly concluded that these sect-appropriate partners were not better matches for their daughters. Whether or not they intended to force their parents' hand by showing them "it could be worse," dating "down" had the desired effect. One woman told me, shaking her head in exhausted disbelief, that when her parents finally met the man from a different religion whom she had wanted to marry for years, they were overjoyed because "they were of the same standard." Other couples highlighted class similarity between their families as smoothing their paths.

Most marriages where status was a concern involved ideas about social hierarchy that didn't reflect vast economic divides. A long-established elite family might object to a marriage to a doctor or engineer, for example, but rarely did I hear about a marriage connecting a professional family to a working-class one. Lebanon's extreme class polarization and segregation stifles social mixing; most Lebanese can't fathom marriage across class extremes. When such couples meet, they rarely marry. Hala was an exception.

————

Before I could set up my recorder, Hala began speaking. "I married Malek, but I also eloped with him." Puzzled, I asked her to go on. But first, Hala wanted to tell me her parents' story. I was struck by how young she looked, given that I knew her adult children. We sat in the living room of her large apartment in an old Beirut building as she spoke effusively.

Hala's parents eloped as teenagers in the 1950s. Her father tried proposing, but her maternal grandfather rejected him because they were too young, financially insecure, and of different religions. When they ran off together, he disowned Hala's mother and forbade anyone in the family from seeing her. The young couple lived with Hala's paternal grandparents until graduating from high school and having their first child. Hala's maternal grandmother and uncles visited her mother secretly. By the time Hala was born a decade later, those visits were no longer clandestine, but her grandfather didn't join them for another ten years.

Meanwhile, Hala's father's career had catapulted him into Beirut's elite circles. Their household celebrated Christian and Muslim holidays and held lavish dinner parties. Hala attended private secular schools, then enrolled in an elite university. Classes had barely begun when she fell in love with Malek, a Druze tradesman without a college education fifteen years her elder. Hala paused her narration. "Before I continue," she said, "let us be clear. This is not a story where religion is the obstacle. It's a story of age and a story of social status. But I fell in love with my husband."

Hala met Malek when he was working at her parents' home. They eloped—or tried to—less than a year later. "My father heard Malek was hanging around me and forbade him from entering the house. I had just turned eighteen. I knew he would never approve. So, I eloped for two hours. I mean, I left my house, we went to the shaykh, Malek converted, and we were about to have a *katab kitab*. But the shaykh knew me. He wasted time while he sent word to my father. We sensed something strange, so we ran. My father sent armed men after me."

Malek's friends hid Hala at a hotel with a female chaperone, but her uncle found her. "We were caught. My uncle told me my father had collapsed; he had a nervous breakdown. He made my mother remove my pictures from the house. He said, 'I no longer have a daughter.' It took only two hours for him to collapse into tears. 'Return my daughter to me and whatever she wants will happen. I will let her marry him, but she will not elope.'"

So, Hala returned home to speak with her father. He told her, "I will approve of your marriage, but you better make it succeed because I'll be the first to blame you if it fails. I won't take pity on you if you've made a bad choice. You will take responsibility for what you have done." Hala nodded.

Hala's father didn't want the world to know his daughter had tried to elope. To save face and protect his social status, he orchestrated a formal proposal. He ordered Hala's uncles and grandparents to attend, and that evening, Malek brought family members over to ask for Hala's hand. Her father accepted on condition she graduate from university. He threw the couple an engagement party followed by a *katab kitab* and gala wedding with prominent guests. Malek declared his conversion to Islam and the couple was married with fanfare. "The train of my wedding dress was six meters long," Hala remembered. "Six girls held the dress."

Despite this public display of approval, Hala's father believed Malek stole her from the family. She has female relatives married to non-Muslims with no drama, but their spouses were from known families. Not only was Hala's father worried about her youth, but he was also upset that Malek was a working-class groom. "It's all about what society will say," Hala concluded. "My father wouldn't risk people saying his daughter had eloped, so he created this whole wedding extravaganza." If the prospect of his daughter marrying a working-class man was bad, the public shame of an elopement was worse.

By publicly lauding the couple, Hala's father used his status to force others to accept an unacceptable groom. He could do so because of that social status. Joulia's father may well have had that kind of power, but he didn't believe he did. His status anxiety paralyzed him, and he needed proof of social approval before accepting his daughter's marriage. Joulia's father is a well-to-do professional; Hala's is among the economic elite.

The Class-Sect Nexus

Social *status* is about more than socioeconomic class. It sometimes seems like Lebanese society is made up of thousands of microcosms, each with its own ideas about who counts as "people of our status." In each microcosm, class, sect, region of origin in the country, education, and family reputation form a tangled set of criteria people use to assess one another. As a criterion on its own, sect is flimsy; blurred with class, it gains strength.

Class and sect have long been enmeshed in Lebanon.[1] Some parents complained about a potential in-law's sect when they were upset about class difference. Others assumed a family was of lower class *because* of their sect, drawing on stereotypes. I lost count of how many interviewees said something like "Maronites are to Roum Orthodox as Shi'a are to Sunni." Depending on the stereotypes you use to decode this analogy, the speaker could be calling Roum and Sunni higher status because they are associated with being professional, urban, and elite, or prioritizing Maronites and Shi'a as warmer and more open-minded because they are less haughty and full of themselves. Druze are often a puzzle, stereotyped as either dangerous or worldly, depending on who you ask. It's possible Isabella's father was skeptical of Fadi's elite status because he was Druze.

Class and status are linked to education in gendered ways. Women's parents usually shunned suitors less educated than their daughters and were pleased if a groom was more educated. Men's parents usually saw a more educated bride as a path to social mobility for their son. One mother revealed her assumptions about sect, education, and status by saying, "My son's wife is Muslim, but she isn't like them. She and her family are very educated. She's doing a PhD, and she's ambitious."

Some Lebanese think that changes in the middle class after the civil war disrupted historical associations between class, sect, and status. A Christian man expounded at length on his idea that professions like medicine, engineering, law, and pharmacy no longer carried as much cultural capital as they once did. He bemoaned the growth of "a new middle class that has wealth with no class." Never explicit, his commentary referred to the recent upward mobility, spurred by education and remittances, of many Shiʻi Muslims. Entrenched stereotypes about Shiʻa—the group most commonly perceived as lower status and lower class—prevented him from allocating the same value to the degrees and careers of Shiʻi professionals as to those from other sects. Another interviewee, a wealthy Sunni woman from Beirut, alluded to the same stereotype about Shiʻa by listing exceptions, families protected by their elite status. "Well, we can marry them if they are from the right family," she explained. "You know, Khalil, Beydoun, Osseyran." A Shiʻi woman who converted to Christianity at marriage shared that everyone in her in-laws' village treated her as lower status even though her family was wealthier by far.[2]

These distinctions appeared in my interviews indirectly. People of all sects used aesthetic and "lifestyle" differences to signal the intersection of sect, class, and status. "Muslim villages always have five mechanics at the entrance with abandoned cars and car parts," a Sunni man complained, "while my [Christian] wife's village is manicured and clean." A mother told me she figured out that her teenage daughter was dating a Muslim when she drained the french fries she was making on newspaper instead of a paper towel. I asked her what that had to do with anything. "*We* use paper towels, everyone knows that," she replied. I must have still looked as confused as I felt, because she continued, "*Muslim* women use newspapers. She learned it at *his* house." Naively, I suggested it might be about expense or an effort to waste less paper. "Of course not," she retorted. "They go to the same school, of course they can afford paper towels. It's because they are Muslim." Others invoked cutlery choice, terms for daily objects, color preferences, and furniture styles.

———

I coincidentally interviewed two women from the same Beirut social circle whose friendship ended when their children married. I met the bride's mother, Celeste, first. She lives with her husband and unmarried children in an upscale new building hovering on an elevated sliver of land at the edge of Ras Beirut. Designed to prevent pedestrian access to its fancy residences, the road thwarted my efforts to access the building by foot without getting run over, so I took a taxi to the entrance. The doorman who buzzed me in to the lobby pushed the elevator button for Celeste's floor. She greeted me warmly in the hallway and ushered me into the living room.

I was engulfed in color. Turquoise, teal, and shades of pink dominated the upholstery and cushions on the sleek furniture. Paintings in stream-lined frames covered every wall, including a portrait of Celeste and another of the family. Multicolored mosaic trays and art objects filled modernist side tables and a grand white mantle. Yellow lilies just starting to drip their pollen scented the air. I noted that turquoise was my favorite color. Speaking only in English, Celeste replied, "I am a *very* colorful person." And she was. A white T-shirt saying, "We should all be feminists" topped a feathery, shimmery, multitiered skirt. Her thick, pale blue eyeliner may have been a skilled tattoo. Vivid rose lipstick, carefully lined, set off bright eyes and blond-streaked hair.

It wasn't until I visited Samia, months later, that I understood how these two mothers-in-law viewed one another. Samia and her husband live in an apartment that has been in his family for generations. The building's facade is yellowed with age and pockmarked with bullet holes from the civil war. It sits on a priceless lot in Ras Beirut close to the sea and boasts both a breeze and an unimpeded view, a rare commodity these days. I rang the bell, and as she buzzed me into the entrance, Samia spoke over the intercom, apologizing that the creaky elevator with its sliding metal door was out of order. I walked up the broad ocher stone stairs to a heavy open wooden door—the metal security door, likely installed during the war, was only closed when the family traveled. Samia greeted me holding a grand-child. Her loose hennaed hair framed eyes rimmed in black kohl eyeliner. She wore a long flowing dress in earthy tones, textured with muted gold fabric braiding. As we entered, Samia passed the baby to an Ethiopian nanny and introduced me to her mother, who was on her way out for lunch. The elder woman was dressed elegantly in a long navy dress with designer bag, heels, coiffured blondish hair, gold and diamond jewelry, and under-stated makeup.

This apartment was also massive but could not have been more differ-ent in style. Beige walls held a few paintings in classic landscape themes and a Quranic quote, all framed in dark gold and wood. Upholstered sofas and Louis XV armchairs in rich multihued and multitextured fabrics sat on threadbare antique rugs in burgundies and earth tones. Side tables of wood inlaid with mother-of-pearl held framed family photos and knickknacks in wood, glass, and crystal resting on beige embroidered doilies. Overflowing bookcases lined the walls. The light here was both dimmer and warmer, a golden glow that contrasted with the white brilliance of Celeste's home.

Not only do Samia and Celeste have polarized aesthetic styles; their arguments about what kind of wedding their children should have reverberated through their social circle. There is no difference of socioeconomic class between them, no difference of status or education. Celeste's husband is Sunni, as are Samia and her husband. Yet each woman explained to me why they view their family as higher status than the other, using irreconcilable criteria in their judgments.

Samia views her family as "typical Sunni Beiruti," a phrase that carries a sense of high status. Her choices of decor and clothing reflect this identity, as does her insistence on speaking only Arabic though she is trilingual. For Samia, being a Beiruti Sunni is a secular identity. I asked Samia what that phrase meant to her, and she explained that they don't pray regularly, they fast intermittently but hold iftars during Ramadan, and they celebrate Muslim holidays. They respect Christianity and their Ras Beirut Christian neighbors and friends but don't take part in their traditions with them. Samia thinks Celeste and her husband are "nouveau riche and vulgar"—an accusation describing their aesthetic more than the source of their money. She thinks Celeste is disrespectful of the norms of Beirut life.

Celeste understands her family as higher status because they are "modern, cosmopolitan, and secular" in contrast to what she described as Samia's "traditionalism." Celeste is proud that she and her husband refused to label their children Muslim or Christian and celebrated all the holidays. "*We* are a secular home!" she declared. "Which is so, so beautiful and gratifying in this society."

The aesthetics of these women's apartments reflect their divergent definitions of both "secular" and "status." Each exemplifies one side of persistent debates about Lebanon's identity as "Arab" or "European." Samia's secularism is "freedom of religion"—with roots in the Ottoman Empire and parallels to the US; Celeste's is "freedom from religion," a French-styled *laïcité*. Celeste suggests that proximity to a European secular ideal elevates status. Samia connects status to a secularism that means "to each their own" while prioritizing Arabic and Middle Eastern forms. In both women's status judgments, sect and class converge and collect a range of meanings. And both are typical—if not in their bold personalities, in their assessments of one another. Celeste's perspective is shared by quite a few Christian parents and calls on stereotypes about Islam. Samia exemplifies ideas held in and about the exclusive social world of Sunni Beirut, ideas that came to the foreground when it came to her other child, Sherene's, marriage.

"This Is Beirut!"

Sherene is a romantic. She and her husband "broke each other's hearts" in their efforts to date appropriate people, but, she said, "at the end of the day, love won." She and Raymond first noticed one another at a university event. She remembers what he was wearing; he asked the organizers about her. By graduation, they were dating, and maintained an on-again, off-again relationship for years. Both were pursuing educational and employment opportunities abroad, plus Raymond is from a less wealthy Maronite family from a mountain town. It took a while for Sherene to believe they had a future.

When they both returned to Beirut and committed openly to their relationship, pressure mounted on Sherene to choose a groom from a "good Sunni family" instead of Raymond. Samia led the protest. Sometimes she focused on their different social worlds. "Who is this person? We don't know him!" Sometimes she invoked the religious prohibition on Muslim women marrying non-Muslims, despite her insistence that she was secular. And sometimes, she said, "If only he were Roum Orthodox from Beirut." Sherene explained, "Raymond didn't check any of the boxes. My mom once told me, 'To marry someone, one of three conditions should be met: honor and lineage, wealth, or virtue and religion.' And for her, Raymond met none of them."

Sherene and Raymond chose to wait Samia out. By the time he proposed, Sherene was over thirty, her father had asked around and been reassured that Raymond was from a good family, and relatives had expressed their support. When Raymond asked Sherene's father for his blessing, he replied, "All I care about is first, you become Muslim, and second, you let Sherene work." Raymond agreed to the second condition but refused to convert. Sherene's father gave his blessing anyway. The couple had a civil marriage abroad and a party back home. Sherene's parents grew to love Raymond. "They never knew him as a person," Sherene told me, soon after their first child was born, "so they were judging him as a package, a profile, as how he'd look to society."

When I interviewed Sherene, and later Samia, I left with a sense that more mattered than sect, but I still thought the prohibition against Muslim women intermarrying was important. As I dwelled on it and interviewed more Sunni Beirutis, I came to understand that status was at stake, not souls.

Munira helped me understand this idea. Her mother is an atheist Christian, and her father is from what she described as "a typical old secular Sunni Beiruti family." For Munira, this phrase meant that family elders might pray, fast, and go on hajj, but for everyone else, it was "an identity." She elaborated, "Growing up, we were definitely Beiruti and Sunni. My family has this Sunni arrogance, big time . . . it's not about religion, it's about 'We are the Sunni of Beirut.' Pray and fast, or don't. Drink alcohol, or don't. No one cares. Everyone does what they please. . . . We have weddings with alcohol, and weddings without alcohol, and if there's no alcohol, and we want to go drink at a bar, no one says anything. It has nothing to do with religion. It is about being *the Sunni of Beirut* . . . I would tell my father, 'You know, you brought us up with absolutely no sectarianism beyond the fact that we're Sunni and we're the best.' He just kind of instilled this pride, it's like people who live in Manhattan look down on people who don't. We're from Manhattan, you're all crap. That was it."

Rarely articulated this clearly, Munira's explanation rings true for many Sunni Beiruti parents who object to their children's marriages. The problem is a violation of hierarchy. Their elitism places Sunni Beirutis at an apex based on assertions of original Beirut residency, political claim to the prime ministership and "founding fathers" of the country, and historical status as nonminority Ottoman subjects. Economic capital doesn't necessarily align. An equally wealthy (or wealthier) Shi'i family remains of lower status, labeled nouveau riche and assumed to have generated wealth in West Africa as opposed to the Arab Gulf, incorporating global racialized hierarchies into this assessment. A non-Sunni or non-Muslim suitor with shared status might be preferable to a Sunni from elsewhere in the country. Beirut's rapid urbanization heightened this Sunni Beiruti identity; as "original residents" felt besieged by newcomers, their identity coalesced.

Several years after Sherene's wedding, Samia told me she still thought her daughter could have made a better match. Repeating her earlier refrain, she said, "It would have been so much easier if Sherene had found an Orthodox Christian instead of this Maronite." I replied that I didn't understand why it made any difference what kind of Christian Raymond was. "When Sherene told me she loved him, I said, 'Look, Roum Orthodox are every-where in Ras Beirut, couldn't you have loved someone from that sect since they are like us?' You can't distinguish a Muslim from a Roum. In the city, we are the same."

Underneath Samia's complaints about religious difference lurked con-cerns about Sherene "marrying down." Roum Orthodox have long been an intellectual and economic presence in Beirut. Samia sees them as part of her social world. In contrast, being Maronite meant being rural, unrefined, and of lower status—never mind that Raymond is highly educated. Of course, there are Sunni villages in Lebanon, and Maronite families who reside in Beirut. That's beside the point. As a Sunni man whose mother fought his marriage to a Maronite woman put it, "In Beirut, every social circle has other social circles within it. So now everyone's a circle within a circle. If [his Maronite bride] had been in just one circle, like, you know, the Roum of Beirut, that would have been enough."

––––––––––

A Sunni-Roum Beirut marriage isn't always easily accepted, but the stories I heard from such couples usually involved mild, short-lived objections. Wael, who is Roum, described his story as "a happy one." We spoke in his office at the company where he met Nahla, though she no longer worked there.

"Nahla intrigued me," Wael began, "but the timing could not have been worse." He had just ended a serious relationship with another Muslim woman, on the cusp of engagement, because her family rejected him. Wael tried to avoid a second star-crossed relationship, but this time, the stars aligned: "What can I say. It was fate. I ended up with Nahla for Secret Santa at work. I mean, that's it! It's a message, it's a sign. That's how it started."

Nahla and Wael never hid their relationship and spent time with both families. Wael's fears of rejection dissipated when he learned Nahla's family included several mixed marriages. Five years later, as financially indepen-dent adults, they decided to marry. They talked through every potential issue. They both wanted a civil marriage. Neither wanted to convert. They would teach future children about both faiths and to believe in God. Nahla agreed to baptize them for the sake of Wael's mother. All holidays would include family gatherings.

Armed with answers to all the questions they could foresee, they informed their families. Wael's parents would have preferred a Christian bride but didn't oppose his decision. Nahla's parents "weren't thrilled" but didn't put up much of a fight. Nahla reminded them that they knew she had been with Wael for five years, and marriage was better than an unsanctioned relationship.

I asked Wael why Nahla's parents "weren't thrilled," given the many mixed marriages in their family. He pointed to status: "No one talked about it, but her family are typical Sunni Beirutis." Nahla is from a group of well-known families that have historically married among themselves. Laughing, Wael described his in-law's social world: "What's his last name? It's not Da'ouq and it's not Itani, so what is it?" Neither Wael nor I have any doubt that his identity as a Roum established in Beirut made for a smoother acceptance than had he been Maronite.

Sherene, Munira, and Nahla are all Sunni women from Beirut. How do we know the religious rule against their marrying non-Muslims isn't the main factor here? Sunni Beiruti families opposed their sons' mixed marriages too. One Christian woman said of her Sunni mother-in-law, "She wasn't excited about me. It wasn't that I was Christian, the problem was I'm not from a big important Beirut family. I don't know if you know about *the families*. You know, they think highly of themselves." Another said, "My husband's mom was unhappy about our engagement because it was a problem for her Beiruti social etiquette." Usually, the fact that future children would be officially Sunni eventually smoothed matters. Not for Sara and Bilal.

————

Sara and Bilal met as students at AUB and decided to get engaged before graduation. "We fell in love," Sara told me. "We didn't mean to, we were just going to be friends, but we fell in love."

The couple thought Sara's family would be the problem. One Sunday morning, Sara left a note for her parents, saying she wanted to marry Bilal, before returning to campus. Her parents followed her and found the couple in the AUB cafeteria. Her father expressed his disapproval, citing their youth, financial instability, and religious difference. Bilal told his parents a few days later. They expressed caution. His father noted Christian women are acceptable marriage partners and their children would be Muslim anyway. Then the parents met and agreed that the couple was too young to get engaged.

Sara and Bilal stayed privately engaged while working on their parents. He emigrated for work, and Sara visited his parents regularly, trying to build a positive relationship. But both families tried to break them up. Sara's parents tried matchmaking. Bilal's older sister stoked his parents' fears that Sara was a social climber and gold digger. Meanwhile, Sara converted to Islam despite Bilal's atheism. She had been a believing Catholic all her life and learned about Islam when they started dating. Convinced of the faith's principles, she converted. Bilal's family still withheld their blessing.

Two years later, Sara joined Bilal abroad and the couple had both a *katab kitab* and a civil marriage. The marriage now a done deal, her family accepted it. When I spoke with Sara's parents a decade later, they told me they hadn't been able to handle the social pressure. The couple's emigration allowed them to avoid telling extended family. Bilal's father also accepted the marriage, but his mother and sister shunned Sara, his sister even rebuffing her efforts to visit. Those relationships were never repaired.

Adding this couple to our Sunni Beiruti stories shows the limits of relying on patriarchal personal status law or sect to explain why parents oppose mixed marriage. The only way to make sense of the reactions of Samia, Nahla's family, and Bilal's mother and sister is to connect them to status concerns. Given how damaged their relationships remained, I couldn't interview Bilal's sister or mother, but he believes they would have accepted his wife were she from an elite family, or at least Roum Orthodox.

It wasn't only Sunni Beirutis. Roum Orthodox families associated with Beirut made similar status claims. Urban status claims also divided sects, albeit in milder form. Maronite spouses complained that Roum in-laws joked about their allegedly uncouth ways; Shi'i spouses vented that Sunni in-laws disdained their families.

Status calculations work in the other direction as well, especially for people whose family values their reputation in their village.

"My Family Is Important in the Village"

When they heard about my project, Zina and Adnan invited me over for dinner. Afterward, we chatted over tea, lounging on their beige wraparound sofa. A glass coffee table displayed books on art and history. It was the kind of interview where everyone forgot about the recorder.

Zina's siblings popped in and out of the room, interjecting comments. Adnan leaned back and gestured; he was the talkative one, interested in social science, and curious about when he could read my book. Zina corrected, nudged, and retorted, filling in gaps or adding her perspective. At first, I tried directing questions to her to correct this imbalance. Once I realized Adnan's Druze family was the problem, I let the conversation flow.

The couple met volunteering at a local NGO as undergraduates. Adnan was clear with Zina that a relationship could never lead to marriage. When I asked why, he shared his older brother's tragedy: After a decade-long relationship, Adnan's mother agreed to meet his brother's Muslim fiancée. Three hours later, the women emerged, eyes red and swollen. The fiancée ended the engagement. Adnan's brother felt doubly betrayed and heartbroken, by both fiancée and mother.

So when he met Zina, who is Shi'a, Adnan explained, "My mindset was that I don't need this headache for me or my parents, and I'm only in my early twenties, so why should I set Zina up for something that isn't going to happen?"

"From the beginning, Adnan was honest," Zina added. "When we decided to date, he said, 'We're together now, but you have to understand this isn't going anywhere.' I was young, and I was like, 'I'm not thinking of the future, I just want to be with you.'"

Whenever the couple felt they were growing serious, they broke up. A few months later, they would cross paths at a party or dinner and get back together. Their parents knew about the relationship. Adnan's assumed it would run its course. Zina's wealthy, transnational family didn't mind that he was Druze, though her mother worried when she kept returning to a guy who wouldn't marry her.

Eventually, Zina wanted more, and they broke up "for real." A year later, they resumed their pattern. By now, Adnan's parents realized Zina kept resurfacing. "I lived in Beirut but visited my parents in the village every weekend," he said. "And we had big problems. Every time, there was a fight. Yelling and screaming about small things, but the relationship was the elephant in the room. We would talk, fight, go quiet, then Dad changes the TV channel, I get pissed, I yell, he yells, Mom yells, and . . ."

"And Adnan's not easy to deal with, by the way," Zina interjected.

"Because they wanted me to give them my word that it won't go anywhere."

During the next "off" period, both Zina and Adnan dated other people. Adnan was jealous. He asked Zina's friends about her and stalked her on Facebook. When he texted, Zina didn't reply.

"I gave up," she explained. "There came a point when I just gave up."

"She stopped believing me."

"I didn't believe him anymore."

"What is it, the baby who cried . . ."

"No, no, the wolf . . ."

"The baby who cried wolf . . ."

"No, it's the boy who cried wolf . . ."

His texts unanswered, Adnan drove to her house. He said he was ready for a relationship and invited her to a music festival. She turned him down. Adnan later texted that the next time he saw her, he would propose. Zina replied that his words were empty.

"I didn't believe him," she repeated.

"Well after all that, who could blame you?" I couldn't help commenting.

Adnan tittered as we spoke years later, but at the time, Zina's rejection shocked him. He enlisted a mutual friend to convince her he was serious. It worked.

"She called the other guy she was dating on the spot and told him to fuck off," Adnan said, now with a genuine chuckle. "And since then, it's been smooth between us. "

It had been years since they met, another four since Adnan began fighting with his parents. It would be another four before they married.

Adnan's parents and grandparents are educated, and his father's professional career positioned him as a village patriarch—a role model, mediator, and adviser on matters from health to politics to inheritance conflicts to personal disputes. Adnan took his position as the son of a man of this status seriously. He understood, and for years accepted, that he was expected to behave properly, hold certain views, and uphold traditions, including marrying a Druze. It took him years to release himself from these expectations.

He never told his parents he was engaged. "You know, there is Reuters in the village. They . . . whoooosssshhh." He spread his arms to convey news traveling far and wide.

A bit dense, I persisted, "So who told your parents?"

"I made a point of telling certain individuals in our village, and they spread the word. I knew if these people knew, then everyone would know. I told them I'm going to marry in Cyprus and that we're fixing up our apartment."

As the news circulated, Adnan completed a graduate degree and found a new job, and Zina—wearing her solitaire engagement ring—oversaw apartment renovations and planned their wedding.

Eventually, Adnan and his father had a frank conversation. "Dad was like, 'So I have to learn from strangers that you're planning to marry?' I said, 'Well, you know, we fought over this one too many times, and I know you disagree, and I respect that, but I'm not gonna go by it, so it's better that we each do what we please.' He said, 'No, you don't know my opinion.' So I asked him, 'Would you go, like every other parent, and ask for Zina's hand in marriage?' And he said, 'Yes.' So, uh, I guess he came around. And then Mom too, she was waiting for him. Like, her role was just to protect him from society."

The next step was for Adnan and Zina to meet with his parents. Encouraging Zina to talk, Adnan said, "You tell her how it went."

"Okay. Well, how was it? It was nice. It was emotional."

"How were you feeling?" I asked.

"I was very nervous. And his mom was very nervous. She told me. I mean, recently, we talked about it again, she and I, and she told me she had been nervous. His dad kept talking about how he was worried Adnan would never go to the village, that he would forget . . ."

". . . the traditions. The belonging . . ."

". . . that it was important for Adnan to maintain the family tradition and participate in village life and do *wajbat* (formal social obligations) and that I would also have to do those things . . ."

". . . to maintain the family status."

Zina reassured Adnan's parents that she wouldn't allow him to neglect his duties, and it was on to the next step.

Adnan's parents and a group of male relatives went to propose to Zina's father. At first, it was awkward.

"We got there, and they were sitting on one side, and we were sitting on the other."

"Yeah, it was very silent."

"Then Zina's dad got up and sat between the men on our side, and my mom went and sat with the women on her side, and they started talking. And Dad did the traditional thing, you know, 'We are here to ask . . .' But then he said, 'And anyway they don't really care about our opinion.'"

"Who said that?"

"My dad, don't you remember? He said we were going to get married with or without them."

"Oh, yeah." Zina smiled.

"Then he continued, 'But we want it to be with our blessing, and your daughter is our daughter now, and our son is your son,' and all that stuff."

"And then they found out how similar they are!" Zina exclaimed. "Like we both have people in [political party]. And my mom got what she always dreamed of, the formal proposal, engagement, wedding, the whole traditional thing."

The couple wed in Cyprus accompanied by an airplane full of family members. "And it was done," Adnan added. "The reaction of the wider community, our village, once Dad accepted, it was all fine."

—————

Adnan and Zina's path was among the longest from meeting to marriage, in large part because social status was important to Adnan, not only to his parents. When he finally decided to marry Zina, all the pieces fell into place, including maintaining his family's position in the village. There were a few glitches. A couple villagers criticized Adnan's father on Facebook, saying that he couldn't be a role model because he couldn't lead properly in his own home. And Zina needed time to adapt to the village. "I felt eyes on me, like I felt the energy was taken out of me, you know?" she explained. "It was to that extent. I left the village feeling suffocated. Then I got more comfortable, and it didn't matter, because I knew everybody was happy, and everybody liked me, you know?"

The couple kept their word about fulfilling duties. Zina remarked, looking at Adnan, "To them, these things matter. That's what your dad was worried about, that these things wouldn't happen if you married someone not Druze." She had the last word before I turned off the recorder: "You know, it's funny, the way he used to talk about his parents when we were dating, he scared me, he made me feel like I could never be close to them or love them."

Adnan chuckled again. Ignoring him, Zina continued, "But they're the kindest people I've ever met in my life. In every way possible. I trust his mom with all my heart. It's amazing what you imagine versus what you actually see."

Zina may well be suggesting that their path to marriage didn't need to be so long. In families whose status hinged on a key role they played in a village, it was more often the marriage of a son that triggered parental protests. An inherited position of patriarchal authority that extended beyond family was at stake. The groom's embrace or rejection of that system of authority affected the outcome of these stories. Another Druze man whose parents fought his Muslim fiancée ignored their protests and eloped. His father welcomed the newlyweds and announced the marriage as a done deal in the village.

Adnan and Zina were young when they met. Farid met his Maronite wife when they were in their thirties. Despite opposition on both sides, by the time they married two years later, everyone was on board. Age worked in their favor. Farid said as much, sharing that he would have acted like Adnan when he was younger. "I used to think a lot about what society will say about me. With time and as I got older, I started caring about what *I think*. I also saw friends marry people of different religions and live a happy life, and I saw relatives married to Druze who had problems." Both Adnan and Farid arrived at the same place—the difference is that Zina was along for the ride, while Farid met his spouse after attaining his independence of mind.

———

Druze parents were not alone in objecting to sons' marriages over status concerns. Maroun explained his Maronite parents' opposition similarly: "It was all about what people are going to say, because my father has a certain status in the village. Everyone knows us, everyone knows me and my parents, everyone knows I'm their son, so they were worried about [his Muslim fiancée]." The key factor here is strong village ties, not sect. Historical patterns of residence and migration mean that Druze and Maronite families are most likely to hold such ties.

Samia, the Sunni mother, indicated that she didn't understand that status mattered outside her Beirut circles when she said to me, "*Layki*, in village areas where Druze, or Maronites, or Shi'a live, you'll find that mixed marriage is easier. But *not for us*. This is *Beirut*." I would hazard a guess that quite a few village parents likewise think mixed marriage is easier in Beirut.

And like Zina, many women who married into villages described feeling like everyone was either staring at them or ignoring their presence. "I will ask a question, and instead of answering me, people look at my husband and answer him," one woman shared. Such discomfort usually passed as villagers and bride adapted to one another.

Samia's "This is *Beirut*!" also associated sects with regions. Maronites, Druze, and Shi'a are assumed to be rural; Sunni and Roum are assumed to be urban. This assertion isn't just about stereotypes linking sects to regions; it is about geography as a source of identity. Beirut versus the village. The South versus the North. The mountain versus the valley. Within its tiny nation-space, Lebanon is replete with regional differences. Just as with status, those differences can be more important than sect. They can be the underlying reason parents oppose mixed marriage.

Remember the ever-expanding concentric tree rings that make up social worlds: a generation married within a village, the next married to people with one degree of difference, eventually a family that includes transnational or interreligious marriage. Several people who empathized with their parents observed that they had skipped a step. "They all married from the same village," one person said, describing her in-laws, "so *of course* it was taboo for their son to marry a city girl from another world." Geography is one way Lebanese map degrees of difference onto social distance, a source of meaning giving sect weight and a factor reducing its dominance.

Six

Unknown Geographies, Unknown People

I was having a coffee at my aunt's house in Beirut one afternoon when her husband told me the story of how his family received their last name. He is from Marjayoun, a religiously mixed region in the South. In the 1800s, several Christian families from a nearby area, Houran, migrated to Marjayoun, fleeing violence. Many were female-led households; husbands had been killed or detained. The residents of Marjayoun named these families after the women leading them. The children of Samara were given the last name Samara, Farha's children became the Farha family, same for Ghelmiyyeh, and so on. For years, the original Marjayoun residents, whether Christian or Muslim, would not intermarry with these families from Houran. Place of origin was more important than sect. This chapter shows how geography factors into ideas about sect and social difference.

The idea that region shapes identity extends back to the Ottoman era. In an interview, Lebanese scholar Mona Harb describes how the French mandate disrupted existing geography.[1] She explains, for example, that Tripoli, now in northern Lebanon, was a major urban hub connected to cities in what is now Syria and its hinterlands. When French colonial authorities made Beirut the center, Tripoli's existing connections eroded as new ones were made. Despite this geopolitical shift, residents maintained pre-French understandings of how places and communities fit together. Today, people in rural northern Lebanon may still view Tripoli as their hub and feel more connected to people in the North and in nearby parts of Syria than to Lebanese from the South or Beirut.

––––––––––

Sima grew up in a village in northern Lebanon. Her parents are Roum Orthodox, distant relatives from the same village. Like her parents, Sima moved to Beirut for university, but she stayed after graduating. The capital was a whole other world.

"Until I went to Beirut, I didn't know there is Shi'a and Sunni and Druze," she told me. "I didn't know there are Roum and Maronites. When people asked me, 'What are you?' it was the shock of my life!" Sima had attended a mixed high school and knew that Christians fasted during Lent and Muslims during Ramadan. Beyond that, sectarian difference was a mystery. Her father was involved with a leftist secular political party, and her family never discussed religion and had Muslim friends. Church was for Good Friday, weddings, and funerals. Prayers were a childhood bedtime ritual.

Despite this upbringing, Sima waited four years to tell her parents about her Druze boyfriend, Akram. Her sixth sense told her they wouldn't be pleased. They had always spoken as though she would naturally marry someone from the North, from a family they knew or at least knew of. Her intuition was right. When Sima told her parents, her mom exploded, "Aren't there any Christian guys to marry? Do you really want people to say a Druze guy came and took you?" To her surprise, her father didn't speak to her for a month. In retrospect, she thinks he was hurt that she hid the relationship from him for so long. During that month, her dad took a taxi to Akram's village three hours away and asked around about him and his family. Once he determined Akram was from a good family, he accepted the match. Her mother followed his lead.

Unusually for Druze living in a village, Akram's parents supported the couple from the start. Akram's strong personality helped, as did the remittances he had been sending them from his lucrative Gulf job. Relatives belonged to the same leftist secular political party as Sima's father, and an uncle had opened the door. Sima had spent the night at their home, waking up to Akram's mom's delicious breakfasts. Marriage was the next logical step. Once Sima's father was on board, the families celebrated the engagement and the couple married in Cyprus.

Social Maps

Sima's father needed to know *whom* his daughter was planning to marry. He wasn't the only parent to investigate their child's potential spouse. Others sent emissaries to meet someone or did informal background checks. Parents' need to know is linked to the idea that their child's happiness depends on marrying someone similar to them. How can one assess the similarity of a total stranger? An unknown person will default as "too different to marry" until similarity can be established.

"I don't know them" is a scary feeling for Lebanese parents. Because Lebanon is tiny, people assume that their extensive social maps are definitive. When someone doesn't fit, alarm bells ring. "How can we *possibly* not know anything about them?" becomes "What is wrong with them?" The unknown carries an assumption of unknowability. Many couples focused on making their parents meet, suspecting (often correctly) that meeting would ease concerns that they were too different to be in-laws. Geographic proximity facilitates knowability but isn't enough. Placing a person also requires determining degrees of separation in a country where two degrees is startlingly common. Do I know your family? Do I know someone who knows them? Do I know someone from your village? Can we trace the ties between us?

"My son's teacher is from your village," my friend told her mother, who was sitting with us. Without missing a beat, and having never met the teacher or their family, her mom explained where their house is located, who their parents are, whom they married, where their spouse is from, whom their siblings married, and their relationships to other people in her social world. People are narrated by others through their relationships. They are placed onto a mental map constructed using kinship, place, sect, and class, plus friendship, professional, and educational connections. New people can be integrated into these maps as one learns about them, often through conversations like the one we were having about the teacher. All this talk establishes commonality and familiarity—things that reinforce the pleasantries of informal service encounters but are crucial when it comes to marriage. One woman described her mother's refrain during arguments: "She kept saying, 'Who's this nobody?' She didn't mean 'nobody' but like 'We don't know him.'"

A group of siblings and their spouses, all in their sixties and seventies, enjoyed a late afternoon reunion; some had emigrated years ago and were visiting for the summer. Conversation inevitably turned to people they know. *"Meen aakhid meen?"* Who has married ("taken") whom? Their gossip begins in their village and circles outward, covering multiple generations, relatives, friends, colleagues, acquaintances. Kin relations are drawn in excruciating detail. Other details include where someone lives or who their neighbors, colleagues, or classmates are. Someone always interjects, "You know [so-and-so] is from [village]." It's never clear what their sources are or how accurate any of it is. They don't use terms like "second cousin once removed." Accuracy is beside the point. "She married the son of the one whose brother married the daughter of so-and-so, who is the son of our neighbor's brother" is a known coordinate on a social map. Every so often, a stream runs dry when someone says something like, "She married a French guy," because the spouse is unknowable.

Social mapping is pragmatic. In communities with common male first names—Muhammad, George, Tony, Elias, Ali—there are multiple men named Muhammad Murtada or George Issa. "No, no, he's the cousin of the guy who was X's neighbor, and he married the daughter of the one with the bakery near the school on the back road" is a way to clarify which Muhammad or George you're talking about. Social mapping is also generational. Older people are prone to these narrations. But many interviewees in their twenties and thirties placed people on social maps; they just used different tools, like social media, to do so. The map and the knowledge it contains *create* the social world in which people live, the social world parents are trying to protect when they oppose a marriage. When a potential spouse is easily placed, conflict about religious difference usually resolves swiftly.

Um Ghassan began by telling me she's been married for over fifty years and apologizing for gaps in her memory.

"What am I going to tell you? It's been a long, long time since I got married . . . what happened, happened."

"How did it happen?"

"The way these things happen."

"Did Abu Ghassan come ask for your hand?"

"Yes, he came and asked. My parents wouldn't give me to him. It's normal. That happens. We got married, and they didn't get angry with me. They talked with me immediately afterward, my mom, dad, and siblings."

"They didn't get angry?"

"They didn't get angry because we all grew up together. My parents liked Abu Ghassan. He grew up with my brothers. Their house was next door. They didn't get upset with him. No one was upset at all."

Um Ghassan is Maronite. Abu Ghassan is Sunni. They live in a mixed village in Akkar, in the North. He's ten years older than her. After years of clandestine flirting, when she turned nineteen, he proposed to her father. When rebuffed, the couple walked to a shaykh's office for a *katab kitab*. Um Ghassan converted because she wanted to be the same religion as her children. With no fuss, the two extended families, already neighbors, merged. "On their holidays, we're all together and on our holidays we're all together," Um Ghassan told me. "It was normal, you wouldn't see a difference. It was like I had married a relative from my religion—normal." Theirs was neither the first nor the last mixed marriage in the village. Provided relations between the families were good, mixed marriages were an occasional, matter-of-fact occurrence. Other people I interviewed who married across religions but within village or region in the mid-twentieth century described the same pattern: proposal, refusal, elopement, and quick normalization. A known, respectable spouse from the same village or region, a spouse with known family roots, mattered more than sect or religion.

With migration to Beirut and other cities, and multiple waves of Lebanese emigration, placing people on social maps has grown difficult.[2] In impersonal encounters around the world, in taxis and salons in Montreal, Bogotá, Detroit, and Dubai, Lebanese ask one another, "Where are you from?" The secular-minded among us dodge this question, hearing it as sectarian code, an attempt to identify our sect. Geography and sect are intertwined, much as status, class, and sect are. This code isn't perfect unless your village is associated with a single sectarian group, but combined with name, appearance, and accent, people make their guesses. During my research, I came to realize the questioner's primary motivation wasn't always (or only) learning my sect. Regional identifications and assumptions are as powerful as sectarian ones.

Coded Spaces

I frequently find myself illustrating Los Angeles's vast distances to visiting Lebanese friends by explaining that LA County is about the size of Lebanon. The latter is graced with more westward coastline, the Mediterranean brighter, balmier, and these days, more pungent with rot, than the Pacific. Six cities, including Beirut, dot its length, merging in towering blocks of unpermitted concrete sprawl filling the foothills of the biblical Mount Lebanon range that separates the sea from a broad valley to the east (see map 6.1).

Imagine layers of colored cellophane laid over this territory, coding regions, sects, and political alliances. With each layer, the mosaic pieces grow smaller and more opaque. Writing about suburban LA County, Wendy Cheng explains how "everyday landscapes" can be "crucial terrains through which racial hierarchies are learned, instantiated, and transformed."[3] Ideas about and interactions with local spaces lead to local ideas about race that differ from racial hierarchies on a national scale.

In Lebanon, ideas about and experiences of spaces lead to ideas about sectarian, national, and racial difference. Longstanding associations link sects and spaces, but what they mean for marriage and other practices varies. Northern Lebanon is a mixed region, but within it, Maronites in Batroun tend toward isolation, sometimes opposing marriages between Maronite villages, while Orthodox Christians in Koura have coexisted and shared leftist ideologies and educational histories with their Muslim neighbors. I interviewed Christians from villages near Tripoli who didn't meet a Muslim until university and others from neighboring villages who attended mixed high schools.

Map 6.1 allows us to compare the religious diversity of a region with the percentage of marriages in that region that are mixed.[4] Some areas stand out: Akkar is religiously diverse with few registered mixed marriages; Baalbek-Hermel has more than its share of mixed marriages given its lack of religious diversity, and Mount Lebanon has fewer than its share. Beirut is a small, religiously diverse governorate in terms of voter registrations, with a disproportionately high percentage of mixed marriages.[5]

The civil war disrupted pluralist residency patterns across the country.[6] Massacres and population displacements changed the overlay of demography and geography.[7] The historically Maronite and Druze villages and towns

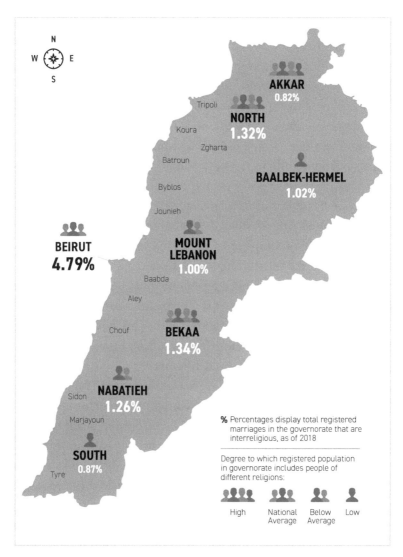

MAP 6.1. Map of Lebanon showing both percentage of registered marriages that are interreligious and degree of religious diversity for each governorate. All data obtained from the 2018 electoral registration records. Map by Kite Creative Studio.

of Mount Lebanon emerged with new populations and ideas about one another. Southern Lebanon's Shi'a, Orthodox, and Druze villages were emptied by Israeli military attacks in 1978 and 1982. The Israeli occupation of the South until 2000 displaced residents to Beirut's suburbs and beyond.

Every Lebanese I've spoken to has ideas about Lebanon's regional identities, assumptions about the sect, social status, morals, and values of the people who live there. Sima's father's discomfort with Akram grew from his origins in an unfamiliar part of Lebanon, an area her father knew only through negative stereotypes of insular mountain people hostile to strangers. And as we heard last chapter in Samia's "This is *Beirut!*" people in the capital scorn those living outside it (and vice versa).[8] Celeste's Beirut-based Maronite father didn't complain when she fell in love with a Sunni doctor, but the doctor hid the relationship from his parents for five years. He was from a poor rural background, and his medical degree represented urbanization and upward mobility. The doctor feared his family would find urbane Celeste "shockingly modern," but in the end, he married her despite his mother's tears. It took years for Celeste and her in-laws to overcome the combination of class and urban/rural difference.

On the one hand, urban Lebanese romanticize the village or mountain town as a haven of traditional stone architecture, fragrant jasmine, fresh produce, a simpler lifestyle, deep family roots, natural beauty, and hospitality.[9] Whether recent migrants or longtime urban residents, many maintain ties to their place of origin, spending weekends there to escape the smog and din, visiting elders, and returning for rituals at the edges of life, baptisms and burials. The state nurtures these roots, registering people to vote by place of origin, not residence. On the other hand, "the stereotype of the Maronite and of the Shi'a just come down from their mountain, or from the regions of Baalbeck and the South, who are 'civilized' by the city and have ceased to crush their kibbeh by hand, is still alive and well in certain circles of Beirut."[10]

Beyond these stereotypes, which ignore multiple histories of urbanization, some interviewees who had lived in Beirut all their lives and married into a family with village ties found the experience challenging. "It's a different kind of life," one woman told me. "Their entertainment is different. They have this relationship with the land, they grow things. They eat lots of fish. They thought I was weird because I didn't like the fish they ate. They have rituals—every afternoon they go to the village center, they walk. For me this was like, 'Okay so what's the purpose?' I didn't understand it. I went once or twice but I didn't want to do this ritual daily and they weren't happy with that. I'd rather stay home and read a book than go walk."

Others echoed this discomfort with village in-laws. "If you want to smother me, tell me to go to the mountain," one said. "I'll feel like I've gone back in time fifty years. I feel smothered, like a fish out of water." Another compared it to Beirut: "Here, if someone wants to come over, they'll call you and ask, 'Can I come over?' There, they knock and walk in the door. They have no concept of privacy. And people leave the keys outside so that others can do that. They enter, like, '*Yalla*, make coffee.'"

For their part, rural Lebanese, like that Sunni doctor's parents, often disparage urban areas and their residents. Anthropologist Michelle Obeid describes how rural residents of Arsal use the word "urbanized" (*mutamaddin/a*) as a criticism of younger villagers who migrated to the city.[11] Villagers bemoan the poor social ties of the city and find living around strangers stressful. Locking a door, an idle coffee pot—these are signs of inferior hospitality.

Beirut itself is many cities in one, a microcosm of the identity dynamics that link people and place across Lebanon. Its contradictions are a favorite theme for journalists, scholars,[12] and novelists[13]: cosmopolitan and sectarian, open and closed, vibrant and violent. The same colored cellophane exercise reveals neighborhoods with powerful identities and associations sedimented into them. Population displacements during the civil war homogenized neighborhoods in new ways by sect.[14] If you ask Beirut residents about their city today, many will say Hamra is one of few remaining mixed areas. They'll explain that Mazra'a used to have more Christians but is now mostly Sunni with Shi'a moving in, that Tariq al-Jadida remains Sunni while Zoqaq al-Blat is mostly Shi'a. The civil war altered people's relationships to identity and space.

Persistent War Geographies

During the war, Beirut fractured, the Green Line separating Muslim residents and militias in "West Beirut" from Christian ones on the "East" side. This association discounts prewar and continued diversity on both sides: Christian residents of Ras Beirut, Shi'i residents of Bourj Hammoud,

Christian villages incorporated into the expanding southern suburb. The Lebanese Civil War wasn't a religious war; it was political. Some of the worst violence was intrasectarian: Christians killing Christians, Muslims killing Muslims, warlords vying for control, political parties claiming turf in street battles. Nonetheless, the war bolstered sectarian boundaries.

Reine Mitri's film *In This Land Lay Graves of Mine* tells multiple displacement stories, people fleeing one area for another in violent population transfers as places were claimed by specific groups. A close friend of mine who lived through horrible intrasectarian violence still couldn't fathom dating someone from a different sect. It took her over a decade to leave her neighborhood to explore other parts of Beirut, to be willing to meet people from elsewhere, even though her war trauma came from violence within her sect. I didn't ask about war experiences, but when interviewees brought it up, I listened to their stories of loss. One woman spent her childhood on the move, living in homes abandoned by other displaced people, using their clothes, their toys, their dishes, all left behind when they too had fled.

Lingering war geographies shaped some parents' responses to mixed marriage. Rita's father refused to meet Mahmoud, her Muslim fiancé. He told Rita to do whatever she wanted without his approval. The couple married in Cyprus with their siblings and friends. It took a couple years for Rita's father to meet Mahmoud, longer to break the ice between them, and even longer for relations to normalize. By the time of our interview, the two men were hanging out regularly.

Rita's father's resistance germinated with the war: Christian friends and neighbors fled Ras Beirut, he experienced sect-based discrimination at work, and sect-based violence rocked Beirut and his village of origin. Rita believes these experiences slammed her father's once open mind shut. An adamant secular leftist, the war convinced him Lebanon would never be secular, Christians were disappearing from the Middle East, and religious Muslims were taking over. The passage of time is not what mended the rift opened by Rita's marriage. Mahmoud thwarted Rita's father's stereotypes about Muslims by drinking and listening to music with him.

I also interviewed a few people for whom the war facilitated mixed marriage because social norms were abandoned. Engagements were shorter because life felt precarious. Pragmatism overruled propriety.

Huda, from a Roum village in the North, married her Sunni Beiruti husband early in the war. He made her feel safe, she told me; he was war's antithesis for her. Huda's mother tried to dissuade her, worried about village gossip, but her father liked the young man and gave his blessing. They married less than two years after meeting in a *katab kitab* and moved to Huda's village to raise their family in its relative safety.

Mainly, however, the war came up in interviews as an explanation for why secular parents, like Rita's father, opposed mixed marriage. The war also motivated interviewees' empathy for their parents or in-laws, explaining why they negotiated patiently or waited instead of eloping. People from Christian and Druze mountain towns where massacres happened said they understood the hatred their parents felt for the other group: "It's in their subconscious. I can't blame them for that." Layers of overlapping trauma, grief, and violence remain, the thick residue of civil war slowing efforts to move past sectarianism, to accept a child-in-law from a sect once feared or reviled.

———————

As she began her story, Celine said, "None of us cared about sect in the '90s, but our parents couldn't forget. They were scarred by war." She met Haitham at the war's end, through an NGO that integrated Christian and Muslim youth in reconciliation efforts. Both are from working-class families. Hers is Maronite from the North; his is Sunni from Beirut.

"We connected immediately," Celine said. "But our timing was terrible. The war had barely ended. I'm from a village where Muslims are considered the enemy." She dated Haitham anyway, hoping her grandfather's unusual open-mindedness would rub off on her parents. The elder had traversed the country doing rural work and had always spoken respectfully about Muslims.

Celine ensured the relationship was conspicuous. Haitham visited her at home, chatting with her parents each time. Her mother cooked his favorite foods when she knew he was stopping by. Her dad enjoyed his company, seeking him out for conversation. But when it came to marriage, Celine's father balked. "He just couldn't handle the idea of his daughter marrying a Muslim."

They tried to convince him for a year, and then set a wedding date, hoping a deadline would compel approval. "The day arrived, and we kept hoping he'd change his mind. Before I left, I told my dad, 'I'm going to get married now. Do you want anything? Can I bring you anything?' He said, 'No, God be with you.' And I left."

The couple took a bus through Syria to Turkey for a civil marriage because they couldn't afford airfare. When they returned, everything was normal with her family.

Two decades later, a cousin eloped with a Muslim man. Celine concluded on a note of frustration that so little had changed: "Lara, I wish people would go to sleep one night, and wake up with a blank white page the next morning. People are going to Mars! And we still hate others because they're different. How are we going to evolve like this?"

At the same time, Celine told me, she had expected worse from her father due to his war trauma. She thinks his genuine regard for Haitham helped. "I'll never forget that he said, 'God be with you' when I left to marry." Perhaps not a blessing for her marriage, but certainly one for her.

––––––––––

Celine and Haitham consider themselves part of the rebuilding generation. They grew up during the war and entered their twenties at its end, ready to seek new possibilities. Those born later were sometimes surprised by the persistent strength of war geographies. Sima, whose father investigated Akram before they married, is flabbergasted by friends who still won't go to a café on the "wrong" side of town. A Muslim who moved to a Christian suburb to shorten his commute vented in irritation at his brother's "What the hell, man? You moved to the Christian ghetto?" response.

Between 1990 and 2005, lines between neighborhoods softened for some Beirut residents.[15] Yet for each person who ventured for the first time to a neighborhood a few miles away, there were several who refused to accompany them. New political tensions triggered by Prime Minister Hariri's assassination in 2005 resharpened those neighborhood divides. The stigma associated with Beirut's southern suburb, long viewed by nonresidents as a Shi'i Muslim "ghetto of poor rural migrants who are ignorant about urban life, and as a space of anarchy, chaos, and illegality," solidified.[16] Hiba Bou Akar describes the ongoing impact of fears of violence or people of different sects on ideas about residency, property sales, neighborhoods, and safety.[17]

The civil war, subsequent episodes of tension since 2005, and each moment of friction in Beirut's history have redrawn the city's maps, literally and in navigational imaginations. Like migratory birds, people know where to go and where to avoid. This isn't unique to Beirut. Most residents of Los Angeles assess neighborhoods using assumptions about "danger" based on stereotypes about the people who live there. Like local urban geographies that led to "regional racial formations,"[18] spatial segregation has contributed to creating sectarian division in Belfast and Istanbul as well as in Beirut.[19]

Belonging and Exposure

Since at least the mid-1990s, some Lebanese have used the word *bi'a* to express (dis)comfort in specific spaces. *Bi'a* translates most literally to "environment," though to better capture the accretion of political, social, and religious meaning into space and identity, I translated it as "milieu" in my 2006 book. Some people use *bi'a* loosely to ascribe similarity and difference. Most use the word to explain why they prefer certain areas of Beirut and Lebanon.[20] "I like going there, it's my milieu, I feel comfortable." "That café has good food, but I'm uncomfortable in its milieu." "How can I go meet his family? They live in the Bekaa! It's a different milieu."

People feel comfortable surrounded by similarity—whether that similarity is visible or imagined, racial or political, or something else.[21] Signs, dress, music, sounds, posters, and graffiti indicate milieu.[22] Identifications with neighborhoods are emotional as much as geographic. Building on Ibn Khaldun's concept of *'asabiyya* (group solidarity, esprit de corps), French sociologist Michel Seurat shows how two Tripoli neighborhoods consolidated around enmity toward the other; neighborhood was an identity and affect more than a territory.[23] In this way, when an interviewee says, "I'm from X," they aren't just locating their origins geographically; they're telling me something about who they are and where they feel like they belong.

There is a difference between knowing one belongs in specific spaces and refusing to go outside those spaces. A person can have a strong sense of identity linked to a place and still explore other areas of the country. Some interviewees identified as from and of a particular milieu while embracing difference, including the milieu of their spouse. Others felt like they and their spouse were part of a special open-minded milieu of mixed families and neighborhoods, islands of acceptance and intermingling in a segregated world. Either way, many attributed their willingness to break the marriage rules to exposure to a diversity of places and people.

"Everyone I know in a mixed marriage has the same history," Nina told me. "It's either at school, where they had a mixed environment that helped them jump over the limits and borders created by society. Or it's at university, when you have more platforms on which to act, freedom to build your personality, and opportunities to be involved with different mindsets and milieus. For my generation, it was the mixture of political milieus that shaped us in the 1990s. We had many causes to work on, with different people, in different environments. We were the generation building bridges after the war."

Nina's view was common among our peers, those of us who came of age in the "Golden '90s." I lived in Beirut then and recall the magical seduction of a city awakening into vibrant chaos, its pent-up creativity and quickening energy—and billionaire money—sanding down war's shards just enough to leave an edgy heart. We were naive in hindsight.

Outside the '90s generation too, many people attributed their mixed marriage to exposure to diversity in their neighborhoods or schools, or later through work or friends. Those whose exposure was late recalled its thrill. One woman called her mom to share the exciting news that there were Muslims in her college classes. "Imagine," she told me, "an eighteen-year-old, calling her mom to say, 'Wow, there are Muslim students here!' For eighteen years I didn't know any Muslims." Others in isolated situations described feeling like they were the odd one out in their family or school, the one always curious about other people.

————

Farah and Michel were an unlikely couple. "I remember, the first time I met Michel, he said he would only get married in a church. He was never exposed. He had only met three Muslims in his entire life at that point!" She couldn't imagine marrying him, wished him luck, and tried to put him out of her mind.

Farah grew up in Ras Beirut in a family that was Shi'a on paper and leftist in practice. Michel was the first in his family to leave their Christian town to attend university—a private institution in another Christian town. Despite

Farah's skepticism, they liked each other, and when their social circles intersected again, they started dating casually.

The only person who took the couple's on-again, off-again relationship seriously was Farah's mother. A year after Michel appeared in her daughter's life, she made a point of getting to know him. Farah's father took longer to decide he liked Michel, but neither parent ever mentioned his Christianity or objected to him as a potential groom.

When Michel introduced Farah to his parents the following year, they said they didn't care about her religion as long as she prayed. Atheism was unacceptable.

With time, the couple's expectations of their relationship evolved. Farah learned that religion was a private matter for Michel, that he wouldn't impose it on her. When Michel's mother told Farah that they expected their future grandchildren to be Christian, Michel told his parents to stay out of it. This confirmed for Farah the changes she had seen in Michel. "Suddenly, I didn't see any crosses. He stopped going to church. He read a lot. I think when he left his environment and took a step back, he realized it was all more of an identity for him than a conviction."

Confronted with possible emigration for work, Farah and Michel decided to link their futures and marry. During the engagement visit, tensions triggered by their mothers' disagreement about the importance of religious practice were defused when Farah's father began pontificating in what everyone agreed was "the most boring lecture imaginable about how all religions are similar." Everyone flew to Cyprus for the wedding. When we spoke several years later, the couple was living in a mixed neighborhood of Beirut, and to their parents' dismay, did not yet have children.

Looking back, Farah mused, "You know, I wasn't really exposed to his world either. I had never talked with someone who wears a huge cross around their neck and has one in their car and goes to church. Christians in Ras Beirut are nonreligious. So exposure to someone Christian and very religious was also new to me."

———

There is a pragmatic dimension to the correlation between exposure and intermarriage. When neighborhoods and lives are segregated, how can a person meet potential friends and partners from different groups? Hence the tragedy, for mixed marriage, when Lebanese University fractured during the civil war. Nonelite youth from all sects, regions, and classes lost an institutional pull to shared spaces.

Exposure—or rather, its absence—is the language people use to explain negative reactions to mixed marriages too: "They were never exposed to…" "The problem was their lack of exposure . . ." Many Lebanese believe that exposure leads to harmony and its lack to bias, that the more "cosmopolitan" and "connected" a family is, the more "open-minded" they will be. They envision certain regions, villages, and neighborhoods as more likely to include open-minded people than others.

"Druze from the Chouf are more conservative than Druze from Beirut, or even Druze from Hasbaya; they're the most receptive to mixed marriages," one person said. "Druze from Baabda are more open-minded than Druze from the Chouf," said another. "Families from Tripoli or Akkar are more open than those from Metn." "Saida is closed, there are so many conservative people . . . but Sour is totally different." Christian regions were pitted against one another: "I grew up in Beirut. I was used to Roum, but the first time I saw Christians in Baabda, I was shocked. I heard this guy with the cross and you know, the slanted God on the cross, and all this French around me."

At least five people who, to my knowledge, don't know one another, described the coast north of Beirut from Ashrafieh to Jbeil as "Marounistan," a place that felt like a different country, ruled by extremist Maronites. Others called this region "LBC country," referring to a Maronite television station. In contrast, Roum Orthodox from Koura described their region as "open-minded," using Maronite-majority areas as a foil. Koura has mixed-religion villages and high schools and left-leaning politics. That said, I can name more than one Roum village that shares the political views and isolationism of "Marounistan." The associations between place, perspective, and sect are inconsistent.

"Mafia" Places

Some places, like Maronite-majority Zgharta, are singled out as especially isolationist. A woman who married into the area was upset that decades later, people still referred to her as "the stranger." When she complained to a friend from Zgharta, her friend replied, "My mother is the same sect as my father, from a village nearby. They've been married for fifty years, and she is still called a stranger in his village! How can you think you wouldn't be?"

And the conversation I had with another couple began like this:

"Where are you from?" I asked the man.

"The North."

"Can you be a bit more specific?"

He sighed. "Zgharta..."

"It's like a mafia," his wife interrupted.

"That's why I didn't want to say I was from Zgharta, because then the entire conversation would be about Zgharta."

"It's like a mafia. All vendettas and guns."

The mafia image also applies to parts of the Bekaa Valley and Hermel. "Baalbek Shi'a are more isolated than Shi'a from the South" is another generalization I often heard. When I asked anthropologist Mayssoun Sukari-yya, who was doing research in a mixed Shi'a-Christian village near Baalbek (which is in the Bekaa Valley), about it, she told me interreligious marriage among those villagers is rare. Muslims there explained to her that they wouldn't marry Christian women out of "respect" for their Christian neighbors and in order to protect them as a minority. They expressed pride in their coexistence and a sense that intermarriage would damage their carefully maintained communal life. In contrast, mixed marriages go back generations in Shi'a-Christian villages in the South where, unlike the Bekaa, the Communist Party once held sway, many emigrated during the Israeli occupation, and that occupation cemented bonds between residents resisting a common enemy.

The most sensationalist images of mafia-like violence are levied at Druze living in the mountains. People regularly warned others that Druze entanglements would at best break their hearts and could end violently. Some Druze I interviewed validated these fears. "We know that many so-called accidents happen in mountain villages related to mixed marriage. The rate of gun violence has decreased recently, but it used to happen a lot," one said.

When the 2013 castration of a man who eloped with a Druze woman went viral in the news, the Lebanese public took it as evidence that Druze were violent.[24] Years later, the incident still appeared in my interviews, whether to explain the fragility of mixed marriage, the dangers of marrying into the Druze community, or the "backward traditions" the interviewee's family had disavowed. Young men in love with Druze women faced inten-sified family concern about their safety in its wake. Friends used it to warn anyone who said they found a Druze woman attractive. "Forget it, she's Druze," they would respond. "Do you want them to cut it off?"

Geography and history explain some of these differences of exposure and some of these stereotypes. Mountains are more isolated than plains. Rates of emigration vary across regions, tied historically to access to a port. Local political structures meant different forms of rule and degrees of con-tact with outsiders. For every interviewee who said Roum Orthodox are closed-minded, conservative, and stuck-up, there was another who said they are secular, educated, and better at coexistence than other groups. For every person who described Shi'a as overzealous, ignorant, and uncouth, another said they are generous, accepting, and kind. None of this is really about sect—or place—at all. It's about people's specific experiences and social influences, about how they relate to other groups and think those groups relate to them. The sheer existence of the stereotypes, assumptions that underscore just how unknown the boyfriend or girlfriend who came to dinner is, fuel parental fears of mismatches and unhappy marriages. It should be obvious that regional images don't hold water. The US South is full of people dismayed, if not terrified, at the turn their milieu took after the 2022 Supreme Court decision allowed states to ban abortion. To assume the loudest voices represent everyone who lives in a place is to abandon anyone who refuses the status quo. Similarly, there are mixed marriages in every region of Lebanon, including those reputed to be the most isolationist (see map 6.1). And in every region, there are parents who embraced those matches and those who fought against them, whether exposed or not.

Diaspora Spaces

"I'm not like my siblings," one woman said. "I lived outside as a child. I was exposed to the world and that changed how I think. This is important. My grandmother always speaks from a village perspective, even though she lives in Beirut, because that's where she was raised. My parents are chil-dren of Beirut, and they think like Beirut. I think differently." Like this woman, many people told me that exposure to the world outside Lebanon facilitated their commitment to a partner of another sect. For their parents, exposure's effects varied and reflected dynamics in the places where they emigrated. Lebanese in diaspora live in diverse societies with their own social dynamics and categories of difference. Diaspora experiences range from mini-Lebanon social worlds to virtually no contact with other Lebanese, from short stints abroad to emigration that may or may not have an imagined return. Strong ideas circulate about how exposure has affected different diaspora places, ideas that held up in most of my interviews.

People who grew up in the Gulf reminisced about nationally diverse communities. The United Arab Emirates, especially Dubai, was a haven for many couples. "Over here in Dubai we are expats but guess what? Ninety percent of the people are expats! Our friends are from all over the world and have different religions and nationalities." Another Lebanese couple who met in the UAE, where both their families lived, said they had an easier time than most mixed couples because "there were no neighbors talking and none of that, 'Ya Latif, what will people say?' reaction from our parents." Julia's Maronite family was different.

———————

Like many Lebanese born during the civil war, Julia grew up abroad. After graduating from a North American university, she joined her parents in Dubai to begin her career. There, she met Basil, a Sunni of Syrian background who had also moved to Dubai to work after living in Europe and North America. "We didn't think about any of it," Julia told me. "We had both been raised and worked and lived abroad and never gave any thought to religion or sect or anything. We just met, really liked each other, and started dating."

Julia's parents were fine with the relationship until community gossip triggered their opposition. They socialized with a Dubai circle of Levantine Christians where mixed marriage was what Julia called a "redline." "It was a no-no. It was talked about. I'm sure my parents' friends commented about me. They must have been saying, 'How can you let your daughter do this?'"

For two years, Julia's parents harped on Basil's official identity: "They kept saying, 'He's a Syrian Muslim, Syrian Muslim. This can't work. Syrian Muslim, Syrian Muslim.'" But Julia didn't see him that way. "Basil's never seen himself as a 'Syrian Muslim.' He's agnostic petering on atheist and doesn't have that sense of national identity," she explained.

For two years, her parents threatened to disown her and enlisted others to their fight: "I would get sporadic phone calls from, like, a cousin who lived far away, asking me, 'What are you *doing*? What are you *thinking*?' And then Mom called my friends for, like, an intervention, and my friends would come speak to me. It was really stressful."

Blindsided, Julia couldn't reconcile her upbringing with her parents' reaction to Basil, because they raised her to be "a tolerant, open-minded, accepting, nondiscriminatory person." Basil tried proposing to her father, hoping that invoking tradition would solve the problem. Her father refused, saying the couple should try living in both Lebanon and Syria to see how society would treat them. To Julia, this suggestion was "ludicrous." Neither had spent much time in their countries of origin, nor did they have any intention of returning to either place.

So Julia and Basil decided to announce their engagement. When it became clear they would marry with or without a blessing, Julia's parents saved face by accepting the match, throwing a party, and attending their civil ceremony. "Once we took the decision out of their hands, they didn't have to worry about it anymore. It wasn't their job to protect us, and they just had to accept it and move on. Then they saw with time that we didn't struggle socially at all. And now," Julia continued, "they absolutely love him. They love him."

The couple continues to live outside both Lebanon and Syria.

———

Julia and Basil didn't expect to fight to marry; they saw themselves as cosmopolitan citizens of a multinational world, the positive result of exposure. Mixed couples living in the UAE liked to contrast it with Lebanon. I heard countless variations of, "The problem in Lebanon is that everyone feels entitled to say things about things that are none of their business. Here, people respect privacy." Problems erupted when their parents' social worlds resembled Lebanon more than the UAE. These stories showed me how transnational in reach the tongues of Lebanese society can be. There are places where the norms of marriage resemble a Lebanon of generations past, places where they have been supplanted by new fears of difference (usually racial) or by aspirational mixing, and places where people seem to live in diaspora and Lebanon simultaneously, what Ghassan Hage describes as "multiple inhabitance,"[25] a process made easier each year by new technologies. Julia's parents fit this last mold.

The few Lebanese Australians I interviewed explained that some Lebanese social circles in Australia are segregated by sect or region of origin. "It's like urban with a touch of ethnicization, not a complete enclave, but pretty isolated," one explained. A Maronite man from Zgharta fell in love with a Shiʻi woman from the South. Both had emigrated to Australia as youth and shared leftist politics. Both families opposed their marriage. His demanded a church wedding; hers refused altogether. So they eloped. His parents accepted their civil marriage; hers waited five years to speak with her again. In retrospect, this man believes his in-laws' resistance grew from their tenacious connections to social networks in their Lebanese village, their "multiple inhabitance."

In sharp contrast, the few people I interviewed connected to West Africa told me mixed marriage was easier there. A woman with family in Sierra Leone explained, "Muslims and Christians, we all lived together as Lebanese; that was most important." A Christian woman, who is from a mixed village and has diaspora ties to West Africa, married a Lebanese Shiʻi man with little fuss. Religion didn't matter because both her village and her diaspora community were relatively integrated. Plus, it was more important to marry someone Lebanese than not. Both these women implied that racial difference is more important in West African Lebanese communities than religious difference. Lebanese in Senegal also have a relatively high rate of interreligious marriages to other Lebanese.[26] Through ethnic unity and anti-Black racism, this diaspora context has brought race to the foreground as the kind of difference that matters most.

What of the United States? Clearly there is the potential for a great deal of exposure. The ethos of individualism might bolster mixed marriage. Anti-Black racism, and racism more broadly, might push Lebanese toward one another. These generalizations should be taken with a shaker of salt because scales of time and geography are vast. Lebanese live in Michigan, California, Pennsylvania, Kentucky, and elsewhere; immigration began long before Lebanon existed as a country. Lebanese Americans overwhelmingly describe Lebanese in the US as more conservative than their relatives in Lebanon. A diaspora time warp leads people to raise their children with social norms from a Lebanon frozen in time the moment they left.[27] As a teenager, every time my family visited Lebanon, my mother insisted that I "dress like a lady," in floral-patterned dresses and skirts. Sure enough, my female cousins often dressed similarly. When I visited on my own, in my twenties, I packed my usual jeans and T-shirts and found my cousins dressed casually as well. At first, I thought this showed cultural change in Lebanon from the 1980s to the mid-90s. Then I learned that every summer, just as the social pressure my mother anticipated filled my suitcase with "Lebanon clothes," my cousins who lived there were forced to "dress like a lady" because their mothers felt pressured by us. My cousin and I found this hilarious, but the time warp affects more pressing issues than dress, including mixed marriage.

Recent immigration to the US is mixed, but most older US Lebanese immigrant communities are Christian and center around the church. A few interviewees grew up in such communities. One described a life organized around Christian holidays: "All of them, we fasted, we had church, there was choir, my mom had a mini chapel in the house." He sighed. "Basically, I was raised like a Lebanese villager." Despite exposure to a wide range of Americans, people from these communities didn't meet Muslim Lebanese until they went to Lebanon on their own as young adults. One person told me, "In my cultural unconscious as an Arab American there were no Muslims. There were only Roum, Maronites, and Druze. Then there's Americans, everyone else." Michelle's Maronite family fit both this picture and the notion of "multiple inhabitance" perfectly.

———

Upbeat, with a friendliness I associate with the US Midwest, Michelle moved to Beirut as a young adult, curious to learn about the place her parents left. In her early thirties, she met Naji, whose chill demeanor tempered her effervescent vibe. His Sunni Beiruti parents knew about the relationship and supported whatever their son wanted to do.

"It was a relief that we only had to deal with one side," Michelle told me. "I had to muster the courage to actually tell my parents about Naji. That was tough." Naji forced her hand by deciding to join her on a trip to the US. "I had to prepare my parents before he came," Michelle remembered. "I told them separately, and neither reacted well. They were like, 'OMG!' because in their mind, a Muslim is gonna come and put a hijab on you. He's gonna force you to do things and you're gonna have to convert, with shaykhs in the middle of everything." The commentary escalated before the couple even boarded the plane. "Where did we go wrong?" "We gave you everything, all we asked is that you don't marry a Jew or a Muslim or a Black person." "How are you gonna raise your kids?" "Are your kids gonna be atheists?" Even Michelle's sister was convinced she would never be able to celebrate Christmas again.

Ever polite, Michelle's parents still welcomed Naji to their home. He brought a bottle of whiskey and drank at dinner with them. Despite this display of similarity, her parents didn't budge. They even invited a priest over to reason with Michelle. She looked him in the eye and said, "I'm not leaving him, you can say whatever you want."

The couple returned to Beirut, and "two years of a cold war" commenced. She continued to visit her family. They knew she was dating Naji, but no one brought it up. "It was 'Don't ask, don't tell.'"

Eventually, Michelle's mother told family in Lebanon, hoping they would change her mind. "I got a phone call," Michelle recalled, "a silly phone call, from my aunt, talking about it like a hypothetical situation. 'If you were going out with someone like X, that would be a big problem.'" The calls continued as the circle of people who knew about Naji grew. "My grandma called my cousin like, 'I'm worried about Michelle.' And it went on and on."

Three years into the relationship, when Michelle's parents were in Lebanon, the couple met with her mom. "I said, 'Listen, I'm not getting any younger. We want to move forward because I want to have kids, so we want to get married.'" Over her mother's protests, Michelle insisted that this was her decision to make. Defeated, her mother invited the couple to the family's hometown.

"I was really happy that day," Michelle said, "because everyone met him, and it was official. Naji officially said, 'I wanna ask you . . .' that whole thing. And my mom was actually happy. My dad tried to play hardball, making Naji defend his values. But then he said okay too. I think they just wanted to be sure that he's a good person."

Naji, who had been listening to Michelle talk this whole time, added, "I think they had given in by then. The switch from no to yes was like a pendulum. The next day her dad's calling all his siblings, and they are flying here to celebrate." They're also well aware that Michelle's age helped her win the fight.

When I asked about their wedding, assuming, based on the couple's general outlook, that it was a civil marriage, they cracked up in unison.

Catching her breath, Michelle explained their laughter. "No, we got married in a church."

"How did you negotiate that?" I asked.

"There was no negotiation." Deadpan.

Naji chuckled, "Negotiate with who? We didn't have a choice!"

Michelle had prepared Naji for this necessity early on. The process was easier outside Lebanon, because Naji didn't have to convert.

Asking them whether they had baptized their child reignited their laughter.

"*Of course* we did. We didn't have a choice!"

"We didn't want to, because we don't believe in it, but it was easier to just do it."

"We did it for peace."

The couple still hears comments from Michelle's relatives, but true to form, they take it all with humor. Naji's favorite is from a cousin who regularly says, "We always wished for the best, but it's okay." They are equally amused by questions, whether good faith efforts to respect Naji, like "Does he eat pork?" or symptoms of limited imagination in an isolationist village. "Is Naji Maronite or Roum Orthodox?" is their favorite.

Ras Beirut

I met Michelle and Naji at a café in Ras Beirut near their home. They chose to live in that area because of its mixed milieu and couldn't imagine leaving. Within Lebanon, no place garnered as much praise as Ras Beirut, lauded as an open-minded haven where people from all over Lebanon mix . . . and match. Formal maps show "Ras Beirut" as a small neighborhood along the coast, but most people I know, and most of my interviewees, use the phrase to refer to a much larger swath of the city (see map 6.2).

This imagined "Head of Beirut" juts into the sea, too rounded to be a peninsula. Two expensive private universities, both with "American" in their names, border its central neighborhood. Students, tourists, and

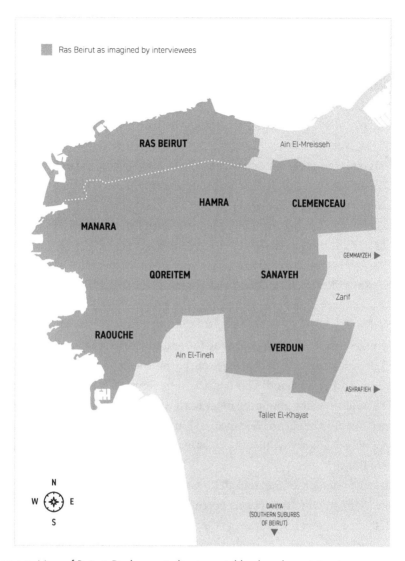

MAP 6.2. Map of Beirut. Dark gray indicates neighborhoods my interviewees included in their imaginations of "Ras Beirut." Map by Kite Creative Studio.

international NGO employees add to its cosmopolitan feel. About 25 percent of the couples in my sample lived in this area at the time of our interview, and others met their spouse there. However, people outside Ras Beirut still described the area as a haven of diversity, imagining that their relationship would be more readily accepted there. Some had relocated to Ras Beirut, or dreamed about doing so, because they saw it as a mixed milieu. Ras Beirut was the litmus test, the sanctuary, the argument clincher, the most succinct explanation for the acceptance of a mixed marriage.

"My parents aren't fanatic at all; they've lived in Ras Beirut their whole lives."

"His dad was open-minded because he lived his whole life in Ras Beirut."

"When I moved to Ras Beirut for high school, I learned that Christians are just normal people."

"My husband didn't meet any Muslims until he came to AUB. He made friends. He got used to us."

"My generation, my friends, we're very mixed—you know, Druze, Sunni, Shi'a, Roum, Maronite, and there aren't any differences between us. . . . Also, let me tell you something, the group I'm telling you about, we all lived in Ras Beirut."

People outside Ras Beirut are the foil, often Christians from "Marounistan," or, since 2005, Shi'a from the southern suburb. "There was a guy who worked with my husband who had to go to Beirut for a meeting, and he didn't know anything about the neighborhood or how to get there," a friend told me, shaking her head. "He lived in Jounieh; it's half an hour away! How is it possible that a guy who must be at least forty can't get around the basic areas of Beirut?"

Another person bemoaned deliberate isolationism. "There are these people living in Christian towns north of Beirut who won't send their kids to AUB because it is a mixed society. But if you won't send them to learn this mixed society, how are we all going to live in a country together? The problem is much bigger than mixed marriage."

The veneration of Ras Beirut as mixed is all the more striking because the area is predominantly Sunni Muslim with a mostly Orthodox Christian minority. Ziad, who grew up in Ras Beirut, was less convinced the area was unique. "Sure, Ras Beirut has a mixed milieu," he said. "But it's not mixed fifty-fifty, it's more like 80 percent Sunni and 20 percent mixed. The milieu is Islam. You see buildings decorated when people return from *hajj*, in Ramadan the drummer wakes people up, when we were growing up, there were fireworks on Muslim holidays.

"There is also a secular aspect, like everyone celebrates Christmas for some reason. There are Christmas trees at schools and the neighbors all have them and buildings even put them up in the hallways. I don't know where that came from."

Ziad's spouse, Mona, grew up in a Christian suburb and today describes Ras Beirut as "home." "I feel a very strong sense of belonging to this area, and a source of pride," she said. "I feel very comfortable here, and I'm very happy in this space."

Ras Beirut is also expensive. It has grown denser over time, seen significant population shifts with violence and regional wars, and been devastated by Lebanon's recent economic collapse. Several interviewees moved out of Ras Beirut, seeking homes in quieter or more affordable suburbs, ideally in another mixed milieu. Badaro was a favorite; its concentration of progressive NGO offices made it feel secular, though prices were rising rapidly even before the economic collapse. A few mixed couples who moved to Christian-majority Ashrafieh felt that area had grown more cosmopolitan than Ras Beirut, a sentiment likely tied to class and negative assessments of Ras Beirut's growing Syrian refugee presence. Most of the time, cost, commute, or convenience determined where people lived.

Jana, who still lives in Ras Beirut, remains convinced it's the most "open" place in Lebanon, where "all sorts of people feel more comfortable because people are more accepting." After a long pause, she continued. "But then sometimes it feels like it's becoming more confined, and then I wonder, Is it my imagination? Am I imposing this perception on this area because I want it to be that way? Or it is really this way?"

Jana was exceptionally thoughtful about her perceptions of Ras Beirut. Most people believed in its capacity for fostering open-mindedness through exposure and were shaken when this process failed. There are just as many parents with high exposure who disown their child for years as there are those who fit the assumption that exposure leads to open-mindedness.

Exposure's Limits

George and Luma's grandmothers are close friends, distantly related, from the same Roum Orthodox village, though Luma is Sunni like her father. George and Luma hung out all the time growing up during visits to their grandmothers. When they struck up a phone relationship and fell in love as teenagers, George's family panicked. One of his relatives asked Luma's parents to tell their daughter to stay away from him, as though she were chasing him. George's parents were so deeply embedded in a closed Christian society that the fact that they knew and were distantly related to Luma's extended family didn't help.

Luma asked her parents to help the couple find a solution. George was ready to marry without his parents' blessing, but she didn't want to elope. At first, Luma's father told George to marry a Christian rather than upset his parents. The couple understood that her dad was trying to respect George's family and give them time to calm down. While they waited, they made their plans. They wanted a civil marriage but couldn't afford it. "We didn't have money to eat, how could we go to Cyprus?" Luma said. "It was crazy, there was no money, we had nothing, so we went for the best practical solution at the time." They planned to have both a *katab kitab* and a church ceremony, registering only the latter.

George's parents were intransigent. They kicked George out of the house and stopped speaking with him. "I was shocked," Luma told me. "I didn't expect it to be this extreme." With that final rejection, the couple decided to forgo the church wedding. With Luma's father's blessing, George converted to Islam, they wed in a *katab kitab*, and emigrated to the Gulf.

Reconciliation took a decade. George's parents first began speaking with George, then Luma, then her parents, then her extended family in the village. When I interviewed the couple another decade after the reconciliation, they had moved to their grandmothers' Christian village because it is more affordable. One of them thinks all is well; the other isn't sure but prefers not to know what people say about them. It helps that their children, though unbaptized, celebrate both Christian and Muslim holidays with family. Some villagers remember that George converted and complained when the couple bought land to build a home. George and Luma do their best to ignore them.

———

Being known to one another's families, a friendship and distant relation between grandmothers, and a village that was part of open-minded Koura before election redistricting shifted regional lines didn't help George and Luma. Exposure hit its limit. Despite how many interviewees talked about exposure, it isn't a binary matter. One is not either exposed or unexposed but has experienced some degree of exposure to some range of places and people. And while exposure may be a condition of intermarriage, it doesn't necessarily correlate with family acceptance of those marriages.

Sometimes, expectations were upended in positive ways. Reem grew up between her Sunni father's Ras Beirut milieu and her Roum mother's Koura village. Her marriage to Shadi, a Maronite from another region, was blessed by both sides. Reem explained, "To tell you the truth, the moment I met Shadi's dad I felt he was an open-minded guy compared to the usual person who lives a rural life. He's so open and exposed to people and to different religions and educated even though he doesn't have a degree, educated through books, through exposure and whatever. . . . He once told me he has this *qawmiyyeh* philosophy, so that's part of it."

Reem's father-in-law disrupted her assumptions that exposure was linked to Beirut and that formal education is a requirement to be open-minded. Her last comment, about his Arab nationalist outlook, tells us that exposure alone was not enough; it was accompanied by a sense of common identity.

When Sima's father got in a taxi to investigate her fiancé, he discovered the same shared political sensibility, a sensibility that holds up collective identity as an ideal. Neither learning more about the fiancé nor newfound exposure to a different region sufficed. The combination of knowing and finding similarity cinched his approval. Other parents who discovered shared leftist secularist politics with their potential in-laws also found it a relief. Both the Syrian Social Nationalist Party (SSNP) and the Communist Party have viewed mixed marriage as a way to move past sectarian divisions.[28] For Roum Orthodox and Druze parents, like Sima's and Akram's, plus many Sunni families from the North, an SSNP connection meant a lot. Shi'i parents who had leaned toward the Communist Party in its heyday— with the exception of that couple in Australia—often accepted mixed marriages unless they faced conservative pressure from extended family.

Had Sima's father not discovered that commonality, would mere exposure have been enough? For couples themselves, exposure to a mixed environment may help, but it doesn't *lead* to mixed marriage. Common friends, shared activities, and similar interests, experiences, and worldviews bring people together. The depth and quality of exposure matters. Psychologists talk about the "mere exposure effect" or "familiarity principle," where the first reaction when someone is exposed to something new is fear. Only with increased exposure *and growing familiarity* does fear change to a positive response. Family requires familiarity.

The form exposure takes can make all the difference. As with the civil war, exposure to different people through violence solidifies divides. Parents who felt rejected by their in-laws worried that the same thing would happen to their children. Parents told stories about friends married to someone "from there" who turned out to be awful. They mentioned news reports, like that 2013 castration, or rumors of houses burned down or women killed over mixed marriage. Muslim parents who faced discrimination at mixed workplaces worried that Christian families would disdain their children. Christian parents from Ras Beirut who saw Muslim neighbors grow more religious worried that Muslim grooms or brides would do so as well. In Lebanon's context of regular insecurity, parents often rely on similarity to ensure their children's futures.

Once in a while, experience worked in the couple's favor. Parents who had seen family estrangements wanted to avoid them. Others accepted mixed matches because they had lent an ear to friends suffering through divorce or abuse at the hands of a spouse who checked all the right identity boxes. My interviewees used this script well, reminding parents of "appropriate marriages" that failed, where women were miserable or husbands were cheating, marriages that revealed how hollow surface-level similarity could be.

———

Mona and Ziad, the couple who discussed Ras Beirut above, grew up in disparate environments. Her family are practicing Maronites who live in a Christian suburb. His are "typical secular liberal Sunnis from Beirut" who fast during Ramadan, rarely pray, always have a Christmas tree, and sent their children to Catholic school. We met in a café near AUB, our interview extending through multiple coffees and croissants. They described their story as "an easy one" with minimal fuss on either side, because by the time they married, they were in their early thirties and financially independent.

My conversation with Mona and Ziad sometimes felt like they were talking to one another as much as to me. They were obviously in love, still getting to know one another, and committed to doing so. Even when they disagreed, their vibe was always, "We're in this together." Tearing up several times, Mona was still processing how her family treated Ziad. He took things in stride, injecting humor into the conversation and making her smile. As we spoke, they remembered obnoxious things Mona's relatives had said, *talteesh* that left no doubt as to what they truly thought about Muslims. I asked for examples.

"Like, her aunt used to say to me, 'You know, you look just like us!' And I would look at her, and say, 'As opposed to the Muslims who have tails?' Like, what?! What?!" Ziad's memory animated his gestures, his voice rising.

"It's like you're the good one," Mona added, just in case I hadn't understood.

"Yeah, exactly."

"'You look like us.' Yeah, like, they have this idea, and he sounds and looks and, you know, listens to music, like . . .'"

"I'm Westernized." Ziad's sarcasm was unmistakable.

"It's exposure. I think for my side of the family, it's a matter of exposure."

"Exposure, yeah."

"They're not exposed to Muslims very much. They're not exposed to people from different sects. I mean, even this area [Ras Beirut, near AUB], they don't really know how to get here."

"They don't come to it. Your family doesn't come to west Beirut and if they do, it's like each one needs a visa to come here, and they are very conscious of being here, but my family, they'll go anywhere."

"That's true."

"Even trying to get your family to come to Gemmayzeh is a struggle," Ziad said.

I interrupt, confused, because Gemmayzeh is a Christian neighborhood known for its pubs and restaurants. Why wouldn't Mona's family meet them there? The couple speculates that maybe it's too close to mixed neighborhoods, or maybe the area's nightlife draws a mixed crowd, or maybe they're scared they'll get lost, their ignorance of Beirut's streets magnifying their fears.

Mona brings us back on topic. "Look, I really think it's because of lack of exposure, they actually have an idea that something will be really different, and then the more they see it, the more they're like, 'Ohhhh,' like, 'Now I get it.' Like when they first met Ziad . . ."

"Yeah, I broke that down actively. I worked on it consciously, like, first, I drink. Second, I . . ."

"But sometimes he makes—sorry for interrupting, Ziad—but sometimes you made it a very big point, I think unconsciously, to display the similarities, to the extent where . . ."

"No, they *always* have asked me, 'Don't you want to drink?' It's like I have to drink alcohol to prove to you that I'm not too Muslim or I don't hate Christians, you know?"

"But I'm not so sure that was actually happening . . ."

"No, no, no. It's actually happening. Come on!"

"No, no, I'm not saying, sorry, I'm not saying that it's *not*, but I'm saying . . ."

"It *is*! It is more conscious than you think it is."

Ziad and Mona agree that her family's bias against him stems from their minimal exposure to other places and people. Mona assumes that the more they "see" Ras Beirut and Muslims, the more they'll see how similar they are to them, putting family tensions to rest. Ziad experiences this as having to prove he's "just like them." Mona thinks Ziad is over-reading sectarian social pressure into the situation and overcompensating as a result. But they agree that exposure only worked *because* it led her family to see similarity instead of difference.

———

Exposure turns an unknown into a known, breaching Lebanon's divided geographies. But exposure has to lead to positive experiences, to new-found familiarity. The new name on the kinship tree has to fit. This can be a long-term struggle. One mother-in-law told me, of her counterpart, "I don't understand what she says. Or what I say is confusing for her. There are terms we don't use or they don't use, herbs we know and they don't, bits and pieces of daily life where you find yourself always saying, 'In your place, how do you do this?' There's always this question mark. Even when it comes to cooking, there's 'you' and 'us,' you know what I mean? If you become family with someone from your same milieu, you don't feel this difference." She had adapted to her in-laws over the years, but our conversation about her child's mixed marriage triggered memories of her initial struggles and thwarted expectations for what life would be like when two families grafted together.

When parents refuse to do the work of bridging differences or when similarity is elusive or social cartography fails, we are left with negative stereotypes. I heard stories from couples who knew in their bones that, despite their own similarities, their families were utterly incompatible. Parents in these stories often said something like, "She comes from a different culture (*thaqafa*). Their milieu is too different from ours." The connection between place and people is explicit in this refrain. "People" becomes "culture"—as though human beings exist in neat boxes, each containing its own, discrete, way of life. I'm of the school of anthropology that thinks pinning everything on the idea of culture, what we call the "culture concept," is one of the disservices the field did to the world. It has become too easy to chalk anything up to "cultural difference." Culture has become a polite way to denigrate difference, a mask hiding racism, sect-ism, classism. Culture becomes the language people use to allow prejudice to shape the meaning of sect. In Lebanon today, "culture" hides Islamophobia and anti-Muslim discrimination.

Seven

Islamophobia and Other Discriminations

When Corinne fell in love with Nader, a Sunni from Ras Beirut, in high school, she feared her Roum Orthodox parents would give her a hard time because her older sister Helena had fought with them over a Muslim boyfriend. "Subconsciously, seeing those fights affected me," Corinne said. "It made me hide things from my parents until I was strong enough to define what I wanted, or maybe just to avoid their interference."

The couple nurtured their relationship through college, all the while maintaining the fiction with their families that they were "just friends." After graduating, Corinne left Lebanon to continue her studies. When she returned over winter break the first year, Nader spent a lot of time at their family home.

"It was clear that we were close," Corinne said. "My dad asked me, 'Is he your boyfriend?' And I said no but then I said, 'Would it be okay if he was?' because I was stronger then and I lived abroad. And Nader is a super nice guy with super secular parents. Anyway, my parents were like, 'Why not? Tell him to come over for dinner.' So he came over . . . and it was like a very soft introduction that he might be more than a friend."

Helena, the older sister, believes their parents had changed by the time Corinne told them about Nader—in part because she herself remained unmarried in her thirties. She described that same conversation differently.

"My dad asked Corinne, 'Are you and Nader friends or more than friends?' She was like, 'Friends.' Then a second later she was like, 'Actually I'm totally in love with him and want to marry him.' And he's like, 'It's okay,' and he laughed and hugged her. It was very easy. I think by then she was old enough. Plus, it was like, 'Our daughter wants to marry her high school sweetheart. That's so cute.'"

Nader's parents were, as you might expect by now, nonplussed. They invited Corinne's family to dinner, and everyone encouraged the couple to marry quickly to avoid premarital cohabitation. Corinne and Nader happily complied.

Corinne and Helena agree that their parents see Nader and his parents as "extra"-secular Muslims. Their mother continues to tell cautionary tales about Christian women who married Muslims. "So-and-so's daughter married a Muslim and now she won't eat gumbo anymore," or, "We thought so-and-so was open-minded but now she is wearing a headscarf." But now, those cautionary tales end with, "But we know Nader's family isn't like that." As Helena explained it, "His parents would drink over dinner. They'd never been to a mosque. All those little indicators that my parents use as proxies weren't there."

"I think the fear is when they think they're going to lose you to the other side," Corinne elaborated. "The disaster stories are the ones everyone talks about, so they worried about things like, 'He is going to take the children because of Islamic law' or 'He is going to marry someone else.' But then it developed into these two tracks, like there is Muslim, and there is *Muslim*. There are secular Beiruti Muslims from good families, and there are *Muslims* who it would be scary for your daughter to marry."

––––––––

"What if he forces you to wear the headscarf?"

"What if he marries a second wife?"

"What if he stops drinking? How will you go out?"

"What if he says you can't celebrate Christmas?"

"What if he says you can't go to the beach?"

Parents asked these questions in many—sometimes tens—of the stories I gathered. Muslim grooms triggered these reactions, though I also heard worries that Muslim brides wouldn't know how to raise children properly.

Because everyone assumes you can tell if a Muslim woman is religious from her clothing, a Muslim bride without a headscarf is more quickly understood to be "just like us" than a groom who must prove it again and again. Women who wear headscarves rarely marry outside their religion.

Interviewees who attributed these comments to a parent's civil war experience or lack of exposure told me they had tried to respond empathetically, however absurd the questions. In their stories, some added a snort of laughter, a head shake, or an eye roll, showing how ridiculous they found it all. But most relived the rage they had felt when they first heard these things said about the person they loved. They called out their parents' biases as bigotry. Some called it racism in English, *'unsuriyyeh* in Arabic. The term "Islamophobia" only came up a couple times, said by people who had spent time in the United States.

I wasn't surprised. In the US, Muslim scholars and writers, and those of us who write about Muslim communities, take it for granted that we must always address Islamophobia and anti-Muslim racism. Having worked in this context my entire career, when I first heard Lebanese living in Lebanon say things I was used to hearing in the US—comments about burkas and "covered women"—my first thought was, Anti-Muslim racism has traveled. Yet I also heard a specific Lebanese Christian Islamophobia where people referred to all Muslims as "Islam," as though the term referenced people and not a religion: "They're Islam." "Of course we have friends who aren't like that, but Islam cover their heads." When I pressed one woman saying such things to me, it became clear that her Islamophobia related to a morass of local Lebanese politics, specifically her hatred of the Shi'i political party Hizbullah, plus geopolitical fears and antipathy toward both Iran and Saudi Arabia, plus US war on terror discourses that appeared in her references to "burkas" or Afghanistan.[1] Her use of "Islam" to refer to Muslims is a mode of dehumanization that refuses to acknowledge the diversity of Muslims in the world. Imagine saying, "Christianity sends queer children to conversion therapy."

Islamophobia travels in multiple directions. While some biased comments came from Europe and the US, they also grew from Lebanese soil.[2] From the early French mandate, while other leaders were writing against new forms of sectarianism in the region, Ussama Makdisi explains, some Maronite Christian leaders "exhibit[ed] open chauvinism towards Muslim

Arabs" as they put forward a "notion of Christian Lebanese civilizational exceptionalism" and "supremacy."[3] These were the men who, along with other elites and the French, laid the groundwork to institutionalize sectarianism in the nascent country. This Lebanese history is as much a part of Lebanese Islamophobia as any external influence. Ghassan Moussawi coins the phrase "fractal Orientalism" to explain how Orientalism is not merely the self-defining gaze of the West on the East but appears within Lebanon, in local ways of seeing other Lebanese through an Orientalizing lens. Fractal Orientalism is a way of thinking about the relationship of transnational and local ideas to one another, of scaling ideas up and scaling them down. Applied to Islamophobia, this image of a fractal captures people pulling multiple stereotypes about Muslims together and spitting them back out onto the people next door as well as those across the country, region, or globe. This chapter follows those biases through various Islamophobic discourses before considering their relationship to racism and xenophobia.

Good Muslims Drink, Just Like Us

"There is Muslim, and there is *Muslim*." Unintentionally, Corinne's analysis of her parents' views echoed another script that is both local and transnational. In the US, this plays out through allies and enemies, good Muslims and bad, Muslims who appear to fit in versus those who don't, Muslims who are useful to geopolitical agendas versus those in the way.[4] For many Lebanese— including many Muslims who view themselves as secular and therefore different from *Muslims*, it comes down to whether the person in question looks and lives like them, or whether they look and act "too religious." It was all headscarves and alcohol.

Over and over, people whose parents eventually accepted their Muslim partner said something like, "When they met, they saw that we're the same. We talk in the same way. We eat almost the same style of food." One mother admitted to me that upon finally meeting her future son-in-law, "I felt like they aren't different from us at all. Basically, to sum it up, they're Lebanese!" Another woman, a wealthy, well-traveled Christian who socializes with Lebanese of all backgrounds, was nervous about a mixed marriage in her extended family until she met the bride's parents. "They were very hospitable, and they are *like us*, a beautiful family, very nice people!"

Parents who "come around" because they realize their future child-in-law is "just like us" aren't changing their stereotypes. They're making an exception for their new family member. The group remains a problem, but the individual can be incorporated into a social map. "She's Muslim, but she's not really *Muslim*." "She's not like them." "He's unusual." "He's Muslim, *but he's just like us*."

Some interviewees hoped that this realization would trickle outward, broadening the impact of their marriage. "My dad is thrilled my husband sits and has a drink with other people," one woman shared. "It's like my dad is saying, 'See! He drinks!' And really, one of my cousins recently met my husband, and said, 'He's very cool, we had a great night together.' So from a drink I feel like my family breached their whole position with Islam. Now they have a case in their home, in their family. They used to hear that not all Muslims are ISIS. But now, they have an actual case in the family. Now, they use my husband as an example when they are talking to other people."

You have likely noticed how frequently alcohol appears in these stories, Muslim men making a point of gifting in-laws alcohol or drinking with them. One couple orchestrated the initial meeting between their families with this in mind. "We made sure to choose the place to meet so they would feel that no one is religious. We went during Ramadan, and we had drinks. We did that intentionally."

Alcohol thwarted other couples' efforts to introduce their parents. "We just can't figure it out," one woman told me, throwing her hands up in defeat. "If I think about inviting my in-laws to my parents' house, then I start thinking . . . you know. His parents don't drink, and my dad, it's all alcohol, so I don't want to put the dads together, because my dad might say something about alcohol. It is neither normal nor healthy that they haven't met each other yet. But truth be told, the risk of an argument is high, so I don't know. Or maybe we just need to prepare a lot, and sit with my dad for around a hundred hours to talk with him and ask him not to make jokes about religion or Mohammad or alcohol, and not to offer alcohol to his dad. And then we'll have to talk to his dad too, and ask him to be patient and not overreact if my dad says something. And both of them are very strong characters, so it's just easier for them not to meet."

Readers in the US might be thinking, But I have family members who drink and family members who don't, and it doesn't matter. Maybe a relative is an alcoholic, maybe they don't like the taste, maybe they prefer to smoke weed. Different relationships to alcohol itself aren't the problem. It may be a logistical challenge, but people adapt and learn and come to know one another. What matters is the meaning people load on top of the difference, the assumptions they make about what someone's choice not to drink means, hierarchies where drinking is better than not drinking or vice versa, fear that refusing alcohol is a sign of something else. In Lebanon, avoiding alcohol is an overt symbol of being a pious Muslim.[5] When both families are comfortable with alcohol, similarity is established. People are saying, "We're not religious, we're not *that kind of Muslim*."

————

While Nader and Corinne were dating, his older brother Hussam met Sophia at a party. Raised in a Maronite family in a Christian suburb, Sophia assumed Hussam was Christian because he was hanging out with a group of Christian mutual friends. When she discovered her mistake, she told him her parents were very conservative and "would probably kill him" if they dated. Sophia laughed as she told me their story. "He was *very* persistent, and we got along very well so I said, 'Let's give it a shot.'"

When Hussam posted a photo with Sophia on Facebook, she went "ballistic," terrified her brothers would see it and inform her parents. She was pleased when one of them instead offered his support. Still, her parents learned about the relationship long before Sophia was ready to tell them. The first time Hussam called her at home, her mom freaked out. "Who is this guy?" Sophia told her Hussam was just a friend, but her mother was suspicious. Unlike Sophia, her mother knew Hussam was Sunni from his name. She began searching through Sophia's Facebook friends until she found his profile and, of course, the photo.

Sophia recalled their confrontation. "First she said, 'This guy, in that picture with you, he looks very cute.' I said, 'Thank you, Mom.' Then she said, 'He doesn't look Christian. What's his name?' But she already knew it! So I told her his name and said, 'Of course he's not Maronite!' And she was like, 'Ahhhhh! Why didn't you tell me?' And I said, 'Of course I didn't tell you, for this obvious reason!' And then she tried to seem cool, and like she was okay with it and just wanted to meet him, but that was just to get information out of me." Sophia thinks her mother's response was milder than expected because she had dated several Maronites "and none of them were good." Her mom liked Hussam when they met, though she still wished he were Christian.

Then Sophia's hand was forced again. Hussam came to the condolence gathering for one of Sophia's relatives, and without knowing who he was, Sophia's father invited him to dinner. Sophia had to explain that they were dating. Despite being the more "open-minded" parent, her father was "a bit stunned." Her parents' concerns revolved around Islamophobic assumptions that Hussam would force conversion or the headscarf or polygamy on Sophia. Still, less than a year after that dinner, Sophia's parents gave the couple their blessing, having seen how deeply in love they were. But they set a condition: an eighteen-month engagement.

The long engagement gave Sophia's parents and relatives time to relentlessly badger her, hoping the relationship would collapse. "They had no shame. Up until the day before the wedding, they were asking me, 'Are you sure you want to marry a Muslim? If you aren't sure, we can cancel the wedding.' There was talk like this until I said, 'I do' in Cyprus."

When I asked Sophia's mother why she didn't want Hussam as a son-in-law, she brought up recent protests over the publication of a caricature of the Prophet Muhammad. "To be honest, I was afraid he would be a fanatic boy," she then said. "But when I met him and his family, and I saw their way of living and their principles, I felt that they don't differ from us at all. He seemed to be very open-minded, his way of living is like ours, their way of thinking and how they behave is like us, they are not different from us. In the end, they are Lebanese. Okay, they are of a different religion, but they aren't very religious. Religion is only on the ID for them. They are secular like us. Of course, I would prefer that he were Christian, but they're happy, so what more can I want, you know?"

Several times during our conversation, Sophia's mother circled back to how important it was that Hussam's family was invisibly Muslim. At one point she said, "Look, if they wore headscarves and prayed five times a day, and their life spun around praying, and women are allowed to do this thing and not allowed to do that thing, *of course* I wouldn't allow her to marry him. I would fight with every limb, but they don't have these things. And as long as there is no external aspect to it, and there is no attitude and he has dinner with us and he drinks as we do and he is not like,

'This is gumbo, remove it,' and 'This is ham, we don't eat it,' everything is okay."

Good Muslims Are Secular, Just Like Us

"They're okay because they are *like us*." What does this mean? A shared lack of headscarves, a shared drinking of alcohol, plus, oddly, eating gumbo—which came up so frequently that it must have been a culinary trend when I did some of my interviews. On top of these visible markers of *not* being a practicing Muslim, Sophia's mother and other Christian parents described their Muslim in-laws as being "secular like us" or sharing their "secular lifestyle." But most of these same Christian parents go to church, at least on holidays; put up elaborate Christmas trees; and want their grandchildren to be baptized. Sophia's mother even told me how important her Christian faith and practice is to her. How can they understand themselves as "secular"?

As Talal Asad has argued, the meaning of "secular" is rooted in a European Christian context.[6] This context infuses my interviewees' ideas about secularism, no matter their background. They all described secular people as more cosmopolitan, open-minded, educated, and modern than other Lebanese. Some people—including some Muslims and Druze—added another idea to this mix: that Christianity is "more compatible" with secularism than Islam. They thought that going to church on Palm Sunday and Easter was still part of a secular lifestyle. Fasting during Ramadan or going to mosque on Eid was not. Even whether a practice counted as religious in the first place differed. People described walking around a church three times then attending Easter services as a "cultural tradition" and going to a mosque for Eid prayers as a religious practice. Several Christian mothers wished their daughter had married a Muslim named Tarek, Ziad, or Karim rather than Muhammad, Ahmad, or Hussein. "We don't display our religion in our names," one told me, as my mind scrolled through common Lebanese names that signal Christianity, like George/Girges, Paul/Boulos, Maroun, or John. A few women complained about Muslim visibility while wearing gold cross necklaces. One's diamond-studded cross reflected the sunlight as she fretted about the increase in women wearing the headscarf in Beirut. "Those women are making Lebanese society less secular." I bit my tongue, fighting an impulse to point out that her cross didn't seem particularly secular to me either.

This idea that Christianity is more secular than Islam dovetails with French unease with Muslim visibility, manifest most obviously in French bans on wearing the headscarf in public schools.[7] Not all my interviewees connected secularism with French *laïcité*. Some connected it to a US-style separation of church and state. Others drew on the multiple strands of secularism (*'ilmani-yya*) that emerge from Arab and Lebanese thought,[8] and from leftist political parties that have disavowed sectarianism since the establishment of the state.[9] As they described their ideas to me, they mixed and matched strands. Admissible belief and practice ranged from atheism to invisible faith. A few supported right-wing Maronite desires to carve out a Christian, Europe-leaning country in Lebanon, but most didn't imagine their nation without Muslims.

Generation mattered. Lebanese who came of age during the 1960s and '70s linked their secularism to participation in leftist political or student groups. Interviewees who came of age after the civil war ended in 1990 associated secularism with postwar activist trends and practices, including support for civil marriage.[10] They shared older leftists' belief that a more secular country would lead to greater gender and socioeconomic equality, less corruption, and even a cleaner environment.[11]

Many such couples identified shared secularism as key to their relationship. As one explained, "[That shared secularist identity] brought us together, in a way. It's on our minds every single day. Each of us is always the staunchest critic of our own respective communities that kind of spat us into the world . . ."

"Due to mainly indigestion," interrupted his spouse.

Other people linked their secularism to nostalgia for prewar Lebanon. They expressed alarm about changes paralleling a global religious revival since the 1970s. Sunni Beirut restaurant owners who stopped serving alcohol in their establishments are part of this trend, as is the religious ideology and rhetoric of Hizbullah.[12] Longtime Ras Beirut residents expressed the most alarm. "All of our peers, our friends who used to drink, they don't drink anymore," Diana, a woman in her sixties, told me. "Now they ask if something is pork. These are friends who graduated from the American University of Beirut, ministers, doctors, educated people, they have the best positions in the country, and they ask if something is *halal*. In the '70s, this didn't exist. In the '80s, we didn't know what *halal* meant."

Parents of all religions whose children attended private secular schools complained about new schedule changes to accommodate students fasting during Ramadan. A birthday party during Ramadan caused a stir on a parents' WhatsApp group because it included a visit to a local mosque for prayer. And as in the US and Europe, the headscarf loomed large in these comments. People mocked women who wore it, or assumed it reflected "extremism." "It really bothers me that there are lots of people who are wearing *hijab* now," one said. "It's so excessive."

Confronting Islamophobia

When Islamophobic ideas about headscarves and alcohol were levied in a fight against mixed marriage, they became weapons. Christian women were often blindsided by their parents' biases. They were forced to face not only their parents' views but also the depth of Islamophobia and sectarianism in their milieu. Crying, one woman described how distant she felt from her family since marrying her Muslim husband: "I think a part of me doesn't really want to face that maybe sectarianism has something to do with it, because, if I do, it really hurts me. It hurts." She began describing what relatives had said to her, then stopped abruptly. "It's really hard to think about the things they said now. It's much more difficult than when they said them. They said these things about my husband, my love. Now these are things they must also think about my children."

Some women had to confront the bias that seeped from their milieu into their own perspectives. Corinne believes her parents thwarted her sister Helena's relationships with Muslims. Helena tells a different version. Her parents and relatives lectured her about how inappropriate it was to date a Muslim high school classmate, but the relationship ran its course until they broke up a few years later. And when Helena fell in love with another Muslim in her twenties, she didn't tell her parents. That relationship ended for unrelated reasons. At the same time, Helena admitted, to herself and to me, the constant stream of information about what kind of person she should marry affected how she imagined her life: "All my life, I basically kept getting comments about what my parents don't want. I'm sure it affected my decision-making on some subconscious level."

Another Christian woman shared her own struggle with ideas about Islam: "You know, at one point, I thought to myself, What if he *does* become more religious? What if he wants to bring more tradition and ritual into our home? I want to support that. I mean, sometimes people go to religion as a way of coping with anxiety, stress, hardships, and also maybe because your identity is always in the process of changing. So let's say at some point he wanted to be more religious? I had this discussion with myself. Could I be okay with him becoming more religious? More practicing? And is that a bad thing? And I thought, Well, it's not a bad thing, if he can practice without imposing it on me. I don't know why I would think that being a practicing Muslim means that he's going to all of a sudden impose it on me. And that comes from fear and anxiety, you know, fear of the other that I grew up with."

Muslim partners and in-laws weren't surprised by what Christian parents said about them. Even if they shared the alarm at religious revivalism or the abandonment of a "secular lifestyle," they were equally critical of the Islamophobia they saw in Lebanese society. Some told me that growing up, they thought Christians were more open-minded, and then as adults, they encountered extremist forms of Christianity which overturned those assumptions.

Muslim parents also expressed concerns based on stereotypes. They worried that a Christian girlfriend was promiscuous or just "playing" with their son and would break his heart, that a Christian husband would force Christianity on their daughter or "make her" wear revealing clothing, that Christian in-laws or villagers would mistreat a non-Christian spouse, or that the inability to divorce would doom their child to an unhappy marriage. Nor were Muslim families, especially outside Beirut, immune to the "just like us" discovery. One woman described her family's initial response to her fiancé: "At first, they acted like he was a weird creature that they wanted to know more about, and they would approach him, like at public events, they would come and ask him completely irrelevant personal questions. They wanted to know where this Christian guy lived and what kinds of things he did in his life. And he would answer, and then they would say, like, 'Oh, you live like us!'" The crucial difference is that when "just like us"—or any of these stereotypes—is uttered by a Muslim rather than a Christian, it doesn't carry the combined weight of local and transnational Islamophobia behind it.

———

Remember Celeste and Samia, the two women of opposing aesthetic styles whose friendship failed when their children married? The crux of the problem was their incompatible ideas about what it meant to be secular. Celeste's "secularism" was mostly Christianity. Christmas, Easter, and church on Palm Sunday, plus traditional sweets on Eid al-Fitr. It was also nostalgia for a lost Lebanon.

"Our generation, oh Lara, you don't know the Lebanon we knew, it was *such* a beautiful Lebanon," she told me. "So we were adamant that we were going to keep the Beirut we knew with all our friends. We were all Muslims and Christians together, no one knew who was what, this one married this one, so what? We were all one. We studied in the same schools; we went to the same universities. Now, all the mothers wear the headscarf. All the girls wear the headscarf. It's different, and we witnessed the change, and it really breaks my heart."

Samia shares Celeste's criticism of the increase in visible Muslim piety via the headscarf in Ras Beirut. But she wouldn't be happy that I have drawn this parallel between their views. Samia finds the increase in headscarves troubling because she believes it is a misinterpretation of Islam. She doesn't wear one but respects female elders who do; it's a marker of age and status. Deeply aware of anti-Muslim sentiment among Lebanese Christians, Samia connected the antiheadscarf bias she sensed in Celeste to global "Islamophobia" (in English) and "sectarianism" (in Arabic). At the same time, while Celeste used Islamophobic stereotypes to describe how Lebanon has changed, she also refuses to move to a Christian suburb because she worries that her husband and children will face anti-Muslim discrimination in that milieu.

Daily Anti-Muslim Discriminations

Mixed couples in Lebanon are rarely allowed to forget their situation. Sophia compared her life with Hussam with the experiences of Nader and Corinne: "We live in Lebanon, and they do not. Everything is against us here." After describing legal complications, she continued, "And people here are always judgmental when they meet me. It's obvious that I am from [a Christian area] from how I look and talk, and then they ask, 'What is your husband's name?' And when I tell them, they look at me as if I committed a crime. It happens often, and I can see judgment in them, like, '*Haram!* How did that happen?' I see it all the time."

Mixed couples confront daily discrimination. For example, their housing struggles are compounded. Long before the current economic crisis, gentrification was pushing people out of Beirut's central neighborhoods. Others wanted to move to greener spaces. The further away from Beirut, the more segregated the area. I heard about landlords in Christian areas who didn't return calls about vacant apartments or refused to rent to mixed couples. Upon learning her husband's name, a landlord told a Christian woman, "We would like to inform you that we do not rent to our Muslim brothers." Another couple heard, "We do not rent to our Muslim sisters." Efforts to pass a law preventing people from selling property to someone of a different sect failed in parliament, but municipalities can take matters into their own hands. The Al-Hadath municipality, just outside Beirut, has an ordinance preventing Christians from selling land to Muslims. Villages can be even more challenging. Several mixed couples who wanted to buy land in the Christian partner's village were discouraged from doing so or blocked by village authorities. In most cases, it wasn't an ordinance but social norms at work. Fears of population displacement and replacement color mixed couples' efforts to find housing in Lebanon.

Once they find an apartment, the doorman or neighbors might refer to a mixed couple as "the Muslim [or Druze, or sometimes Christian]" and "the one married to the Muslim [or Druze, or sometimes Christian]." Other hassles ensue. Several people were questioned when they tried to set up a service for their home. A telephone company employee asked a Muslim man trying to install a phone line, "What are you doing here? Why are you registering a phone line with us in this neighborhood?" His Christian father-in-law had to intervene. Filing government paperwork is another hurdle. When a woman marries, she must file papers to move her registration as a Lebanese citizen from her father's family registry to her husband's. The public employees filing this paperwork often opine on the marriage. A woman with an obviously Christian name heard, "Ouf, [you married a] Shi'a? What happened to you? Inshallah he's wealthy."

When Sophia said, "Everything is against us," she was talking about legal and bureaucratic hassles as well as the feeling of being judged for her mixed marriage. Other people shared similar feelings. They told me about colleagues who scolded them and clients they lost. Some avoided former salons or stores. Friends made cruel comments. One woman was stunned when a close friend responded to her engagement news with, "What a waste!" Still stinging, my interviewee continued, "I said, 'What do you mean, "What a waste"? Am I being liquidated? Eliminated? What do you mean?!'" Intrusive questions were common. Several Muslim women were asked if their Christian husbands were circumcised, a question they found offensive, embarrassing, and sometimes bewildering.

Even in urban areas, strangers commented on mixed marriages. When a store owner an interviewee had known since childhood interrupted a conversation to say, "Wait, *you're* the one in a mixed marriage?" she was shocked. "I kept thinking, How is he standing there, thinking about my marriage out loud like that?" Another woman told me about a shopkeeper who congratulated her on her visible pregnancy and then said, "We need to have more Christian babies." She replied, "Oh, but you know this baby isn't going to be Christian!" A glint in her eye, she told me, "The shopkeeper had no idea where to look or how to apologize, but I had fun!" And a man laughed, "The street we live on in Beirut, it's like they have our file, it's like there are undercover police. Once, the hairdresser said something to me, about emigration or something and how hard it was, and then he was like, 'Would it be hard even though you are Christian?' And I was thinking, How did he know that? So I'm sure the whole street knows we're a mixed couple. The hairdresser, the concierge, the baker, the grocery store owner. We joke about it, like we're being watched."

When commentary seeped into social gatherings, it could be an unpleasant wake-up call to the extent of Islamophobic and anti-Muslim views in Lebanon. Muslim women sometimes found themselves caught in conversations where guests who didn't know they were Muslim said terrible, bigoted things about their religious group. Many of them called it out. "Do I look different than you? I am Muslim; do I look like a bad person to you?" After an uncomfortable silence, the usual response was, "Oh, we have lots of Muslim friends!"

Anti-Muslim bias even marred a playdate at one woman's friend's house. "This other woman there was talking about how her kids' school was moving closer to Beirut. And she was nagging like, 'How am I going to take my kids down there?' This is an educated person. And she was saying, 'How are they going to mix with all those Muslim students?' All 'Muslims Muslims Muslims.' She kept saying, like a thousand times, 'Muslims are not like us. Muslims are not like us, not like us.'

"And I was silent, silent, silent, and finally, after she was done spewing all of this, I couldn't take it anymore. I stood up and said, 'Look at me carefully.' I turned around and said, 'Do I have a tail?'

"She was shocked. She said, 'No.'

"'Do I have animal ears?'

"'No.'

"'Do you see anything in me different from you?'

"She froze and was like, 'Why are you asking me all this?'

"'Please, just tell me, am I different from you?'

"And she said, 'No.'

"And I yelled, 'Because I'm a Muslim!' She didn't know where to look, she was so embarrassed."

My interviewee used a racist idea that non-Muslim Lebanese sometimes say to dehumanize Muslims (or Shi'a) to call out the other woman's bigotry. Few people invoked such racist ideas explicitly in our conversations, or talked about religions in Lebanon as races, but ideas about the racialization of religious groups hovered just beneath the surface.

Islamophobia and Racism

I have argued, alongside many scholars, that Islamophobia in the US is a form of racism, highlighting the structural aspects of this form of discrimination, its intersections with anti-Black racism and xenophobia, and the racialization of Islam during and before the war on terror.[13] Sarah Gualtieri shows how immigrants to the US from Greater Syria linked race and religion in the 1920s, viewing marriage to a white ethnic as a way to assimilate into whiteness and calling both Christian-Muslim marriages and Syrian–non-Syrian marriages "interracial."[14] Junaid Rana explains how European ideas infused colonial racism in the Americas in ways that racialized Muslims.[15] Sylvia Chan-Malik, among others, connects Islam in the US to communities of color, highlighting Islam's roots as a Black religion in this context.[16]

These US-specific histories don't hitch rides to Lebanon on the backs of Islamophobic ideas.[17] Despite the power that European and US-based ideas hold for many Lebanese of all religions, the fact is that Lebanon is a Muslim-majority country in a Muslim-majority region. One reason Islamophobia is more accurately called "anti-Muslim racism" in the US is because it is systemic, not merely an individual bias or "phobia" that can be shed through education or exposure. In Lebanon, sometimes Islamophobia works like structural racism—women in headscarves are routinely denied jobs in certain neighborhoods, for example. And sometimes Muslims are racialized in dehumanizing ways. But it is neither consistent nor systematic; there is no stable hierarchy of sects to sustain a clear structural inequality.[18]

Plus, collapsing Islamophobia into racism in Lebanon deflects our attention from Lebanese racism against African and Asian migrant laborers and domestic workers, discrimination that brings race, nationality, and class together. Racism in Lebanon has a different history than in the US; its structural persistence isn't built on settler colonialism and enslavement. In her dissertation, one of few works on race in Lebanon, Sumayya Kassamali suggests that Lebanese ideas about race emerge from a combination of European racial ideologies and "local anxieties and discriminatory associations."[19] European ideas about white supremacy join local discrimination built on histories of Lebanese trade practices in Africa and participation in the slave trade, racial labor hierarchies, and the abusive *kafala* system that brings domestic workers from Ethiopia, Sri Lanka, Indonesia, and elsewhere into Lebanese homes via "sponsors" who control their labor and mobility, often by taking their passports. The migrant workers who sometimes brought coffee or cleared the table during my interviews are employed via that *kafala* system.

Race, class, and nationality intersect powerfully. Black American basketball players on Lebanese teams are celebrities. Ethiopian domestic workers are barred from some swimming pools. A Lebanese might marry an Asian American professional with relative ease but never a migrant domestic worker from Asia. And most parents would likely fight a marriage to a Black American professional more stridently than an interreligious one, despite class parity and the prospects of a US passport.

Both racism and Islamophobia are linked to Lebanese desires to be associated with Europe, and, by extension, with global whiteness. The *kafala* system connects Lebanese sponsors to global whiteness through their participation in global circulations of racial labor exploitation.[20] Christianity is another bridge, mistaken as somehow quintessentially European,[21] an internalized hierarchy of religions and world regions that places colonial Christian Europe at its apex. In the 1970s and '80s, many young Druze men studied in the Soviet Union and returned with Christian wives from Russia and Ukraine. These women were greeted with respect, embraced into families, assimilated into village life—even in conservative Druze villages where marrying outside the sect was anathema. Whiteness smoothed their path, until new associations of Eastern European women with sex work took hold after the civil war.

Lebanese have even adopted European markers of Christianity. In Orthodox villages in the 1950s or '60s, decorated Christmas trees were rare displays of wealth, cosmopolitanism, and connections to Europe. There is something painfully ironic about people from the world's oldest Christian communities looking across the sea to define their Christianity. We can understand it as a reach, in the 1950s, for modernization by connecting to Europe, plus the influence of Protestant missionaries and return émigrés who had lived in the US. Today, it is a reach for racial status, to be counted as part of a global community of white people, a longing for European whiteness that grows as Christian political power in Lebanon wanes. Being Christian and being white cannot be separated in the imaginations of many Lebanese, even when they don't use the language of race.

A few people I interviewed imagined phenotypic differences between Christian and Muslim Lebanese, global colorism laid onto sectarian difference. Ali Kassam describes how women who wear the headscarf are racialized in contrast to the "ideal" light-skinned, blue-eyed Lebanese woman.[22] Several of my interviewees related their irritation at constantly hearing, "You don't look Muslim." Others had internalized these associations of physical appearance with religion. "I don't look Muslim," one woman told me, "and I'm very proud of my looks because I can advocate for Islam, even though I'm not a fanatic or anything." When I asked her what made her look non-Muslim, she pointed to her blondish hair and sleeveless top, characteristics potentially shared by Lebanese women of all religious backgrounds. Another said, "What's funny is that before we got married, my friends didn't believe that my husband is Muslim! They kept saying, 'It is not obvious!' I know it is because he is blond and he is very cool." Lebanese attempts to count as white in the world are also racist efforts to distance themselves from being Black or brown, from nations viewed as "lower" in a global hierarchy.

Thinking about Islamophobia as it intersects with nationality, class, and ideas about race brings us to another discrimination pervasive in Lebanon: xenophobia. When imagining themselves as among the white nations of the world, Lebanese of all sects force not only migrant workers out of the nation but their Levantine neighbors as well: Palestinians and Syrians.

Xenophobia

In *The Ninety-Ninth Floor*, a novel by Jana Fawaz Elhassan, a Lebanese Christian woman and a Palestinian Muslim man meet in New York City. As Majd and Hilda narrate their relationship, the identity issues that emerge connect to politics and histories of violence. At different points in the novel, both describe their love for the other as love for the enemy. Majd was injured in the 1982 massacre of Palestinians at the Sabra and Chatila refugee camps in Beirut, massacres carried out by a right-wing Lebanese Christian militia under the supervision of the Israeli army. Hilda is from an elite political family affiliated with an adjacent right-wing Christian political party.

"Can you imagine if I was in your house and I was speaking to your mother with a Palestinian accent? She surely would collapse," Majd says to Hilda.[23] Later, he thinks to himself, "Perhaps in Hilda too I used to see an attempt to avenge my displacement, an attempt to prove to the old Christian enemy—her family—that I, a Palestinian they had tried to annihilate, had now returned: through the heart of their daughter and the heart of their very home."[24]

Toward the end of the novel, Hilda visits home, where she tells a woman who has worked for her family for decades about Majd. "I wanted to tell her that I was in love with you, a Palestinian, but whenever I started to move my tongue, it betrayed me. Finally, I gathered up my courage and shouted in a loud voice, 'Laurice, I'm in love with a Palestinian guy. I'm in love with a Palestinian man, Laurice.' I said it just like that, as if the words were racing to come out all at once. My hand slipped away and she looked at me, shouting back, 'You're mad.'"[25]

The novel concludes with Hilda announcing to her family, just before she returns to New York, that she has met a wonderful man and is in love with him. As she concludes her description of Majd, she says, "Oh, I forgot to mention that he's of Palestinian origin and that his injuries resulted from shrapnel that wounded him at Sabra and Shatila." At that very moment, an impromptu delegation interrupts their conversation—her father has just been appointed to the Lebanese cabinet—and Hilda slips away and into a taxi to the airport.[26]

————————

Even though I limited my focus to mixed marriage among Lebanese, it would be irresponsible to ignore Lebanese xenophobic opposition to marriage with Palestinians and Syrians. These dynamics link histories of political violence to ideas about nationality, which are in turn linked to borders that European powers drew in ways that didn't align with local understandings of territory. Southern Lebanon is part of the Galilee. The North connects to Syria. But just as sectarianism has done its work and filtered into identity, so has nationalism.

Many Palestinians came to Lebanon as refugees after they were violently expelled by European Jewish militias in mandate Palestine before Israel declared itself a state in 1948. Wealthier Palestinians and Christian Palestinians were often granted Lebanese citizenship, the latter for the same reason Armenians were welcomed—they added Christian numbers to the population. Other Palestinians, most of them Muslim, lived in abject poverty in refugee camps, and many continue to do so. They face legal and structural discrimination from the Lebanese state, plus Islamophobia and xenophobia, especially from Christian Lebanese, many of whom blamed Palestinians for the Lebanese Civil War.

These layers of religion, class, nation, and politics appear in Etel Adnan's classic of Lebanese literature, *Sitt Marie Rose*. The titular character is a Christian Lebanese woman kidnapped and executed by a Christian militia during the civil war for doing humanitarian work with Palestinian refugees and falling in love with a Palestinian Muslim man. Her love interest is assumed to be both non-Lebanese and non-Christian, and her sexual betrayal of sectarian community is equated with political betrayal.

There are quite a few marriages between Lebanese and Palestinians with Lebanese citizenship, generally within the same religion and class. Most marriages between Lebanese and Palestinians without citizenship are between two Muslims, often low-income couples who met in their urban neighborhood.[27] When middle-class Lebanese families are involved, the stigma of Palestinians as refugees (even if they now have citizenship) rears its head. If class parity can be proven, problems often resolve. One Lebanese woman married to a Palestinian shared that as soon as she explained that her father-in-law was well-established in his professional career, people opposed to their marriage accepted it. Even where there is no opposition, *talteesh*—that snide banter—ensures that no one ever forgets there is now a Palestinian in the family. Lebanese family members balk at hearing Palestinian idioms or accents. Family debates, no matter the topic, will reference the in-law's Palestinian identity, even when irrelevant.

There are also quite a few Lebanese-Syrian marriages within the same religion, both among elites and among families who live along the border the French mandate drew. Outside those border communities, many Lebanese find marriage to Syrians anathema, a reduction of status. The Syrian occupation that began during Lebanon's civil war and continued until 2005 meant that many Lebanese knew Syrians as either young soldiers manning checkpoints or wreaking havoc in their villages, or as migrant laborers.[28] After the Syrian uprising and civil war began in 2011, the image of Syrians shifted, and many Lebanese viewed them as the new unwanted refugees, a drain on the country's resources.

The Lebanese state discriminates against these noncitizen residents. Palestinians are barred from many professional fields and can't own property or businesses. Syrians are subject to violence and banned from public spaces, including schools in some towns. When a Lebanese woman marries a Palestinian or Syrian (or anyone non-Lebanese), she cannot pass citizenship on to her husband or their children. This means that her family members are subject to that legal discrimination. They need visas to live in Lebanon and permits to work there, and laws limit their ability to inherit from her.[29] Lebanese anti-Palestinian and anti-Syrian sentiment is so strong that every time the government comes close to changing the law and allowing women to pass citizenship on to their spouses and children, the "problem" of Palestinians and Syrians potentially becoming Lebanese through their wives thwarts the process.

When marriages are multiply mixed, by both nationality and religion, nationality takes on magnified meaning. A mixed-religion marriage can exacerbate other kinds of difference, amplifying family objections. A Lebanese Christian woman married to a Syrian Muslim man believes nationality was the bigger problem for her parents: "Had he been Lebanese Muslim it would have all passed over much, much, much more easily. The Syrian component triggered my family's reaction." Lebanese married to Palestinians concurred that nationality had compounded objections. One queer woman told me her Lebanese partner asked her not to mention to her family that she was half Palestinian, because her partner's parents were right-wing Maronites.

May's Palestinian Catholic family has Lebanese citizenship. She met Emad, a Sunni Beiruti, at work. When the civil war began, Emad found a job in Kuwait and proposed to May. May's father objected because Emad was Muslim. May retorted, "But this is not how you raised us, we were raised to value the person as he is, his brain and how he thinks, and now you are talking to me about his religion?"

"I know," replied her father, "but when it comes to marriage, it's different."

May's reply was ready: "Baba, if I meet a Christian here in Lebanon, you know, they are all *quwwad* and *kata'ib* (Lebanese Forces and Phalangists, both right-wing political parties/militias). I will meet someone who hates Palestinians, and that would be much worse than marrying a Muslim. Emad and me, we grew up in the same part of Beirut, we have the same culture, the same neighborhood, the same university."

This conversation continued every morning over coffee for three months. May consistently explained that she had far more in common with Emad than she would with any Christian Lebanese man. Her arguments convinced her parents to meet Emad. They liked him, but her father still hesitated. Emad's family sent a bouquet to May's parents with "Jesus" written on it, trying to show that they accepted May as a Christian. Six months later, May was restless. The war prevented her from commuting to work. It was time to marry and move to Kuwait. This time, when Emad spoke with her parents, they accepted the match.

May believes that her father's fears were magnified because they were Palestinian—despite their Lebanese citizenship, they were living in an adopted country during a time of violent upheaval. Both May and her father knew viscerally that being Palestinian in Lebanon, even if Christian, even with citizenship, was a risk. May thinks her father would have worried no matter whom she wanted to marry. By focusing concern on the right-wing—and therefore anti-Palestinian—leanings of most Lebanese Christians during the war, she asserted that marrying a Lebanese Christian amounted to marrying the enemy.

Like May and her father, Palestinian Lebanese experience Lebanese xenophobia and when it comes to marriage, often worry about it. One person explained, "Being Palestinian Christian neutralized the sectarian dimension of identity. Like sure, we were Christians, but if we went to Ashrafieh, it was uncomfortable." Another explained that her father didn't care about her fiancé's religion but was terrified her in-laws would reject their family because they were Palestinian. And one story involved a couple who were not only Palestinian and Lebanese, Muslim and Christian, but also from families that were publicly polarized. Their romance was based on their shared perspectives, and they had the kinds of relationships with their parents where they could assert their will, but family gatherings would never be simple. These were stories I gathered in passing, from friends, or where I hadn't known that one partner was Palestinian until the interview began. I suspect the dynamics suggested here apply more broadly, and that Lebanese-Syrian marriages are on the rise. I hope someone else researches their effects.

––––––––

The last three chapters have taken up the most common factors that drive parental objections to mixed marriage, all factors that underlie, fuel, and sometimes masquerade as sectarianism: status concerns, regional differences, lack of exposure, and anti-Muslim bias. It's time to address the elephant in the room: What about faith? What happens when religious difference *is* at the crux of a matter, when people believe that souls are indeed at stake?

Eight

What about Faith?

Maysa and Antoine are both believers. A Shi'i Muslim who has always lived in Beirut, Maysa attended public schools and the public Lebanese University, eventually completing a master's degree. Antoine grew up in a poor farming family in a Maronite village. A first-generation college student, he moved to Beirut to study and stayed to work. Fate brought them together when Maysa appeared in Antoine's office as his new intern. Despite their decade-plus age difference, they clicked and began hanging out after work. When her internship ended, they continued to date.

The couple waited a year to tell their parents. Antoine's family wasn't thrilled, but he was in his thirties, financially established, and everyone assumed any children would be Christian, so all they did was comment, "Why marry a Shi'a? Why marry beneath you?"

Maysa's soft-spoken parents told her that if she married him, she should leave home and never return. They were upset about both religious and age differences. As a believer, Maysa understood she wasn't supposed to marry a non-Muslim, but she also questioned the basis of that rule: "I wondered why God wouldn't want someone to be happy, even if that happiness meant marrying someone of a different religion. I'm not extremely religious, but it's not like I ignore religion. I pray and fast. It was hard for me. I had to make a decision against what was normal."

She was taken aback because her parents had always been open to Christian friends and holidays: "It was like this rule became important all of a sudden. My parents suddenly wanted to prove that they're real Muslims."

Maysa's parents didn't want to be accused of having left their village in the South to raise unruly and improperly Muslim children in Beirut. "I know I was hurting their social image. That was the only thing I sympathized with." Maysa's siblings—and she has many, mostly older—were divided. Some said she should marry whomever she wants, some shared their parents' concern about family reputation, and some believed it was forbidden for her to marry a non-Muslim.

Caught between feelings, faith, and family, Maysa quit her job, broke up with Antoine, and joined relatives living in diaspora. Antoine was devastated. Seeing his misery, his sister called Maysa and put Antoine on the phone. He convinced her to return. "I made a new plan for my life without telling my parents," she explained. Her parents knew she was with Antoine but ignored it.

The couple's openly secret relationship persisted for six years, Maysa's resolve growing stronger. "What is forbidden grows more sweet," she observed. Three years into it, her father passed away. Another three years went by.

One evening, sitting in front of the television, Maysa's mother looked up from her cup of tea and said, "Okay, invite him over." Time, loss, and worries that Maysa would never marry had softened her resistance. Maysa wasted no time. Two weeks later, the couple married. "We didn't get engaged. I didn't meet his parents. He didn't meet mine. We just got married, because we had been waiting for six years!"

Maysa's family thinks the couple had a civil marriage in Cyprus. They didn't. After donning a white dress, she left home with a celebration *zaffeh*, but instead of heading to the airport, they married in church. Maysa accepted it as a condition of being with Antoine.

Once they finally met him, Maysa's mother and siblings liked Antoine. They avoid disapproving relatives in the South. On Antoine's side, because Maysa got baptized to marry, most people believe she is a Christian and treat her as an outsider to the village but part of the religious community. Maysa finds the few who persist in seeing her as Shi'a amusing because publicly, she is for all intents and purposes Christian. The couple is raising their children as Christians in a mostly Christian household with a mother who practices Islam privately. They celebrate Christian holidays with Antoine's family and Muslim holidays with Maysa's family. Antoine acknowledges Maysa is Muslim, but she is uncomfortable praying or fasting in front of her in-laws. She dreams of emigrating and raising their children far from sectarian and religious pressure.

————

Maysa and Antoine are unusual among my interviewees. Few had pious families and fewer still practiced their faith. Most were raised by nominally religious parents. They were taught to believe in God and celebrate religious holidays. Elders often practiced their faith, parents sporadically did, and no one made them do any of it. Others were raised in nonreligious families, leftist or communist, with parents who went against the grain of society, hiding alcohol in mugs at family gatherings, being "an atheist in the closet," or fighting with relatives who tried to impose religion on their children. And no matter how they had been raised, by the time they met their spouses, most of my interviewees had a lax, nonexistent, or hostile relationship to religion. They were professed atheists, agnostics, or broadly spiritual. Some associated religion with "brainwashing"; others respected but didn't share their family's or in-laws' beliefs. For some, religion was a matter of intellectual curiosity; for others, it was about diverse cultural traditions and multiple holidays celebrated with food and family.

People like Maysa and Antoine who practice their faith are less likely to marry someone of a different religion. Couples where both spouses believe and practice set themselves apart from other mixed couples, describing themselves as "a *truly* mixed marriage." One woman explained, "If neither of us practiced our religion, we would both be of the same sect, the sect of 'no religion.'"

These "truly" mixed marriages are the only ones that I would describe as "interfaith," marriages where difference is reflected in each spouse's beliefs and practices. When faith matters, it becomes something that couples, and their parents, must negotiate. Despite Maysa's official conversion, she remains a believing Muslim. Her marriage to Antoine appears "not mixed" on paper but is an interfaith marriage in practice.

Interfaith Marriage

Just like couples who might say "Neither of us sees religion so it doesn't matter," interfaith couples prioritize their similarity and shared values. While parents and society often assume that shared values require practicing the same religion, for these couples, it instead means having the same ideas about God and faith. An unmarried woman in her midtwenties articulated this perspective beautifully. She's willing to marry anyone except an atheist: "He doesn't have to believe in any kind of god, but if he doesn't believe that there's something bigger out there, and it could be really the most abstract of higher powers, I wouldn't be able to get along with him." Another explained, "The bigger issue is with an atheist. If I'm a religious Christian and you're a religious Muslim, people can at least see the beauty of faith. It's a worldview issue, a common connection through believing in something bigger than you." Exceptions among my interviewees include a nonbeliever whose spouse fasts during Ramadan and a person exploring multiple religious traditions whose spouse is an atheist. But for most couples, religious *difference* doesn't matter; *degree* of faith and commitment does.

Some interfaith marriages failed over disagreements about how to raise their children. Others worked because the couple had preemptively agreed how to manage religion in their family life. One mixed family celebrated and practiced both traditions, and whenever there was a potential conflict, they held a vote. During a December when Christmas and Ramadan coincided, the family voted to have a Christmas dinner during *iftar* time and to make an exception to the "no wine during Ramadan" rule for that evening.

Maysa's story reminds us that gender inflects the power each spouse has in an interfaith family. Women often make sacrifices to marry for love, face pressure to hide their religious commitments, or conform to their husband's faith in raising their children or in their public presence. For example, after Aya eloped with Yusef, they spent years negotiating religious practice. Their children understand that their mom is Muslim and their dad is Christian and learned about both religions. They were baptized, despite Aya's reluctance. They attend secular schools and celebrate all holidays at home. Aya prays and fasts regularly; Yusef attends church each Sunday. Aya told me, "Sometimes I think to myself, How did I marry a Christian? I still fast, and sometimes I pray. He doesn't like to see me praying, but I tell him I don't mind when he goes to church, so he can't mind when I pray." Aya doesn't regret her choices, but she feels at a disadvantage given how sect and religion are inherited in Lebanon.

Dalal, a Sunni woman, married at twenty-one, unusually young for a college student in the 1990s. Before Elie proposed, he asked her what religion their hypothetical children would be. "Maronite, just like you," Dalal replied, confused. "What else would they be?" Looking back over a decade later, she now understands how her choices as a young woman were constrained by patriarchal family structures. She also had a church wedding, left college when their first child was born at Elie's insistence, and gave up her dreams of working when the kids began school because he disapproved. Elie's parents continue to pressure Dalal to convert, saying she won't inherit anything from Elie otherwise. "I don't care if I inherit or not," she told me, "I don't want to convert. To this day, I have not converted, and I will not convert." Maintaining her identity in this small way is how Dalal stakes out a space for herself amid her many concessions to patriarchy.

Line is better positioned to maintain space for her faith and views because she married at a later age, after agreeing with her partner that each would keep their respective religious practices private so that "no one will impose anything on the kids." When we spoke, their children were young, and they had just begun figuring out how to "focus on the common and shared values of both religions." Yet Line still thinks her children will inevitably be exposed to Christianity more than Islam. She seemed resigned to this disparity, stuck in a patriarchal system that laid an imbalanced groundwork for any negotiations within their marriage. "I knew what I was getting into," she sighed. Their children had recently taken part in the Palm Sunday procession. Line insisted that their baptisms be private ceremonies. And she was holding the line for secular mixed education despite the excellent parochial school near their home.

In all these cases, practicing or pious in-laws added to the pressures women who married into the family faced. The more pious one's in-laws, the more likely they are to impose their faith on their grandchildren. One might expect that more pious parents are also more likely to oppose mixed marriage. But parental faith affected responses to mixed marriage in a variety of ways, some unexpected. My interviews challenge the assumption that faith leads to objections to mixed marriage. Self-declared "secular" parents were just as likely to object as pious parents. And pious parents sometimes found that their faith helped them accept their child's choice of spouse.

Faith-Based Parental Responses

Marie grew up in a Maronite mountain town where "Christians married Christians." After graduating from Lebanese University, in her midtwenties, she met Rami on a night out with their overlapping social circles. By the time they began dating a few years later, Marie's parents already knew Rami as one of her friends. Anticipating opposition, she didn't volunteer that they had begun a relationship, or that he was Shiʻi Muslim.

One afternoon, out of nowhere, Marie's mom asked her if she was dating anyone, saying it was time for her to think about marriage. Marie took this opportunity to tell her about Rami. When her mom exclaimed in joy, Marie laughed. "Do you know that Rami is Muslim?"

Elation flipped to shock, then the questions began. "Why?" "Can't you find someone else?" "Will people accept it?" "Would he be willing to convert?" By the end of the conversation, Marie's mother remained upset, but said, "You know what I would prefer, but you have to make your own decisions and take responsibility for your choices."

Now Marie had to tell her father. After a series of similar questions, he began sharing examples of mixed marriages that had ended in divorce. Marie replied with examples of Christian couples who had divorced. Unmoved by her argument that all marriages face challenges, her father stopped speaking to her for two weeks. Her older siblings came to the rescue. They decided to get to know Rami and then, if they liked him, to intervene. Meanwhile, Marie's mother was bemoaning the idea of non-Christian future grandchildren as a catastrophic future. But her mother also prayed regularly. She began asking God to help her accept Rami.

Once Marie's siblings gave Rami the green light, he began to spend time with their parents. Marie's mother continued to ask God for help and within months, they accepted the match. The couple agreed to have a priest bless their civil marriage. Rami was fine with a church wedding, but Marie didn't want him to convert. After their wedding, they settled in Marie's hometown, where they were welcomed even though Rami is one of the few Muslims in the area. They haven't baptized any of their children, but they mainly celebrate Christian holidays, albeit as social rituals rather than religious ones.

———————

Faith sometimes fueled parents' opposition to mixed marriage. Druze parents feared their child would forfeit burial rituals. Muslim parents feared for their daughters' souls. Christian parents feared their children would abandon their faith (even if they had already done so). All parents worried that daughters-in-law of a different religion wouldn't raise children properly in the father's faith. For Maronite parents, this took on added importance because many viewed the "Christian family" as a pillar of both faith and social standing.

These worries made sense when one or both potential spouses were believers, but if they were both atheists or agnostics, these worries reflected parental assumptions or desires for their child rather than a concern that took seriously their child's worldview. As we saw in chapter 3, civil marriage was sometimes the bigger problem. And some parents saw mixed marriage as the last straw in their child's separation from their religious community. For them, the problem wasn't the bride or groom, but what that person represented in their child's trajectory. Mothers who had hoped a spouse of the same faith would bring their children "back to religion" were especially devastated.

At the same time, faith provided support for parents. I don't know the extent to which prayer helped Marie's mother accept Rami as a son-in-law, but she wasn't the only mother to rely on her faith as a source of strength in the face of her child's mixed marriage. Belief in God could be a space of commonality with new in-laws, bonding parents against a nonbelieving couple. Prayer could provide comfort or strength, piety a bulwark against social approbation. When Wael, a Roum man, announced his engagement to a Sunni woman, everyone accepted his decision to his face. Then they went and harassed his mother about it, asking her how she could accept a Muslim daughter-in-law. His mother's faith helped her through that pressure. As Wael observed, "The only one of them who is actually religious is my mom, the only one who just said, 'Do what makes you happy.' It was people who are just socially religious, who only go to church on holidays, they are the ones who had an issue." Douaa's mother also used piety to help her confront social pressure.

————

Douaa was excited to share her story with me because, she said, "It's a happy story." A Shiʻi Muslim, she grew up in the Shiʻa-majority southern suburb of Beirut and attended a Christian private school followed by Lebanese University for both her undergraduate and graduate education. Douaa's parents are deeply pious and have been open-minded about all their children's spouses. Her brother married a Christian in a civil ceremony with no drama. And when Douaa met Paul, a Christian from Zahlé, neither family objected. Paul was over forty, the two are from similar class backgrounds, and his pious Christian parents were just thrilled that he was marrying at all. Douaa's family defied religious tradition and supported her. She attributes this support to her parents' education and exposure to diversity. "They have seen the world. They have friends from all religions. And maybe it also has to do with the fact that they are both a little artistic, so they don't care what other people think, they don't need to follow the rules."

I asked Douaa's mother, Fatima, about her stance. She is a practicing Muslim who prays, fasts, and has been on the hajj. The first thing she told me is that she appreciates Paul's mother's piety: "Her faith is similar to my understanding of faith. Faith is practice in everyday life, in my relationship with my neighbors, with my relatives, with my kids, the way I deal with people at work, this is religion to me. And it is the same for Paul's mother." Fatima then echoed her daughter's emphasis on the relationship between open-mindedness and education. "*Alhamdulillah* [gratitude to God], our entire family is educated, for many generations back, so this open-mindedness comes from there." She told me a story about how, when she was young, she and her cousins asked their grandmother whether it would be okay to marry a Christian man. Their grandmother had pulled a gender reversal on a commonly accepted Muslim tradition.

"We used to joke and say, 'Teta, if we loved a Sunni guy, what do you think of us marrying a Sunni?' And she had said, 'There is no problem, we are all Muslims.' And then we had told her, 'If we loved a Christian guy, what would you say?' And she had said, 'They are people of the book as well, so it's okay.' We had thought she would be angry or say, 'What are you talking about?' And not at all, on the contrary. So always, in our family, our relationships are built with the human qua human. We don't care about religion; we only care about morals and how people treat one another."

Fatima was well aware that her approach was more open than that of many of her peers. She deliberately went about supporting her daughter's engagement. To confirm her understanding of the extended family's perspective, she discreetly polled relatives. Reassured that there would be no hassles within the family, she devised a strategy to manage broader social pressure. She consulted with the office of the late Sayyid Muhammad Hussein Fadlallah, a key religious reference for many Lebanese Shi'a.

"I called his office," Fatima told me. "And I told the shaykh there the situation. First, I explained she wants a civil marriage. I myself am absolutely for civil marriage because it is a hundred percent valid, because in Islam, marriage is a declaration and consent between two people with a judge or a cleric to make the contract. And in Cyprus that is exactly what happens. Okay. So I asked the shaykh, 'As a mother, can you reassure me that from a religious perspective, civil marriage is sound and valid?' And he said, 'It is one hundred percent sound and valid.'

"And then I told him she wants to marry a Christian. He asked, 'How old is she?' I said, 'She is thirty-three.' He said, 'In principle, it is a problem for a woman to marry outside Islam.' I asked, 'What's the problem?' He said, 'The problem is if he forces her away from her religion.' I said, 'In civil marriage, each person keeps their religion.' He said, 'Okay.'

"So I asked, 'As a mom, what am I supposed to do?' He said, 'You're not responsible for anything. She is thirty-three, and you don't have any religious responsibility for her. She is a grown up. She makes her own decisions.'"

This conversation gave Fatima the confidence to respond to social pressure. "I confronted anyone who said anything to me with that conversation. I told them, 'I consulted a religious authority and he said such and such, so let God judge us Himself later on.'"

Douaa and Paul's story is one where their mothers' faiths facilitated acceptance of their marriage. Neither Douaa nor Paul practices their faiths the way their families do. Christine was one of the few people I interviewed who herself was religious. She and her mother exemplify the complex but ultimately positive role faith could play.

Christine's Story

Christine grew up attending weekly Mass and kept the habit after moving from her village to Beirut for university and then to work at an NGO. Sometimes she goes to church or a saint's shrine to light a candle in supplication or pray for guidance. She fasts during Lent, marking her forehead with ashes each year on that fateful Wednesday. Christine was raised in a family so deeply embedded in the Maronite community that it was rare for someone to marry outside the sect, let alone outside the religion. Even marrying a Roman Catholic would generate gossip and concern.

All her life, Christine assumed she would marry a Maronite and raise Maronite children in a Christian family. So when she met Hassan, whose name marked him as Shi'a, she hesitated. Hassan did not. They were at an antigovernment protest, marching with a group of friends and colleagues against the corruption of the sectarian political system. Hassan knew immediately that Christine was "the one." He saw her compassion and their shared politics: a distrust of sectarian institutions and a commitment to social justice. Despite sharing his feelings, Christine's faith held her back.

As the protest movement grew, Christine and Hassan kept running into each other at meetings and demonstrations. First they looked forward to those encounters, then they began planning them. As their friendship deepened, periodically Christine would tell Hassan she needed to take a step back from the developing relationship. "I need to go and think about us." Hassan never understood. "What do you mean you need to go and think?" She always saw him again, a few days or maybe a week later.

Months passed. Christine's mother, Therese, began to wonder what was going on with her daughter. Always thoughtful, Christine was now moody, preoccupied. Therese's concern grew when she sensed Christine was interested in someone. Perhaps her daughter's silence about this unknown romantic interest meant she was conflicted about it. She tried asking if there was indeed "someone."

After several denials, Christine finally told her about Hassan. Perplexed and angry, Therese asked, "How can someone like you, a believer, do this? How will you live this way? How will you raise your kids?" She couldn't accept the idea of Christine dating someone who wasn't Maronite, let alone Christian. These questions pinpointed the issues triggering Christine's hesitation and added to her uncertainty. Christine grew sad. She told her mom she wouldn't do anything without her by her side, but that she was struggling because she loved Hassan a great deal. The conversation ended there, for a while.

Therese is also a fervent believer. A slight woman with a caramel glow unassisted by any makeup, her presence is both kind and commanding. Torn between Christine's obvious unhappiness and her desires for her daughter's future, she mulled over Christine's confession and their life in a mixed society. She turned to her faith and prayed: "Oh God, I don't know. I put this situation before you. This is Christine's life, and I don't know what to do. It's very difficult for me. I put myself before you." After a few days of prayer, Therese found her heart softening. She felt like a different person, a person who might be able to accept the situation.

Therese took this change as a sign that she couldn't be responsible for the decision about whom her daughter married. She worried that if Christine didn't marry Hassan, she might not marry at all, as she was already past thirty. To absolve herself of this responsibility, she went to church to hand the problem over to God: "Oh Lord, I am putting this relationship on your altar." As she stood from her prayer, Therese felt God working inside her and felt certain that the hand of God was involved in her daughter's life path.

Christine's father had passed away years before, and she was close to one of her maternal uncles. Therese consulted this uncle as well and was surprised by his response: "For Christine to be in this situation," he told her, "is a call from the Lord. He wants to see people in Lebanon coexisting." With both her brother and God at her side, she agreed to meet Hassan.

Hassan came to her home for a visit. Over coffee and a plate of homemade anise cookies, Hassan and Therese clicked. They spoke for hours that day, and on future visits, about life and work and faith. When we spoke, Therese told me that Hassan helped her see the universality of Christianity: "I don't accept that Christ came only for Christians. I know that our Lord came for all people and that there are things in Islam that are very beautiful. We are shutting them out. I am not like this. I saw commonalities. I saw that Hassan is a person who searches for God and loves in Christine her faith. I saw that Christine can live her Christianity with him."

Despite her newfound respect for Hassan, Therese was still worried. She fretted about her grandchildren's as yet unborn souls if they weren't baptized. And she knew she would face "a hundred wars with a hundred people" if the couple married. Christine herself was still mulling over these matters and hadn't yet committed to Hassan, despite his multiple proposals. Decisions had never been easy for her; her capacity for empathy meant she moved through the world able to understand multiple sides of any situation. She worried about how her decision would reverberate in her extended family, among people she loved, in circles where she was respected. She worried about how to raise children who were both Christian and Muslim. She consulted with her maternal uncle, who said, "No matter what happens, I trust you. Even if things don't work out between you two, this is a very important relationship for you. It's clear that it's a crossing point, and we'll see what happens." She also consulted a priest who counseled her to pursue the relationship, assuming that if she did, Christine would learn that there were other reasons she didn't want to be with Hassan. Instead, Christine decided to take a longer break from Hassan and dedicate herself to figuring out whether she had the courage to pursue their relationship to its logical endpoint of marriage.

By this point, Hassan had had enough. He told Christine he was done. He didn't want to see her anymore. It took Christine three months to commit to Hassan in his absence from her life.

"It took our relationship to be broken," she told me, "for me to break out of the ideas I had, from the system I was raised in." To be with Hassan, Christine had to work on herself and move beyond her own stereotypes. She had always thought of herself as open-minded, and only now was learning what accepting sectarian diversity meant in Lebanon's social context.

Her mom helped. Seeing her daughter's misery, Therese spoke to her frankly. "I dreamt and dreamt that you would leave him, but now I need to tell you that Hassan is not someone you can give up. Christine, you can trust him. This is a person for whom you have destroyed the world, a person you love, that's it, it's done, you cannot walk away from it. I have never seen a love that changes, transforms, and hits people like this."

Once Christine had decided she couldn't live without Hassan, accepted her mom's blessing, and mustered the courage to fight the coming social battles, she discovered that she first had to fight to get him back. It took her a few months to convince Hassan to even speak with her again. It took a year to rebuild their relationship, this time on a foundation of mutual commitment.

Their mothers met and became fast friends. Therese was thrilled to find her pious counterpart in Hassan's mom. Not only did she pray and fast, but she also went to talk to the Virgin Mary at a shrine near their house whenever she was worried about something. She had done so when she saw Hassan wounded by Christine's hesitations. For Therese, "This was proof that Hassan's family is open-minded, that they are believers in a way that doesn't conflict with our beliefs."

When the couple finally decided to marry, their immediate families, and Christine's uncle, were just waiting for them to set a date. But Christine's extended family still had to be told. The plan was to start with more open-minded relatives who lived in Beirut. The grapevine had other ideas. Some family members in the village panicked. One prayed for the relationship to end. Another visited local shrines, asking for divine intervention. Others called Christine and pressured her to end it. So Therese took matters into her own hands. She went to the village and summoned all their relatives. Smiling, she voiced her support for her daughter and the couple. She told them Hassan was worth one hundred Christians. She told them Christine was living her Christianity and would continue to do so. And she said, "We know how much you love us, but this is Christine's life. We asked all the questions you're asking, and we expressed all the concerns you're express-ing, and we determined Christine will be able to live happily with Hassan."

It took time. There was argument, objection, a loud call to God, an ac-cusation of shame. Therese silenced them all: "No one loves my daughter more than I do. You all know how cautious she is. Do not worry. This is a good thing." Everyone came around save one relative, who announced she would pray for the relationship to fall apart and did so loudly until the day of their wedding in Cyprus.

The last time I saw Christine and Therese, they were taking turns rock-ing the couple's infant son. Over their first year of marriage, Christine and Hassan had each reached toward the faith of the other. Hassan attends Mass sometimes. Christine fasted during Ramadan and attended weekend *iftars* at her in-laws' home. They circumcised their son.

As Christine set a plate of her mother's amazing anise cookies before me, I asked about baptism. I knew the ritual was important to her, and that Hassan didn't mind as long as the child's official sect remained Shi'a. But they both worried about how his parents would feel. As Christine thought,

Therese spoke up: "We'll baptize him discreetly. This is an addition to his life. He'll be raised in two beliefs, and later on he'll choose whatever he wants." When we last communicated, Christine confirmed they had celebrated a discreet baptism and remained on their path to raising a family in both faiths.

————

Christine and Hassan live in their faiths *and* live an antisectarian life. Their marriage, alongside all the stories in this chapter, shows that sectarianism and religiosity are two separate concepts, ideas and practices that are as likely to be opposed to one another as they are to coincide. Falling in love with Hassan helped Christine see the insidious ways sectarian ideas creep into notions of religious community. For Therese, faith helped her embrace Hassan as a son-in-law as they grafted their families together.

Decoupling sectarianism from religion is more radical than it may at first appear. Once disentangled, religious faith remains the province of one's relationship to God, and sect becomes a secular category. In other words, decoupling sectarianism from religion removes God from sect, despite the best efforts of the Lebanese state and religious and political leaders to keep them intertwined. Sect becomes just another form of social difference. Unless someone is a believer, this distinction doesn't matter. If you don't believe in God, the rules and differences and practices are all human created. Many Lebanese, however, believe in God. To insist that their faith does not require sectarian discrimination may well provide the keystone for a nonsectarian future.

Religious difference was less important to family opposition to mixed marriage than status or regional differences, lack of exposure, and Islamophobic stereotypes. Social pressure shored up each of these concerns. The weight of social pressure falls most heavily on mothers, brides, and even female relatives. The fallout mixed marriages can leave in their wake is gendered.

Nine

Shunning Is Powerful

As Tamara tells it, her Maronite mother was eleven years old when she started working in a hospital in Beirut. Raised in a poor, conservative family, her mother never learned to read and write. At fifteen, she fell in love with Tamara's father, a Shi'i Muslim, and married him via *katab kitab* without converting. This was the 1930s. Tamara has heard that her mother's parents were initially livid but grew to love their son-in-law. Her father's parents took longer to come around; many relatives on that side never accepted her mother. Tamara's parents lived happily together, madly in love, raising her and her siblings with both religions. Officially Shi'a like their father, at age eighteen, each was asked to choose a faith.

Tamara also married young. At "almost seventeen," she fell in love with Simon, a Maronite man fifteen years her senior. So she chose her mother's sect and was baptized into Maronite Christianity. "Then we eloped," Tamara told me, "even though my father had no problem with it. My parents came to church for the wedding."

Puzzled, I interrupted her story. How was it an elopement if her parents were present? Why did they elope if she had already converted? What was going on?

Laughing, Tamara filled in the details. She explained that her parents liked Simon, but he didn't formally propose. She left her parents' home without their blessing and moved in with Simon's family before the wedding.

I was still confused. Her story thus far suggested her father would have accepted a proposal. Tamara explained, "We thought about this a lot. I talked with my dad about it too. I didn't want him to lose his dignity. *I* wanted to be the one held responsible for my marriage, not my father."

Tamara told Simon not to propose because she knew her Shi'i relatives— her father's side of the family—would disapprove. They were already trying to arrange a match for her. When she overheard someone ask her father if they could bring a groom over to meet her, she told Simon they had to elope. She thought she was helping her father save face with his family by taking the decision out of his hands and freeing him from the untenable position of being caught between her happiness and the expectations of his parents and siblings. But her father was angry. It took a few months for Simon's family and Tamara's maternal relatives to convince him to attend the wedding.

As she had expected, Tamara's paternal relatives cut her out of their social world, except for one paternal aunt. "I love this girl," she told the others, "And I love my brother, and she's his daughter, so I'm going to her wedding." This aunt was shunned for a time for defying the family. Simon's extended family also opposed the match despite Tamara's maternal heritage and conversion. She learned the extent of their disapproval decades later, when Simon passed away and they tried, unsuccessfully, to block her inheritance.

The newlyweds lived near Simon's family and continued to celebrate Muslim holidays with Tamara's parents. It wasn't easy, especially at first, as gossip and snide comments persisted, behind their backs and to their faces. "For around five years, I was really tired, I was tortured, but I really loved Simon and wanted to live with him forever, so I stuck with it." Misty eyed and missing her late husband, Tamara said, "We were prepared for it. Simon used to say, 'The moment we enter our home, we have to completely forget everything, and whatever happens and whatever they say, we will love each other.'"

———

Tamara's story includes several ways social pressure shapes decisions about mixed marriage: people cutting ties with family members, eloping to support a parent, facilitating reconciliation, gossiping, and trying to block inheritance. Social pressures like these carry a heavy emotional toll, especially for women. They compound fears of losing emotional support, relationships, family ties, a sense of home, and economic and social networks. This chapter brings these effects of mixed marriage into focus and shows how people manage the fallout.

Nearly everyone I interviewed mentioned feeling the burdens of social pressure. Outside the home, unnatural pauses or biting comments are reminders of what is at stake. A woman's hairstylist froze when she mentioned her daughter-in-law was from a different religion. She never went back. Neighbors snidely asked, "What, she couldn't find anyone other than a [sect] to marry?" Relatives dispensed silent judgment, blame, and melodramatic declarations like, "If it were me, I would have jumped off the roof!" Social pressure is one reason Lebanon's sectarian system is so persistent. A recent study found that people were more likely to sign a petition calling for dismantling the sectarian system if their names were kept confidential.[1]

Shunning is social pressure weaponized. People fear losing their place in a social world made up of small, tight-knit, and sometimes competitive communities. Mixed marriage disrupts these social worlds, potentially with both economic and emotional consequences. Disownment is also social pressure weaponized, with painful consequences, especially for women who feel simultaneously guilty about the pain they caused their parents and betrayed by those parents' inability to prioritize their daughter's happiness.

Emotional Tolls

Aya and Yusef were raised in conservative religious families, hers Shi'a and his Maronite; both remain believers. Luck and mutual friends brought them together one afternoon at a Lebanese ski resort. Aya noticed Yusef looking at her, so she walked over and asked what he wanted.

"I'm asking about you, asking whether you're single or not," he replied. She told him she was.

"Will you marry me?" he asked, laughing.

They started seeing one another. Aya's strict father didn't allow her to date or even stay out past dinnertime. Her mom would call to warn her when it was time to head home so he wouldn't notice. But when her mom asked about Yusef, Aya denied the relationship. She didn't want to start what she believed would be an impossible conversation. Until Yusef, she had avoided even speaking much to non-Muslim men. The couple kept trying, and failing, to break up. They even tried setting each another up with appropriate marriage partners.

Five years later, they were still together and in their early thirties. Yusef said, "That's it, we're clearly meant to be, and we have to marry. Figure out how you're going to tell your parents."

"I *can't* tell my parents," Aya replied. She wasn't brave enough to face her father and opted to elope. The couple found a home and furnished it, made reservations, and completed paperwork. Describing that time to me, Aya paused, lowering her head to hide her tears. Then she took a deep breath, looked up, and said, "I don't like to think about that time in my life," before continuing her story.

Aya turned her phone off when she boarded the plane to Cyprus. Once she and Yusef were married, she turned it back on to a flood of messages asking her to return home and have a *katab kitab*. Her mother panicked about what people would say. Her father called Yusef and informed him they had an appointment at a shaykh's office for the *katab kitab* once they returned. But the couple had already had a *katab kitab* in Cyprus, because Aya wanted to marry before God. They even had the documentation to prove it, but Aya's father insisted they go to his shaykh. When the Lebanese shaykh said Yusef had to officially convert and register the *katab kitab* instead of the civil marriage, the couple refused.

Aya's father didn't speak with her for years.

After another long pause, Aya told me she's blocked out memories of those years, that there are things she would prefer not to dig out of the recesses of her mind. I didn't press. Her tone brightened as she shared how her mother forgave her and visited regularly. Even after she had two children, Aya's father continued to insist on a registered *katab kitab* in Lebanon. Aya even consulted with religious reference Sayyid Muhammad Hussein Fadlallah, who told her to ignore her father's demand.

Years went by. When Aya's mother passed away, her father formally greeted the couple at the condolence gathering. A few more years passed. After a brief hospitalization, Aya's father called her to begin repairing their relationship. He remained unhappy about the marriage but became a loving grandfather. Aya married believing that her father would deny her any inheritance, but he has decided not to disown his grandchildren.

Aya was the first person in her extended family to marry a non-Muslim. Two of her male cousins have since married Christian women, and when we spoke, one of her female cousins was engaged, with her family's blessing, to a Christian man. Aya opened the door, but at significant emotional cost.

––––––––––

My interview with Aya was difficult. I tried to stop her several times, turning off the tape recorder and asking her to please not relive traumatic memories on my behalf. But she insisted on sharing her story, both because it felt cathartic to do so and as a cautionary tale. She wanted people to stop romanticizing elopement. "People say to me, 'Wow, you were so courageous.' And I tell them, 'No, I wasn't. I was a coward, because I didn't want to face my parents.' People only see the romantic side of it. They don't see the sacrifice I made. It wasn't a good thing."

Looking back on their initial fights with family, many people described them as lonely and stressful times. Like Aya, some blocked out the worst of it. A disownment or long silent treatment could shred the roots connecting kin. Even when connections were revived, traces of damage remained as callouses reminding people of the arguments, silences, tears, and insults that filled the space between them for a while.

Callouses also formed around the words an objecting parent had said about their child's partner. "I was really, really, really hurt," one woman told me, "because this brought out something in Mom that I wasn't aware existed, all this racism . . . I never thought it was so entrenched in her." Others felt betrayed when parental objections contradicted their upbringing. I heard many variations of "I was raised to be independent and open-minded, how could my parents just retract that?"

Dania, who had always been close to her father, was shocked, confused, and hurt when he rejected a proposal from Yehya, her longtime Christian partner. Yehya recalled her father's response: "He flat out said no. And we were flabbergasted and devastated. And her dad was like, 'You know, it is nothing personal. I love you very much. You are a great guy. But it can't happen.'"

"This was a very unpleasant reality check," Dania added. "My dad is agnostic, you know, he doesn't pray. . . . None of these things mattered all my life, and then suddenly it became an issue? And we were like, 'What just happened?'" Flummoxed by her father's response, Dania came to understand that he had caved to pressure from Sunni extended family. From her perspective, "the world went mad" because her father had spent his life standing up for his beliefs. For several months, Dania refused to speak with him. When her father suggested to Yehya that they elope, hinting that he'd accept their marriage afterward, her rage only grew.

Worried the situation was damaging Dania's relationship with her family, Yehya volunteered to convert to Shi'i Islam, noting that it didn't matter to him and choosing a different Muslim sect to emphasize that it was on his own terms. Yehya told Dania, "We're confronting the entire flow of history right now. We're really going against the grain, and apparently, we don't even realize it, so we can't fight all of that." It took a while for Dania to accept the conversion, which contradicted her principles, but it appeased Dania's atheist father, who gave them his blessing. Dania's tears during our interview held both her anger at her father's betrayal of their shared secular values and her empathy for the social pressure she imagines must have precipitated it.

———

The most painful moments were when people lost a parent before repairing their relationship with them. Like Aya, Mariam had tried to marry within her sect, refusing to date anyone who wasn't Christian, preferably Syriac. When she met Ahmad, she was clear that she would only date him for temporary fun. But for reasons she couldn't articulate, Mariam kept seeing Ahmad, while constantly fretting about it.

A year later, she abruptly ended the relationship: "I developed a lot of feelings for him, and it was getting serious, so I decided I needed to break it off." A few months later, Mariam met "a guy with the perfect checklist: Christian, a good career, good finances, good looking, every scenario that a girl would want." She took this "perfect man's perfect timing" as a sign from God, but despite her efforts, the new relationship didn't last long. Mariam couldn't get Ahmad out of her head, and the "perfect guy" turned out to have all sorts of flaws.

This experience taught Mariam to question her "checklist," but she still wasn't ready to fight her parents. "I waited another year and then I knew deep down that Ahmad was the one. I had a sense that he was still out there for me. I couldn't stop loving him." She called Ahmad and asked him to meet her at a café.

When Mariam told him she wanted to try again, Ahmad replied, "I don't want to get back together if you can't take things seriously for what's next . . . either we fight together or we forget this."

Mariam committed to Ahmad and the fight ahead. Step one was telling her parents. "Dad, Mom," she said, "Ahmad is the one. He's my fate. He's my soulmate."

Her father froze in silent shock. Then he walked out of the room. That was the last time Mariam spoke with him. A few months later, the couple arranged a meeting to discuss marriage with him, but a week before they met, Mariam's father passed away.

Crying, Mariam told me, "I just miss him a lot. I suffered a lot at the beginning. It was so hard because he wasn't talking to me before he died." The tragedy reverberated through her relationship: "I had a reverse reaction after his death, and I didn't want anything to do with Ahmad. But he stayed supportive." Ahmad's unwavering support confirmed that he was the right person for her. Her siblings supported her, and her mother told her to do whatever made her happy. The couple married in a quiet civil ceremony eight months later.

Mariam takes comfort in the fact that her father met Ahmad once, briefly, before he died. She wasn't the only person I interviewed who lost their father during a family conflict. In one case, relatives blamed the woman for her father's death.

The emotional tolls of conflict over mixed marriage disproportionately affect women, in part because they are responsible for emotional labor in their families. Mixed marriage is a direct challenge to *paternal*, more than parental, authority. Grooms and fathers also feel the pain of family rifts, but the patriarchal structures of decision-making and authority shape the emotional consequences of fights about mixed marriage. Women were more likely to share deep feelings of guilt with me. Damage to father-daughter relationships was especially painful. Sons continue the family line, so daughters are more likely to be disowned. Perhaps understanding these gendered patterns, many women were less willing to risk their family relationships than men, unless they believed that there was no alternative. Empathy for their parents, and especially for their mothers, inflected their stories. "I feel bad for my mom," one woman said, "because everyone asks her who I married, and she has to tell them."

Shunning as Weapon

The mere fear of being shunned can mobilize parents against a mixed marriage. Recall that "What will people say?" was the most cited parental concern across my interviews.

Wissam's Druze parents were among those motivated by this fear. Aware of their social milieu, when he and Nadine decided to marry, Wissam proceeded with care. He orchestrated an informal encounter between Nadine and his mother to ensure that Nadine wasn't an unknown entity when she later came to dinner. Afterward, Wissam mentioned marriage as a possibility, giving his parents time to adapt. He patiently listened to their anxieties for a year.

"It is as if two things were happening in them at the same time," Wissam told me. "My mom once described it like she's living an internal conflict between her self who wants to be happy for her son and her self who was raised in this environment that requires marrying from the same sect, and these two things are both strong in her, but she doesn't have the courage to let one defeat the other." Wissam's father was also worried about how people would treat the couple. He cautioned Nadine that Druze outside Beirut might snub her.

In their ambivalence, Wissam's parents eventually told the couple to just get married with their private approval but no public acceptance. When relatives learned through social media and word of mouth about the marriage, they reacted as expected, with silent judgment and drama. Wissam's parents' refusal to publicly support the match saved many of their relationships.

Wissam was the first in his family, and only the second person he knows of from his village, to marry a non-Druze. Other relatives had left people they loved, buckling under social pressure. Given this context, Nadine appreciates how her in-laws handled the situation. "I never felt rejected," she told me.

"They were wise and welcoming. His mom said that she wouldn't be at his wedding but 'Go live your life.' It was quite generous."

As we have seen throughout this book, parents of all sects feared being shunned as the result of their child's mixed marriage. These fears are intensified for those, often but not always Druze, who are embedded in family- and sect-based economic networks.[2] For a person of any sect, the smaller and more closely knit their social world, the more likely it is that they will fear shunning or experience its social and economic consequences. Complex Lebanese inheritance laws mean that property may be jointly owned by siblings and cousins. One or two people in a family network may be authorized to act on behalf of the group and hold the purse strings that control distribution of funds from property rents or sales. People who might have helped someone find employment may refuse to do so. Invitations may be withheld. And while many parents learn that their fears were unfounded, every story where networks do break down after a mixed marriage reinforces those fears.

––––––––

Loulwa grew up in the Druze mountain town from which both her parents hail. By the time she met Issa, whom she described as "the man of my life," she was in her early thirties, the primary breadwinner in her household. A few months into their relationship, she invited Issa and a friend to join her and her mother for lunch in the village. Afterward, sitting alone with Issa on the balcony, sipping coffee and gesturing to their surroundings, Loulwa's mother remarked, "Loulwa knows her position in all of this." When Issa asked what she meant, she replied, "I mean that our house is open to everyone, but she will never marry anyone who isn't Druze." By his account, Issa pushed back gently, and they had a frank, polite conversation that concluded amicably when Loulwa and their friend rejoined them. Then, as the guests were leaving, Loulwa's mother whispered to their friend, "Listen, you tell him I have access to people who can assassinate him."

In retrospect, the couple understands this statement as part jest and part indication of just how upset Loulwa's mother was. But that day, it infuriated them. Years later, Loulwa laughed as she told the story: "We were thinking, What on earth? Is this real? Is this a mafia thing? How dare you threaten someone? Oh my god! It was unbelievable. And she *doesn't* have this access. It's not like she's a mafioso and has guns." That lunch was the only time Issa saw Loulwa's mother before they married.

When she understood the depth of her mother's objections, Loulwa hesitated. She didn't want to hurt her. But that night, she woke up choking, feeling like she was suffocating at the idea of losing Issa. The next day, she shared her feelings with her mom and explained that she was going to let the relationship with Issa run its course, with marriage as one possible outcome. She also decided to help her mom cope with the situation by taking responsibility for telling extended family about Issa. "I was taking the bullets with my mom, or on her behalf, so she wasn't alone," Loulwa explained. Her relatives panicked, saying all the usual things, including emotional blackmail. "No decent girl would do this. What will happen to your mom?" they said. "No one will ever speak to your mom again."

Meanwhile, Loulwa kept talking to her mom about Issa. Outright fights faded to rational arguments. When a friend advised her to "face her mother with love," she was skeptical, retorting, "I am telling you, she says things to me like, 'It would be easier for me to learn that you have cancer than for you to marry a non-Druze.' And you want me to face her with love?" But over time, Loulwa took her friend's advice and adopted an attitude of compassion toward her mother's outbursts, learning to understand them as rooted in fear. "From then on, whenever my mom said something stupid or hurtful, I would smile and tell her I love her and just accept that this is where she comes from and it might take time."

As her mother's responses softened, Loulwa said, "I won't be with any other guy, but I also won't marry Issa without your blessing." A few months later, her mom said, "Okay Loulwa, you're an adult, you know what you're doing. I trust you, and I trust your judgment. If he's making you happy, just stop wasting your time. I give you my blessing. Go ahead and get married." That was her limit. She didn't attend the wedding in Cyprus but invited the couple out for dinner afterward.

In this case, fears of social repercussions were justified. With few exceptions, extended family shunned both Loulwa and her mother. Five households refused to speak with them for years. Loulwa eventually reconciled with all but one person, understanding her relatives' reaction as an effort to prevent their own children from following in her footsteps. She did in fact open the door, and quite a few of her cousins have taken up the fight.

———

Threats of shunning rarely came to full fruition as they did for Loulwa and her mom, but stories like hers reinforce the idea that it *could* happen. Many interviewees understood their parents' fears. Like Tamara, in her decision to elope, and Loulwa, in proactively informing relatives, they not only empathized with their parents but tried to redirect social opprobrium onto themselves. Another woman told her mother to give anyone who questioned her marriage her phone number: "They can call *me* about it. It wasn't your choice, it was mine, so just give them my number. I will deal with it."

While fathers worried about reputation, mothers bore the brunt of backlash from relatives, friends, and neighbors. They were the ones on the phone or at the neighbor's house fielding questions, being scolded, or overhearing gossip about their child. As one person told me, "The mother is blamed for everything." Trying to protect one's mom didn't always work. People sometimes congratulate the person getting married, and then call their mother to berate her about it.

The experience of widowed mothers, who often fought mixed marriage with all they had, highlights this parental gender difference. The weight of potential family censure added to the weight of facing a major parenting moment without their husband. It was a heavy load. Widows who supported a mixed marriage usually had their brothers at their side, sharing both responsibility and burden.

Gendered Social Burdens

Joanna was the third generation to marry outside her sect. She is the daughter of Tamara, whose story opened this chapter. When Joanna fell in love with Ribal, a Druze man, Tamara cautioned her, "Your journey will not be one of flowers, it will be one of thorns. You must remove these thorns with Ribal, and if you can't, don't go further because it won't be easy at all." When the couple decided to marry, Tamara supported them. When she stood by Joanna publicly, as a widow, and gave the couple her blessing, their relatives on both sides followed suit. Tamara was a rare mother who could block interference with her child's marital choice. Her experiences shaped her backbone, and her mixed marriage cemented her stance with the strength of precedent. But her warning to Joanna presaged the battle the couple faced with Ribal's mother, Dia.

Dia had also lost her husband a few years earlier. Aware that this would double the gossip she faced, Ribal waited until the couple was ready to marry before telling her. He would be the first in the family—other than an uncle in the US married to a white woman—to break the rules. Ribal told me, "My mom literally went into a nervous breakdown when I told her. She started having spasms, and crying, like it was a medical reaction." Dia refused to see Joanna for the next few years.

Although Dia remained overwrought, the conversation she had with Ribal changed over time. At first, she maintained it was a sin to marry a non-Druze. Ribal pointed out that he and his siblings had been raised without religion, and that when they had asked, as teenagers, what would happen if they married a non-Druze, the response had always been, "It wouldn't be ideal, but it's your decision." Confronted with this contradiction, Dia's position evolved, and she acknowledged that social pressure was behind her objections.

Amid Dia's continued arguments, Ribal proposed to Joanna on a European vacation. He had already obtained Tamara's blessing. Dia cried when he called with the news but agreed to have lunch with the couple. The meal was uneventful, but the next day, her tears resumed. She complained that Joanna wasn't worth the fuss. "She isn't even that good-looking." This was her final strategy. Dia had moved from guilt ("Why are you doing this to me? Your dad passed away, why do you want me to suffer like this?") to concern ("You'll end up divorced, why do this to yourself?) and was now trying personal attack ("Fine, it's not about religion, but I don't understand what you see in her.").

Ever mindful of his mother's tenuous social position, Ribal drew on reserves of patience to try to lift weight from her shoulders. The eldest son of an only son, Ribal had inherited patriarchal family authority. When he informed his paternal aunts about the engagement, they voiced mild concerns. Afterward, his mother heard far worse from them. Dia also faced pressure from her own parents and siblings, plus the broader village community. She held firm for months, refusing to see Joanna again. Eventually, something shifted, and Dia "just faced the reality that no matter what she did, it really wasn't going to change anything."

When the couple sensed this change of heart, Dia and Tamara met for drinks at Chez Paul, a café in Gemmayzeh. The two widowed mothers bonded. Dia cried and tried to convince Tamara that the marriage was a bad idea. Tamara surprised her by sharing that both she and her parents had had mixed marriages. Bewildered, Dia asked Tamara, "If you suffered from your husband's family, how can you allow your daughter to do the same thing? How can you *not* have a problem that she is marrying a Druze?"

Tamara replied, "Because I suffered and was eventually able to change the perspective of most of my husband's family, I think it is her decision. Just as I fought my battle, let her fight her battle!"

Later that evening, Dia warned Joanna that she would always be the outsider. "No matter what you do, no matter how much they love you, you will remain the one who isn't Druze, someone intruding in the family."

When Joanna replied, "Ribal is worth it!'" Dia gave up her fight.

A year after their engagement, Ribal and Joanna married. Dia attended their civil wedding ceremony abroad and the party in Beirut. Belatedly finding her backbone, she hosted a traditional Druze open house, or *tahani*, for congratulations in the village. Despite expecting a small crowd, she wanted to show society that she wasn't ashamed of her son and that she continued to fulfill her social obligations.

———

Dia and I met at a café in a Beirut mall about a year after Ribal and Joanna's wedding. She had just come from work, but we talked for hours, as if our conversation energized her. Or perhaps we just hit it off. I'm closer in age to her than to her son and was clear that I was interested in her perspective. Whatever it was, Dia was warm and self-reflective about her behavior. She explained that she and her husband were both more open-minded than their families and had raised their children abroad without adherence to sect. When her husband passed away, Dia and her children moved back to Lebanon. That's when the social pressure began.

"My husband wasn't here to support me and support any diversion from the norm," Dia explained. "If he were still alive, it would have been much easier because we could have handled the pressure together. But I wasn't ready to take it all on myself, to take the blame, to take all the, you know, the pointing at me.

"You know, until I was forced face-to-face with the reality of their marriage, I wasn't going to change my mind. To tell you the truth, from the moment I felt the relationship was serious to the moment it became a done deal, I was very negative toward Ribal. I was hoping that by putting pressure on him, I would be able to change his mind. To be honest, I also felt that it would protect me from society, that people would see me fighting, saying no, refusing to give Ribal my blessing. So society would say, 'She did what she could.'"

She was right. Eventually, Dia's family saw her anguish and encouraged her to accept Joanna so as not to lose her son. Dia attributes the show of support she saw in the end to her strong stance against the marriage. "They all understood that I did what I should do but couldn't stop him. If in the beginning I had said, 'I have no problem' and threw a wedding for him, of course they would have boycotted me and stopped talking to me. Instead, my brother, for example, he said, 'My sister, I will come and stand by you.' When he saw me upset and suffering, he said, 'My sister, I'm against everything that Ribal did, but I'm standing by you.'"

Besides mobilizing family support, Dia had another motivation for her resistance. She didn't want her other children to marry non-Druze. To make matters worse, her daughter was dating a Christian at the time.

"I'm happy Ribal is happy, I love Joanna," she said, "But, if you ask me, 'Do you want your other son to marry a Christian?' I would say no. And I cannot compromise with my daughter. I knew she was watching to see what I would do with Ribal, so my battle was indirectly with her."

Right before Dia and I met, she told her daughter that I was interviewing her for my project. "Are you going to tell her you gave Ribal a heart attack?" her daughter replied. Sighing as she told me about their conversation, Dia said, "I caused a crisis for my son. I was very harsh on him."

I replied that it had also been hard on her.

"There wouldn't be a night where I wasn't crying," she concurred. "I used to wake up with my pillow full of tears."

Circling back to her status as a widow, Dia mused, "If my husband were still alive, all this wouldn't have happened. I can't be 100 percent sure, but I think that, if Ribal had said to him, 'I love this girl and will not marry anyone else,' he would not say no. Maybe he would have stood by his son and been able to face people in a stronger way."

She teared up. "I didn't want to be looked at in society, because I'm alone. I didn't want to be the odd woman out. . . . I don't like standing out as the *gharib* [stranger/outsider] in my society; this is where I live, these are the people I drink coffee with every morning. I don't want to be *gharib*. Not because I'm traditional, but because I'm *alone*. I don't want eyes turned toward me. Let it be my son's choice, not my choice, you know?"

————

Dia's repeated use of *gharib* captures the feeling of being an outsider, stared at if not shunned, gossiped about if not ignored, lopped out of society, uprooted. Parents can be punished for their children's violations of the social rules, suffering damage to the social worlds upon which their own wellbeing depends. As Dia notes, opposition may well be the key to holding relationships together. Many parents oppose a marriage, tell people they did so, embrace the ensuing sympathy, and then, as soon as it's all a done deal, accept the situation. "I did what I had to do," they say. "*'Amilt illi 'alayyi.* I did what I could. I did my part." Some parents were transparent about this strategy, explaining it to the couple or asking them to wait a while before coming to visit, to give their social world the appearance of a consequence before reconciling.

Carla's Maronite parents were among them. They didn't object to Eyad, her non-Lebanese Sunni boyfriend, until civil marriage was on the table. Suddenly, they acted surprised, as though they hadn't seen the relationship develop over several years. Her mother worried about how family and friends would react, about village gossip. Her father demanded a church wedding. In time, the couple convinced Carla's parents to accept her decision. They understood the demand for a church wedding as "a form of plausible deniability," a claim that either they didn't know Eyad wasn't Christian, or that he had converted.

To maintain this plausible deniability, Carla's parents gave the couple their blessing but didn't attend the wedding in Cyprus, proving to society that they tried to oppose the match. Years later, Carla and Eyad still don't know which relatives know that Eyad isn't a Lebanese Christian. "Maybe no one knows. Maybe everyone knows but it's one of those things you don't talk about. And it really doesn't matter to us," Carla concluded.

Dia couldn't hide her knowledge that Joanna wasn't Druze. As a widow, it was crucial that she objected to the match, to prove that she could fulfill parental responsibilities in her late husband's absence. A parent who can say "I did my best to stop my wayward child, but in the end, I love them and can't break my own heart by disowning them" is more likely to be received with kindness than one who does not appear to make the effort. It was no small thing that her brother stood by her. Even when mothers were able to stand up for their children, they often drew on the patriarchal backing of their brothers. Fathers were far more easily able to take public stances of support.

A Patriarch's Final Word

Ranya and Sami didn't even know they were from different sects until their third date. They met at a Beirut beach club and took a while to exchange last names. Ranya knew her Roum Orthodox parents expected church weddings and baptized grandchildren, but she told her mom about Sami because keeping secrets wasn't her style. Her mom met and liked Sami but was unhappy that he was Muslim. For months, she presented arguments against the relationship, using every single Islamophobic stereotype listed in chapter 7. Sami reasoned patiently with her, repeatedly explaining that Ranya would always make her own decisions and that he wouldn't impose anything on her. For months, Ranya's mom's attitude shifted with an unknown tide. Some days she seemed fine with the relationship. Other days she told Ranya she would stop speaking with her if they married. Ranya finally asked for help from one of her mom's closest Muslim friends, who convinced her to support the couple.

Sami and Ranya began planning how to approach her father. Behind the scenes, her mom prepared the way. Ranya's dad surprised her one day by asking about Sami: "Are you happy with him? Do you want to stay with him?" When she said she was indeed happy and knew she wanted to marry Sami, her father just listened without response. As soon as Sami proposed, he gave his blessing and took charge of the situation. "He met with everyone in the family," Ranya remembered. "And he just told them, 'My daughter is getting engaged. He's not Christian, he's Muslim, and he's from Beirut. I met him and I like him, and they have my blessing. If anyone in the family has an issue with that, then they have an issue with me. They should deal with me.'" Relatives attended the engagement party and the wedding celebration that followed their Cyprus civil marriage. "Once he took this supportive stance, that was it," Ranya told me. "I love my dad for that."

––––––––––

A parent's capacity to use their own position to squelch broader family protest depends not only on gender but also on birth order among their siblings—reminding us that patriarchal connectivity is about both gender and age. Most of the time, when a father publicly supported a marriage, everyone else fell into line and embraced the new couple, at least to their faces. But some fathers didn't have that kind of authority.

An elder male could thwart a father's support or divide a family. Social pressure to oppose a mixed marriage can force female and younger relatives to take stances against their own judgment. Aunts who attend weddings despite family decrees are scolded or temporarily shunned. Some patriarchs forbade women in a family from seeing or talking to a daughter, granddaughter, sister, or niece. Some women ignored these rules, keeping surreptitious communication lines open.

Like Ranya and Sami, Lena and Alex didn't think about sectarian difference when they began dating. He had asked, early on, where she was from, but misheard the response, thinking she had named a mixed Christian-Muslim village instead of her Muslim town. Given his stereotypes about how Muslims looked, it never occurred to him that Lena was Shi'a. By the time he learned, they were already in love. For her part, Lena had never thought about it. Her parents weren't religious, her father had leftist politics, and she had already deleted her sect from her Lebanese identity card as part of the antisectarian activist movement.

When Lena introduced Alex to her father and said they were just friends, Alex contradicted her: "Your daughter wants me to introduce myself as her friend. But I am not her friend, I love her, and I am a Christian, and I want to marry her. And I can marry her now. So you either tell me, 'You're welcome to do so,' or we will elope."

Lena's father's exclaimed, "Yes, of course!" He wanted Lena to be happy, his leftist side was pleased, and he liked Alex a great deal. But as soon as they began discussing the formalities of a proposal and informing extended family, he lost control of the situation.

Lena's grandparents were conservative Muslims on both her mother's Sunni side and her father's Shi'i side. For them, such a marriage was impossible. Her parents' generation split. Half sided with Lena and her parents, half with the elders. "All hell broke loose," Lena told me. She tried to help her parents respond to the onslaught by explaining that she didn't have to convert because they would have a civil marriage. It only made things worse. Relatives began presenting Lena with acceptable grooms; she refused to meet them. One grandmother badgered Lena's mother, accusing her of complicity in making Lena's future children bastards.

Lena tried asking people to discuss the matter with her instead of with her parents. Instead, her relatives stopped speaking with her entirely. Her grandfather kicked her out of his house when she tried to visit. Her father's family decided to disinherit him if the marriage took place. And a villager unrelated to the family posted on Facebook that Lena should be killed for living in sin.

Sectarianism entered the fray when Lena's paternal relatives blamed her mother. "This is her Sunni mother's fault," they said. Her mother responded by enumerating years of grievances: Her father-in-law calling her "Aisha" instead of her name to make a sectarian point. The family funerals that included Ashura lamentations cursing Sunnis.

The moment that hurt Lena most was when one of her uncles, the patriarch on that side of the family, forbade her favorite grandmother, who lived with him, from speaking with her. "One time," Lena remembered sadly, "we were on our way somewhere, and I saw my uncle's car, and I went hysterical. I told Alex that my grandma is in that car, so he parked next to it and my grandma was in the front seat and my uncle's wife was in the back seat. . . . My grandmother saw me and blew me kisses and then she told me to go away so my uncle's wife wouldn't see me. That's when I really felt I had been treated unjustly. I always remember that feeling, it has a burning sensation, especially to lose time with my grandmother. I am very attached to her."

Throughout this nightmare, Lena and Alex remained strong. Their parents exchanged visits. The couple was formally engaged. And to try to calm matters, they married twice. They registered their Cyprus civil marriage with the state and also had a *katab kitab* without filing the paperwork. The *katab kitab* appeased elders to a certain extent, though most relatives still obeyed Lena's uncle and didn't attend the celebration.

With time, even that recalcitrant uncle began speaking with Lena again, but callouses remain. To prevent Alex from inheriting from Lena, her father's inheritance went to her uncle. More poignantly, when we spoke, Lena remained upset that she had lost time with her grandmother because of patriarchal power in the family. And in this case, the intensity of family opposition slammed the door to mixed marriage shut. "No one dares now," Lena concluded our conversation. "No one dares."

The Other Side of Social Pressure

The stories above have also hinted at social pressure's positive effects. While Lena's story shows the influence and power held by many senior male family members, I also heard stories where age played a greater role and grandmothers could leverage their status as elders to support mixed marriage. A few grandmothers played pivotal roles in convincing a family to accept a match. Others facilitated post-elopement family reconciliations. Aunts and uncles were also key sources of support. Maternal uncles sometimes advocated for their nieces, and paternal uncles held sway with their brothers. Aunts advised couples or provided a safe haven in their homes. When parents fielded phone calls of congratulations amid the barrage of criticism, their social fears were eased.

Positive social pressure was the crux of Zaynab's story. She grew up in the South with practicing Shi'i parents until the Israeli invasion displaced her family to Beirut. After dating Nadim—a Druze man ten years older—for a year, the two were ready to marry. All of their parents rejected the match, but to their surprise, it was Nadim's father who did so most stridently, despite Nadim being in his thirties and multiple existing mixed marriages in the family. The couple decided to wait until at least one set of parents gave their blessing. Siblings and relatives came to the rescue, reasoning with the parents on both sides. Zaynab's came around first; Nadim's followed months later. Family members rarely united to support a couple like this, but individual support was common.

Even without initial support, many parents—especially those who held their heads high and embraced mixed couples—found that rather than being shunned, their social worlds followed their lead. Razan was the first in her Druze family to marry outside her sect. When she told her mom, after the usual protests, her mom admitted that her worry was the extended family. But when her parents blessed her engagement, most relatives replied with congratulations.

Displays of social support for parents reassured them that their families and social circles wouldn't shun them if their child broke the rules. A few parents threw over-the-top weddings to prove to society that their child had made an excellent match. Describing her daughter's lavish engagement party, one mother explained, "It was like I was telling them all, 'See, my daughter took someone deserving of her.'" Social reassurance—whether in the form of phone calls of congratulations, a brother or family member standing with them against others, attendance at a wedding, or simply the continuation of existing relationships as though nothing had changed— countered the fear of being shunned. Once parents were on board, debates turned to postwedding matters, and especially their mixed grandchildren.

Ten

Mixed Families in a Divided World

Rana and Hisham invited me to share a delicious meal with them during our interview. They also wanted their children to join us. The teenagers already knew that their mom's family were Druze who had lived in Ras Beirut for several generations and that their dad had grown up in his Maronite family's village. But they hadn't heard the whole story, and Rana and Hisham thought this would be a good opportunity for them to do so.

When they met as graduate students in the US, Rana tried to figure out Hisham's sect.

"I was blunt in a bad way," she admitted. "And really, I think about it now . . ."

"She *and* her friend," Hisham interjected.

"Now I think," Rana continued, "How could I do that? We asked each other, you know, 'Where are you from?' And he said, 'The North.' And I found that, like a little bit challenging, vague, like he was being vague on purpose. That's Hisham!"

"It was a loaded question!"

"Yes, but we were open about it, and you didn't want to say! Then my friend asked, 'From where in the North?' And Hisham wouldn't say. And then, um, we asked something really bad. One of us, I don't remember who, asked, 'Are you eligible to run for president?' Because you know, that means you have to be Maronite."

"See!" Hisham exclaimed "It was a loaded question! They might as well just have asked, 'What are you? Maronite?'"

We were all laughing, the stage set for what would be a fun evening.

Rana didn't learn Hisham's sect until her friend called a few days later with the discovery that he was indeed Maronite. Despite their initial conversation, neither cared about sect, and they began dating.

When they met Rana a few years later, Hisham's parents were happy she was Lebanese, unlike his previous girlfriend, and just wanted him to settle down, marry, and have children. The couple explained to their kids that this quick acceptance of mixed marriage by a religious family from their region of Lebanon was unusual, and that Hisham's father was swayed by Rana's high level of education.

Rana's parents, however, were dismayed. "There were two reasons for their displeasure: being Maronite, and where I am from." Hisham started laughing again. "One is easier than the other. Being Maronite is a bit better."

"Why?" The teenagers joined the conversation, now intrigued.

"It's like a mafia," Rana explained. "They think it's like a mafia. But they didn't say anything because they didn't know I was going to marry him."

"*Hel-lo!*" Hisham couldn't stop laughing.

"They learned I wanted to marry you when . . ."

"Later . . ."

"Yeah, they were upset later."

"What do you mean 'upset'!? Your brother called!"

"What is going on right now?" one of their kids exclaimed.

It took a minute for Rana and Hisham to catch their breaths. Rana tried to clarify their timeline. "Okay, he has a point. They learned we wanted to marry later and that's when they got upset, but when they first met him, they gave him a warm welcome and everything."

"No! Wait, she skipped something!"

"I swear I can't remember!"

"She told her parents when we started getting serious, and her father opposed it. Naturally, a guy from my town, a Maronite, still studying, no job, of course he opposed it! So, her brother calls . . ."

"Really?"

"Yes, really! When we were at our friend's place. How can you not re-member? And her brother talks to me . . ."

"What did he say to you?"

"You were *there*! I think he said something like, you know, 'This has gone on for a while, and you two aren't moving forward, and you shouldn't be to-gether.' Moral of the story, the parents . . ."

"Mom and Dad . . ."

"Yeah . . ."

"No, my dad didn't know, just my mom."

"Yeah okay, anyway, they didn't approve."

I needed to clarify. "So they raised the issue through your brother?"

"Yes!" they said in unison.

Their daughter wanted more. "So when all this was happening, you knew Grandma and Grandpa were upset?"

"Yes, she knew, she cried . . ." Hisham spoke first.

"I pushed it to the back of my mind . . ."

"You started to cry."

"*What?!*"

"You started to cry! How can you not remember?"

"I swear I forget. I cried? Really? Did my parents know that I was upset?"

"I don't know, but your brother was talking to them too."

"Okay." Rana took up the narrative thread again. "So then we reassured my parents that we weren't getting married, right?"

"Yes, we said that just to reassure them."

"But *did* we want to get married? I can't remember."

"Why else would your brother call?"

Hisham and Rana clarified that her brother's intervention happened while they were still graduate students, uncertain about a timeline to mar-riage. Then Rana picked up the plot again, explaining that they each made the independent decision to return to Lebanon and found work in Beirut. By the time they were ready to marry, they had been together a decade, Rana was in her early thirties, and both she and Hisham were employed. Her father gave his blessing.

The only relatives who opposed Rana's marriage were older, professional, educated women. Shaking her head, Rana said, "They are supposedly so

open-minded and intellectual, and they said, 'What's wrong with not getting married at all, like us?'"

"Meaning, if you can't find a Druze man, then don't get married at all?" I
asked, noting the teenagers' shocked expressions.

"Exactly! That's what happened to them. None of the men they met
were Druze, so they didn't marry."

Hisham's family wanted a Maronite Church wedding. Exploiting their
Maronite chauvinism, Hisham responded by suggesting they go to a Roum
Orthodox priest who would marry them without Rana's conversion. "So
they said to me, 'Stop with your jokes. Just go get married in Cyprus.'" As
Hisham described how family and neighbors were stunned that his father
had accepted a civil marriage, their son interrupted: "Wait, what's the difference between civil and sectarian?" Explanations ensued before the story
continued.

A few days before the couple flew to Cyprus, Hisham and an entourage
of relatives visited Rana's family to propose. Rana remembered being nervous about everything, including what to wear that day. "But," she said, "I
was so happy!"

"Why were you nervous?"

"My poor parents didn't know what you're supposed to do. My mom was
stressed because we rarely hosted big parties. They split up, the men sat in
a room, and the women in another room. Then, Hisham's mother got up—
she's a social butterfly. She knows how to . . ."

One of the teenagers interrupted. "Why were men and women in different rooms? Is that a Druze thing?"

"For the proposal," their dad replied, "when you ask for someone's hand
in marriage."

Rana went on, "Suddenly, Hisham's mother stood and said, 'Rana!' And
I was like, 'Oh dear, what's happening?' I was scared. So I stood up. My sis-
ter-in-law told me to relax, and they dressed me in gold. And I got all red, I
was like, 'What is this? They're buying me?' They were putting all this gold
on me." She laughed. "Anyway, it was . . ."

The other teenager jumped in: "Is that also a Christian thing or only
Druze?"

"It's a Lebanese thing."

"No, it's an Eastern ritual."

"Oh no way, I didn't know that."

Other rituals also bewildered Rana, who took part in good humor. When the couple returned from Cyprus, they visited Hisham's family in the village. "I was supposed to stick dough to the door. There is this dough . . ."

"Yeast dough."

"It must stick . . ."

"Then she had to stick coins on, in the shape of a cross."

"And then you have to crack a pomegranate—it's a sign of fertility. You have to step on it with your shoes."

Rana and Hisham's children listened intently, hearing many of these details for the first time. Rana and Hisham had worked hard to raise them with secular values while maintaining loving relationships with both extended families. Our conversation showed me that their efforts had succeeded. When I asked what they did about religion in their home, their son pointed to the Christmas tree visible in the adjoining room. "That's it," he said.

When they think about parenting, my interviewees often thought about their own childhoods and how they had learned the sect-based scripts people use to collapse all kinds of difference in Lebanese society. They wanted to raise their children differently. Many told me that raising mixed children in Lebanon was the hardest thing they had ever done. As we will see in this chapter, parents must navigate life as a mixed family in a context that tries to impose set categories and ideas onto them.

Raising Mixed Kids

Some mixed couples taught their children to believe in God and talked about both "petit Jesus" and "petit Muhammad." Their kids might say both the Lord's Prayer and Al-Fatiha before they slept or fast during Ramadan using the methods of Lent—giving up chocolate or sweets for the month. Others focused on shared values unlinked from faith: "I really don't care what they believe in. I'm interested in making sure that when they see an elder, they help him. That's it. If they want to pray kneeling, that's fine. If they want to pray standing, that's fine. If they want to meditate, no problem. If they want to do yoga, that's fine. If they don't want to pray, I don't care. It's just a detail. It's just a lifestyle."

Secularized, hybrid, holiday traditions were common: family gatherings, shared meals, and when appropriate, gifts. Christmas trees were decorated with snowflakes and lights. Sometimes the non-Christian partner was far more enthusiastic about decorating a tree, viewing it as a fun activity rather than a ritualized obligation. A few Druze-Muslim couples celebrated Christmas enthusiastically, noting that Muslims believe in Jesus as a prophet.

There were certainly exceptions—mixed couples raising their children in one religion, usually that of the husband. Atypically among my interviewees, a Muslim woman insisted her children be raised as Christians like their father because she believed they would be confused otherwise. She hired a private religious tutor and insists her children go to church every Sunday with her mother-in-law. Another couple is raising their children to identify as Muslim like their father but celebrates mostly Christian holidays. "My husband is a very bad Muslim," this woman told me. "People will ask me things like, 'Why didn't you buy your kids new clothes for Eid?' And so I will have to go to him and be like, 'Did you know we were supposed to do that?' And he'll be like, 'Yeah.' So I'm like, 'What do you mean, "Yeah"? How am I supposed to raise them in both religions if you don't tell me what I'm supposed to do on your side?'" Here we see patriarchy placing responsibility for religious education on the mother's shoulders.

————

No matter what parents try to do, it is virtually impossible to avoid religion in Lebanon. Schools incorporate it into curricula, neighbors ask questions, classmates begin practicing it, and relatives insist on teaching it. During that dinner with Rana, Hisham, and their teenagers, Rana told us that when their daughter was a toddler, a neighbor's six-year-old tried to teach her the opening verse of the Qur'an. Another person told me about a neighbor who had interrogated her five-year-old son:

"What religion are you?"

"What do you mean?"

"What do you celebrate?"

"What do you mean?"

"Do you celebrate Christmas?"

"Yes."

"Do you celebrate Ramadan?"

"Yes."

Frustrated, the neighbor told him to go ask his mother "what he was." Furious, my interviewee went next door and scolded the neighbor before explaining to her son that "Mama was Muslim and Baba was Druze, but everyone is human and nobody is different or better than anybody else."

Questions often began between the ages of seven and nine—just as schools add religion to curricula or classmates begin to fast or pray. Teachers at parochial schools asked children about their religion because they needed to sort them; for example, Muslim students in Christian schools are exempt from religion classes. At secular schools, religion also entered the curriculum at around this age. The WhatsApp group chat for parents at a private secular school in Beirut exploded when a social science unit about world religions prompted questions from their nine-year-olds about religious identity.

One woman witnessed her nine-year-old's confusion as she drove him and a friend home one day during Ramadan. "I unconsciously opened a water bottle and took a sip," she told me. "And my son's friend gasped, 'Aunty! You're not fasting?' So I said, 'No my dear, I don't fast, I am Christian.' And then he looked at my son and asked him what he was, and poor kid, he looked at me clueless. So I said, 'It's okay, *habibi*, you're Muslim.' And then this kid looks at my son and asks him if he is Sunni or Shiʻa! Can you believe it? So again my son looks at me like, 'Mom, help?' So I answered that his father was Sunni. And can you believe this kid's reply? He's like, 'It's good you're Sunni because I wouldn't be your friend if you were Shiʻa.' Honestly, at that point, I wanted to stop the car and go strangle his parents."

Religious peer pressure is part of the daily struggle of raising mixed kids in Lebanon. Children came home from school with ideas prompted by classmates, like, "Will I go to hell if I eat ham?" or "Can we go get palm leaves at church on Sunday?" Another WhatsApp group chat of parents imploded over a birthday party that included prayer at a mosque after an *iftar*. Some mixed couples don't allow their children to fast. A woman who initially forbade her ten-year-old from fasting changed her approach when her husband suggested their son might fast just to rebel against her. She told her son he could fast as long as he did it for the right reasons, to feel deprivation and empathize with the poor. When he learned this meant no junk food or chocolate, her son decided he was too young to participate.

Other parents allow religious practice to unfold on its own. "We let our children figure out their path slowly," one father told me, "while trying to steer them toward friends who are like us, who are mixed or don't practice." So far, this couple thinks their approach is working. Their daughter had recently asked to fast during Ramadan with her friends. Her parents said she could fast after breakfast, because she was only eight and needed energy for her school day. She only lasted a few days. Parents of teenagers observed that their kids had gone through a phase of religious experimentation. "But eventually, they want to go out drinking, so the people who don't drink move to a different clique, you know? Or the ones fasting during Ramadan are sleeping all day, but my kids are doing stuff with other friends. It works itself out eventually."

Trying to avoid such peer pressure, mixed couples often wanted to send their children to secular schools, but that's an option only available to the wealthy. While some 70 percent of Lebanese students attend private schools, the more affordable ones are run by religious organizations. Plus, type of school doesn't necessarily eliminate religious pressures. Elite and upper-middle class students at the secular American Community School during the postwar 1990s poked fun at one another's sects using offensive language.[1] At the elite and secular International College, tensions regularly emerged when Christian students from a primary school in an isolated town joined the Beirut campus for secondary school, bringing with them forms of Christian chauvinism new to students in Beirut. And school was only one locus of pressure. Extended family, especially grandparents, added to the maelstrom of influences mixed couples try to control.

Fending Off Family Interference

By the time they became grandparents, most parents who had fought against a mixed marriage had changed their perspective. Some even apologized to a daughter- or son-in-law for giving them a hard time. Yet as grandparents, they still tried to insert their religious preferences into the mixed family dynamic.

Lina and Karim were both expat kids whose parents fled the civil war and returned in time for them to attend high school and university in Lebanon.

Lina's parents liked Karim until they learned he was Muslim. Lina responded by saying, "Don't worry, he's not really Muslim, he's an atheist," which upset them even more. For a few years, Lina's parents tried many of the tactics we have seen to convince her to leave Karim. Whenever the pressure got to her, she suggested breaking up. Karim always refused and held strong. In the end, Lina explained, the fact that Karim "stuck around through all my parents' whining and me trying to break up with him proved them wrong." Still unhappy, Lina's parents accepted her decision and the couple married with everyone's blessing in a civil ceremony destination wedding. They moved to Dubai because they feel comfortable in its expat social world.

Flash forward a decade, and Lina and Karim are grappling with their mothers—the grandmothers of their children. Lina's mother's interventions are typical of many Lebanese Christian grandmothers faced with non-Christian grandchildren. Laughing, the couple shared an example with me.

"My mom always wants to baptize the kids because she really does believe in Jesus," Lina said. "She feels like you should baptize your children so God protects them. So she'll go pray for them all the time. She's like, 'I prayed for your children by the way.' I'm like, 'Okay, thanks, Mom.' It can't hurt. I'll never forget when I accidentally spilled wine on my son and my mom was like, 'Oh he was baptized, thank you Lina.' But she's come to terms with it. She understands that if we're going to baptize our kids, then we're also going to take them to the mosque; it has to be equal. . . . But when we left the kids with her last year when we went on a holiday, we came back and turns out she took them up to Mar Charbel the first day. The second day she took them to Harissa. She did this like religious world tour with them."

"She took them everywhere," Karim continued. "They came back with slappers, those wrist bracelets, with the superman logo, but with a *J* for Jesus instead of the *S*. And they don't know what it is. They just have fun picking it up and slapping it on their hands."

"We get home, and I see my kids fully Christianized, and I'm like, 'Mom, what the heck did you do?'"

"Bracelets and shit!"

"She's like, 'What? I'm teaching them, and you know what, I asked God to protect them. You should be thanking me.' I'm like, 'Oh my god, okay.' So, I took everything and gave it to our nanny. I mean, it's harmless, but it annoys me. Because I really don't want to expose them to it yet. And I was so stressed. Like now my children are going to go see their other grandma and she's going to ask them what they did with my mom, and my children will be like, 'Oh, we went and saw Jesus.'"

"It's like an arms race with our religions. The peace between the families," Karim concluded.

————

Karim and Lina weren't the only couple contending with a grandmotherly "cold war." Samia and Celeste, the former friends who fell out as mothers-in-law, continue their tug-of-war around their shared grandchildren. Celeste might throw a dinner party during Ramadan that begins before *iftar* and invite Samia, knowing that she can't attend. Samia might refuse to participate in a Christmas gift-giving ritual. Many mixed couples described grandparental efforts to mark their children as "their" religion. They declined gifts of cross jewelry or Ayat al Kursi, or stored them to give to their child once they had grown up.

Grandparental endeavors to shape grandchildren are neither unique to Lebanon nor specific to mixed families. I have a white friend in the US who complains about having to undo her evangelical Christian mother's attempts to "brainwash" her children after every visit. Such meddling is magnified in Lebanon's sectarian context. It can threaten the fragile balance between families or disrupt couples' efforts to maintain a secular home. From the start, many parents' objections to mixed marriage are about the threat the couple poses to their imaginations of the future. Before they marry, most couples agree that each person should manage their own parents, so that in-law relationships remain pleasant. Once they have children, arguments or questions take material form as gifts or visits to religious sites. Some couples diligently maintain balance, ensuring that if their children "go with Jeddo to church," they also "go with Jeddo to mosque." Others set firm boundaries with parents, despite the hurt feelings this may cause. As one person put it, "We have a two-person marriage, which is not the norm in Lebanon where everyone is always involved and knows everything. Our parents learn only the headlines, even for small things. Like if we are buying a new refrigerator, we tell them afterward or let them just see it in our house." Most couples figure it out as life goes on.

A newlywed couple was prompted by my questions to discuss how they would handle such interference. The husband was nonchalant. "That's the beauty of it," he said. "Their grandmother will secretly try to teach them something. Their grandfather will secretly try to teach them something. And then the kids will secretly realize they're all idiots. It will be fine."

His wife disagreed. "No, I want to know beforehand. Until our child is a certain age, I need to be aware, I need to be informed, I need to be asked."

"That's too controlling."

"The other option is offensive. It shows their real feelings about me. If there was an excessive attempt to make our kid more your religion, I would feel like they don't want the child to be like me. This applies the other way too. If my family tried to make our child more my religion, I would also be offended, because maybe they are saying they don't want the child to be like you."

"But they think they are doing it out of love. They are doing their best to care for their grandchild by teaching them what they believe is right."

"You don't see the underlying hostility that comes with that?"

"If it comes with hostility, they aren't aware of it. They don't see it that way. From their point of view, they're bringing you all the love, the best form of love they have, which to them is the ultimate truth."

Most of my interviewees agreed with both these ideas: that grandparents' actions stem from love and that those actions overstep boundaries. It sometimes began before a child was born.

Names Matter

Grandmother drama from Karim's side appeared when it was time for the couple to name their first child. Karim began this story: "We're very pragmatic. So, number one, our children's names shouldn't be identifiable as any religion. Number two, our kids are second-gen expat kids. Our parents think and speak in Arabic. We think and speak in English. We wanted to give our kids international names. We wanted names that work in Lebanon but aren't typically Lebanese or Arabic."

"So, in the hospital after our son was born, we were just like, 'Okay, we'll name him Marc,'" continued Lina. "And Karim's family went apeshit. They got pretty pissed off about it. I didn't realize the name was so Christian. We saw it more as Marcus the Greek, Marc as short for Marcus."

"But in Lebanon, I guess there aren't many Muslim Marcs." Karim started laughing.

"So that name did *not* go down well. And we knew they were pissed off, like in an instant. Karim came to the hospital looking upset. I'm like, 'What's wrong?' He's like, 'Yeah, they're not happy.' I'm like, 'Okay, let's go to Google.' It's not like we even fought back. It was just like, 'Okay, fine, I get it.' So, I was in the hospital bed and we just Googled top boy names for both Muslims and Christians and got a list of six names. I remember one was Mikhael, one was Daniel, one was Ryan, one was Adam, and Zayn."

"That's why a lot of people in our situation, mixed couples, they pick names like Adam. That's the number one mixed-religion name these days, Adam. It's very conciliatory. It's like, 'We give up, we just want to make everyone happy. We're naming him Adam because we don't want to hear shit, not because we like the name.' It also happens to be Western and Arab and international and Christian and Muslim and no one can fucking say shit about it. We didn't want to do that. We wanted to pick a name we actually liked."

Lina added that the pushback to their original choice "kind of left a bad taste in my mouth because I always thought everyone was open-minded. I thought it was fine, but then all these *feelings* came out. Like the birth of our son opened these doors, literally twelve years later, that were like, 'Ahhh, okay, underneath it all, you *are* a bit annoyed that we married.'"

"Why do you think it came up then?" I asked.

"I think for my mom it was that up until that point the scorecard was equal on both sides," Karim replied. "No one imposed any more than the other side. Maybe with the naming issue it felt like that status quo had been broken."

"She felt like I was trying to Christianize her family."

"It was like 1–0 basically."

"But it was still hurtful, because I had a really open-door relationship with them."

"I think it was also because she would have had a lot of explaining to do to her friends. Like, 'What did you name your first grandson?' 'Marc.' 'What?'"

In the end, Lina and Karim chose a name that felt neutral and was relatively acceptable all around.

———

Naming matters in Lebanon, *especially* for boys. When I asked women if they knew someone they had just met was Muslim or Christian before beginning to date them, they often replied, "Of course, his name was Omar" (or Muhammad or Ali or Charbel or Simon or George). There are religious names for Lebanese women: Zaynab, Fatima, Marie, Christiane, but many women carry one of the myriad two-syllable neutral names that dominate Lebanon's social landscape and have filtered into all the country's communities (i.e., Rana, Rola, Rima, Lana, Lara, Lama, Lina, etc.).

As a result, most mixed couples try to name their sons in nonreligious ways. Some try "international" or American names like Jed or Ryan. Couples laughed about how their parents would sometimes find Arabic translations or pronunciations for these names, so Jed became Jad, and Ryan became Rayan. Others sought names that worked in both religions. Adam is, as Karim noted, a popular choice. In earlier decades, Yusef (Joseph) was common. And like Lina and Karim, quite a few couples didn't realize the Christian connotations of an "international" name until after they announced it. One couple chose the name Danny and kept it a secret until the baby was born, imagining the fun of a big reveal. They were stunned when the Muslim side of the family accused them of choosing a Christian name. They changed it to a neutral Arab name, like Sami or Hisham or Walid. Another mixed couple chose Luka, somehow missing the connection to the Christian name Luke. They held their ground. Other couples preempt discussion. One chose a neutral Arabic name, announced it before the birth, and threatened to change it to either Charbel or Muhammad if anyone objected. Their strategy worked.

A "Christian Family"

"Teta put water on us at church!" was one of the most common signals of grandmother interference. Quite a few Maronite grandmothers informally baptized their grandchildren. Parents found out when their kids reported on their day with Grandma. Grandmother-conducted baptisms don't change anything about a child's official identity. They reflect the grandmother's belief in the divine protection baptism imbues, assuage her concerns about the child's soul, and signal her desires for a "Christian family."

When Sana met Marc, she thought to herself, What do I want with this disaster? She wasn't worried about her Sunni family. A sibling and several cousins had married non-Muslims. Her gut feeling was that Marc's family would pose a problem. Nevertheless, the couple fell in love and married in Cyprus. Not only was Marc the first person in his extended family to marry a non-Christian, but he was also the first to have a civil marriage. His parents' objections centered around the concept of a "Christian family." I asked what that phrase meant, and Marc explained, "It's a pillar of the Maronite faith, a family that goes to church at minimum on Christmas and Easter, ideally more often, and that has church rituals for marriage, baptism, communion, and the fortieth day memorial mass. It's a family that is *known* to be Christian." Marc thought his family was normal, but from Sana's perspective, they were especially conservative. Before marrying, the couple agreed on how they would handle religion: they would baptize their children but allow no religious practice afterward.

In Lebanon, baptism is more than a religious ritual.[2] If the officiant records it with the state, baptism marks an official change of sect. No one knew whether baptism mattered for future legal situations. Some people thought unbaptized children with a Christian father would have inheritance problems. Others thought children born outside Lebanon with a Christian father had to be baptized to be registered with the Lebanese state. One couple baptized their Muslim children thinking it would ease their future emigration to Europe or the US.

When the husband is Christian, patriarchal social norms mean that baptism is taken for granted unless the couple objects. A few non-Christian women I interviewed accepted this as a social reality they couldn't fight. "Of course my kids were baptized," one told me. "I mean, they're technically Christians, what can I do about it?" In line with this patriarchal norm, Christian in-laws tried to suppress the influence of Muslim daughters-in-law on their children. One Sunni woman recalled that her Maronite mother-in-law told her, "We don't care if you ever become Christian, but we insist that the kids will be." Upset, she reported the conversation to her husband, who reassured her, "If my mom wants to have Christian kids, she should give birth to them. She has no right to interfere with our children."

Not all husbands were as willing to stand up to their mothers. Another Muslim woman told me that for years her in-laws have refused to acknowledge that she isn't Christian. Her husband agrees that this is a problem but won't speak with his mother about it. Baptisms could alienate non-Christian mothers. One cried at each of her children's baptisms, experiencing it as a ritual that moved them further away from her. Another felt "traumatized" when the priest wouldn't allow her to hold her baby, who was crying because people he didn't know were dunking him in water. Others were upset when their husbands reneged on premarital agreements to not baptize their children.

Most Christian men married to non-Christian women baptized their children in discreet ceremonies without the usual Lebanese fanfare. They viewed baptism as a necessary compromise to maintain the peace, and often insisted, as Sana and Marc did, that there would be no further religious rituals or education. Non-Christian mothers sometimes didn't attend the ceremony or tell their parents about it.

Rana and Hisham, the couple whose teenage children joined the interview, agreed to baptize their first child, but when their second was born, Hisham balked at another baptism, saying that the first one had been the compromise. A decade later, Hisham told us at dinner, gesturing to his son, "This guy here saw his cousins being baptized and he comes and says to me, 'I want to get baptized.'"

"He was ten years old," Rana added.

"Nine."

"Nine," the teenager confirmed. A brief pause, then, "Wait, I said, 'I want to get baptized?'"

"Yeah, you said, 'I want to get baptized.'"

"Do you remember why?" I asked the son.

"Well, my cousin was pressuring me a lot, being like, 'Well, why don't you get baptized?' So then I guess I asked, and Dad was like, 'Sure, why not?'"

Baptized Muslims

When she fell in love with Hussein, Stephanie anticipated trouble from her Christian parents and spent six years saying "whatever it took" to get to the goal of marrying him with their blessing. Among her parents' many conditions was that the couple baptize their future children. Hussein agreed, and his parents said that wouldn't be a problem. But when their first child was born, Hussein's parents changed their tune. "Now they were hell-bent against it," Hussein said. "I think they hadn't thought it through earlier as an actual scenario." The couple, who had no opinion on the matter, was stuck between two polarized sets of in-laws. They compromised by baptizing their kids in a private ritual with only Stephanie and her immediate family present.

Baptism was a common compromise couples made to obtain the blessing of a bride's Christian parents. These rituals were usually private, sometimes even hidden from the non-Christian grandparents. Because these baptisms weren't registered with the state, these children were officially Muslim or Druze, like their father, but baptized, like their mother. Some couples saw this as a way to facilitate their children's ability to choose their sect when they turned eighteen. And indeed, I interviewed a woman who was Muslim like her father but could marry her Christian fiancé in church because she had been baptized as an infant.

Sectarianism thwarted one couple's plan to quietly baptize their children to give them options and some of their mother's heritage. Ignorant about religion, they went to a famous church with gorgeous architecture and asked the priest to baptize their child. He refused because the mother was of a different Christian sect. "You have to go to your own church," the priest explained. So the mother took the baby to a church of her sect, but the priest demanded to speak with the child's father. When the couple returned together, they explained their plan to let their children choose what they wanted to be as adults. After much discussion, the priest agreed not to register the baptism. "Who are the godparents?" he asked, ready to begin the ceremony. The couple had brought Christian friends with them, but the priest rejected them as godparents because they were from a different sect. Frustrated, the couple gave up.

We've seen this sort of hassle before when mixed couples tried to have symbolic, unregistered religious ceremonies in addition to civil marriages. The control Lebanese religious authorities wield over every aspect of personal status is driving many couples away from religious ritual or symbolism altogether. Personal status hassles also shape mixed couples' futures when marriages fail or when a spouse passes away.

Legal Constraints on Futures

Because children "belong" to a different sect than their mother, women in mixed marriages who don't convert face an extra layer of discrimination when child custody is disputed, whether in divorce or because their husbands have passed away. In most Lebanese personal status laws, mothers retain physical custody up to a certain age and then must "return" the child to their father. Shi'i women keep male children until age two; Sunnis and Druze until age twelve, and Roum Orthodox Christians until age fourteen. The age for female children is generally a few years older.

Physical custody is only one part of the problem.[3] No Lebanese mother is considered the legal guardian of her child. Only fathers or male relatives can hold that status, unless the male guardian grants a mother legal guardianship. This means that mothers can't do things like open bank accounts for their kids, travel with them without permission, or register them for school. When a mother is widowed, guardianship passes to her husband's closest male relative. And if a widow is a different sect, her in-laws can challenge physical custody more easily in court. Custody is the primary reason women convert, especially if relations with their in-laws are tense.

Layal learned this lesson the hard way. She had married the love of her life with the blessings of both her Sunni parents and his Roum Orthodox family; they were all from the same elite Beirut community. It never occurred to Layal to convert; neither she nor her husband cared about religion. When two of their children were still minors, tragedy struck and Layal's husband passed away. Suddenly, Layal had no power in her children's lives. "It was like I didn't exist," she explained. "Nothing was in my name. I couldn't do anything legal for my own children." Decisions like where to send them to school were taken out of her hands as her in-laws asserted their control. When her daughter was accepted to a summer program abroad, her in-laws used their authority to prevent her from traveling as a minor. When her grief finally subsided enough for her to think straight, Layal consulted a lawyer. He presented conversion as the solution. But Layal's father was still alive, and she couldn't afford to lose her inheritance. She was working long hours to support and educate her teenagers, and while her late husband's future inheritance would pass directly to her children, she couldn't access that wealth. Layal's in-laws finally agreed to help with school fees, but they tied that financial assistance to their absolute control over educational decisions.

Layal's story isn't only about child custody and guardianship. It's also about inheritance and efforts to keep wealth within a family and a sectarian community. Once again, each sect follows a different inheritance law.

Christian sects follow a civil law under which men and women are supposed to inherit equally, but people can supersede this law with a will, changing allocations or disinheriting a child. Christian families regularly use wills to prevent women who marry non-Christian men from inheriting property so that property is not later inherited by their non-Christian husbands or children. Druze may choose to write a will or follow Sunni law. Under both Sunni and Shi'i personal status law, sons each inherit an equal share, while daughters inherit half a male share. But if a Sunni has no sons, the deceased's patrilineal relatives inherit a portion. If a Shi'i Muslim has no sons, the daughters divide the full inheritance. This is why Sunni Muslims without sons often convert to Shi'i Islam. Most crucially, non-Muslims cannot inherit from Muslims—meaning that a non-Muslim wife cannot inherit from her Muslim husband, and a non-Muslim mother cannot pass assets to her Muslim children.

Reem's Sunni Beiruti father and Roum Orthodox mother fell in love just as Lebanon imploded into violence in the mid-1970s. Reem's paternal grandmother and uncles never accepted Reem's mother because she didn't convert when they married. When her father passed away, his family tried to take custody of Reem's youngest sister. Her mother converted to Islam to keep custody until her youngest turned eighteen, then converted back. Reem's uncles also tried—and failed—to stop Reem from marrying her Maronite fiancé, a match her father had blessed before he died. And they tried to block Reem and her siblings' inheritance, an effort that also failed because they are Sunni like their father.

The more material wealth and property a family holds, the bigger the problems posed by inheritance. But even couples who aren't wealthy, but have a home or other assets, worry about what will happen if one of them passes away. Some women wait until they have inherited from their parents to convert. Many couples write house deeds in both their names and set up legal paperwork to ensure assets will pass to their kids. Paperwork is expensive. Wills and other transactions and documents require legal assistance. They can also be challenged in court. Inheritance taxes or other taxes sometimes need to be paid upfront. Many a plot of land in a Lebanese village is co-owned by well over ten individuals, who may live on multiple continents, as inheritance processes have continued over time. A surprising number—nearly half—of my interviewees didn't know how inheritance would work for them or their children. Figuring it out or consulting with a lawyer was often on their to-do list. No one wants to think about death and the issues that follow. Fewer still had given much thought to where and how they would be buried.

Most people avoid thinking about their own funeral. In the US, estate planning professionals suggest making one's wishes known to loved ones. Decisions must be made: Which cemetery? Burial, cremation, or perhaps a tree pod? What kind of ritual? In Lebanon, burial is the only legal option, and while not technically a matter of personal status law, it falls under religious jurisdiction because cemeteries are linked to specific sects. Mixed couples are as much of a social problem in death as they are in life. Logically, burial weighed on the minds of older interviewees, while younger couples hadn't even realized it was a problem.

Burial kept one of my interviewees up at night. "I always think about it, always," she said. "What will happen? My children follow their father's sect, so they won't be with me, and that doesn't matter, but maybe it does, I don't know. It's something that I think about and think about." She sighed. "But at the end of the day, I'll be buried with my parents, and he'll be with his parents, and as for our kids, after a long life, inshallah, they'll be with their father, unless they want to figure out something else. It's their choice."

Like this woman, many people just accept that each spouse will return to their natal family graveyard. But they aren't happy about it. "The simple solution is that we won't be buried together," one person said, "and that's sad. My mom and dad will be buried in the same place, but we won't be. It is not cool, imagining that our children have to go to two different places to visit us after we die. It doesn't make any sense."

Others thought this option wasn't even possible. A Muslim woman told me she doesn't think she can be buried in a Muslim cemetery with her natal family because she married a Christian, but she can't be buried with her husband because she didn't convert. She's heard that cremation is possible through the American University Hospital but is worried that no religious cleric will pray over someone who is cremated. Throwing up her hands, she exclaimed, "Fine! Let them burn me! What else can I do?" If she had the resources or land, she could arrange a private family plot. That doesn't solve the problem, for believers, of ritual or prayer, but at least it's a resting place. Another woman who ruminated about these matters suggested, only partly in jest, to her husband that they buy a small bit of land beside their house for their burial. Others with resources have used connections and bribes to resolve these problems. A few couples had even discussed starting a petition to the government to create a nonsectarian cemetery. Alongside inheritance, burial sometimes prompted women to convert later in life.

————

Many mixed couples cultivate nonsectarian and inclusive lives and homes, ignoring the world around them until it intrudes, unwelcome. "If we pay it no attention, it might just go away." They were aware they lived in what they called a "bubble." The term wasn't a criticism of their lifestyle. Many couples felt that their bubble was crucial to their ability to protect themselves and their children from some of these daily reminders that they differed from most Lebanese families. Some thought that perhaps they were even changing Lebanon in the process. This is one of the biggest questions that lingers from my research, the question left unanswered at the end of many of my conversations: Is mixed marriage having a broader effect on Lebanese society? Are these couples, as many of them imagine themselves to be, harbingers of a more inclusive future?

Conclusion

Can Mixed Marriage Change the World?

When Sama and Ramzi married, neither family interfered. Their story is one of a close friendship turned romance when they were in their thirties. Aware they were upending multiple social rules, Sama and Ramzi went about their lives privately. When it seemed appropriate, they met one another's families. Their parents expressed reservations about the atypical aspects of their relationship: Sama is older than Ramzi, and this would be her second marriage. While both were financially independent, Ramzi didn't look like a traditional "provider" on paper. Rather than ask for blessings or permission to marry, the couple informed everyone that they were engaged and invited them to the wedding. Today, Sama and Ramzi live in Ras Beirut and send their children to private secular schools. They manage the legal hassles thrown up by the Lebanese state by consulting lawyers and dotting their i's and crossing their t's as much as possible.

How typical are Sama and Ramzi? Only a scant 15 percent of the people I interviewed told stories of no family opposition. The reasons for this ease varied, but usually included at least one of these factors: the people getting married were over thirty years old; the families were elite; the couple shared leftist and secularist politics with their parents; both extended families already included multiple existing mixed marriages; or, in a handful of interviews, the mixed marriage was a second marriage. On the one hand, 15 percent doesn't seem like much. Then again, it may be meaningful in this sectarian context. Perhaps "only a scant 15 percent" should read instead as a point of excitement. Fifteen percent of my interviewees could break the marriage rules easily!

Recall also that most Lebanese avoid mixed relationships or break up under pressure. For two Lebanese to follow through with mixed marriage, they have to believe the labels of sect don't matter enough to stop them. In this sense, my interviewees are outliers; as couples, they aren't the norm in Lebanon. But they do represent a significant trend, a subculture within Lebanese society eschewing marital norms and slowly changing ideas about who is *not* too different to marry.

In this third decade of the twenty-first century, Lebanese are talking about mixed marriage more than ever before. It's in the news and on social media. When a lavish mixed Lebanese wedding—the video a visual and auditory pastiche evoking Christian and Muslim cues—went viral in 2019,[1] social media responses ran the gamut from calling the bride a sinner for marrying a non-Muslim in a civil marriage to praising the couple for being a good example for future generations. I found a third pattern in the comments both interesting and telling: people wondered why others were making such a fuss, claiming that mixed marriages are "normal" and not worth the commentary. That third pattern evinces this growing subculture of Lebanese who renounce sectarian categories. A few of my interviewees even claimed membership—tongues firmly in cheeks—in "the nineteenth sect," a phrase we hear periodically among antisectarian Lebanese and activist groups.

Tenuous Bubbles

"Accept me as I am, and I'll accept you as you are. I don't want to fight with anyone. I'm not defying the system. I'm not defying people. I'm not defying society . . . I'm just trying to be! I'm just trying to do what I believe in, smoothly, without fighting with anyone, without creating any problems. Just let me live how I like, and you live how you like. And we can live in parallel, neither interfering with the other's affairs."

As she described her desire for the future, this woman's voice shook with frustration. Her imagination of a "nineteenth sect" was about separation, being able to live without sect-based social pressure or personal status laws, to raise a mixed family however she and her spouse chose, to create a life outside dominant social norms.

Others saw a "nineteenth sect" as a step toward broader social change. "We are both activists," one told me, "and we believe that *this* is how change should happen. Real change is made by people. Our marriage was about a real change. We implemented what we believed in."[2] Interviewees like this person were sometimes puzzled when I explained that my project wasn't about civil marriage. Their commitments to secularism blinded them to the possibility that a mixed couple might marry in a religious ceremony. Some were reluctant to talk with me, eventually sharing that they didn't like thinking about their marriage as mixed because it forced them to face the ugly realities of Lebanese society. Some claimed to be "sect-blind": "I don't see sect." Others refused this claim: "I think it's important to be secular but to acknowledge and embrace difference rather than ignore it."

The constant thread in my interviewees' descriptions of a nineteenth sect or growing subculture was the idea that it was a space or milieu where they found other people like them. As one put it, "It's about lifestyle, priorities. It's not just religion, it's everything, knowing people who are gay, knowing people of a different race, it's a package. We never fit in, but at the same time we have our environment where we *can* fit in." The most obvious "bubbles" were outside Lebanon. Distance improved in-law relationships, allowed couples to cultivate new traditions, and protected them from gossip. Ras Beirut residents also cultivated such spaces. "This is my world, and I love it," one said. "I know what's happening outside our bubble, I know there's fanaticism and hate, really I know, but I choose not to see it." Another shared, "I feel like we live in a different zone. We've even filtered out friends who don't share our view, so we ended up with a small network of people who are like us, a lot of mixed marriages. We created that comfort zone for each other." For some, this segregation was necessary for their survival: "People like us, you have to form your own bubble to manage to live in this country and defy the system."

Bubbles are temporary havens. Lebanese outside the country remain connected to family in Lebanon and visit regularly. Ras Beirut friendship bubbles don't encompass daily life, work, and extended family. After telling me about her "little cocoon of people," an interviewee continued, "I'll think

I've forgotten what it's like out there, but then something will remind me." And when they looked "out there," many people saw their bubbles moving further and further from center. The divide between Lebanese for whom sect matters and for whom it doesn't is growing. Mixed couples feel that widening rift keenly.

There's a contradiction here. In the twenty-first century, as many Lebanese double down on sectarian ideas, more Lebanese are open to mixed marriages than ever before. Mixed couples are part of a larger social milieu where people are working to cultivate spaces and communities that *feel* antisectarian, despite the legal and institutional structures that trap them. They are building spaces and communities where sect doesn't matter. The question remains: Will this have a broader effect?

A Recent Story

"Our story is boring." In my experience, this is often a promising start to an interview, so I encouraged Nathalie and Omar to tell me their story anyway. Expat Lebanese for most of their lives, they met in Dubai where they both worked. Both were believers, Maronite and Sunni. After many evenings hanging out as friends, Nathalie asked Omar whether there might be more to their relationship. "It's not going to happen," Omar said, remembering a Christian ex-girlfriend who left him instead of fighting her Islamophobic family. Nathalie slammed the door behind her.

Nearly a year later, Nathalie and Omar reconnected on a vacation with mutual friends. They took a side trip together. Sharing the narration as if with one voice, they continued: "Long story short, there was only one room on the whole island, and it had a king-sized bed."

"But nothing happened. We slept, and woke up hugging each other."

"It was magical. We had waited a long time, and we had really fallen in love a long time before, but we feared it, and we were too old to take big risks."

On both sides, their parents expressed concerns that faded after the first meeting. Omar's parents saw how much sense the couple made together. And Natalie's dad told her that Omar was "the one."

Omar proposed to Natalie at sunset on a beach two months later, then asked her father for his blessing.

"I love your daughter, and I won't marry her if you don't want me to."

"I have some concerns," her father replied. "We see these guys on TV with the long beards."

"Honestly, I'm scared of that shit, too. Those aren't Muslims, I don't know what they are."

The two men compared prayers and religious values, finding commonalities. Hours later, impatient, Nathalie interrupted them: "When are you going to be done?"

They told her it was all fine and to join them. "And that was it!"

Bringing the two families together was next. The couple was nervous leaving their parents alone at a restaurant to talk. But when they returned, "It was like they didn't realize we had even left!"

"Yeah, we got back, and they were like inviting each other over for sleepovers!"

"This is honestly what peace is, getting people to love each other and respect each other, no matter how you pray. That was the beauty of it."

Once everything was settled, Nathalie and Omar just wanted to get married. And they did. Three times.

"We went to Cyprus, and it was really romantic."

"Her mom was like, 'You're not married yet,' so we had separate rooms at the hotel."

"And we were both thirty-five years old!"

"And then for the *katab kitab*, we didn't really know what to do. We went to the court, and it was like paying the electricity bill, like you take a number and then a shaykh would come."

"And he was mumbling a speech and talking to my dad, but whatever, we made a fun day out of it."

"And then we had a big beach wedding."

"The only thing I wanted was my dad walking me down the aisle. And the woman doing the ceremony was like a poet, she talked about how we met, and it was very romantic, and she quoted one of my favorite childhood books."

Fairytale ending in hand, they concluded our interview, saying, "We hope we spread some positivity!"

Not such a boring story after all, it turned out.

Sites of Social Change

Nathalie and Omar are among the most recently married couples I interviewed. No doubt you'll recognize some of the factors that smoothed their paths: age, geography, and personality among them. They tried to avoid ending up together, but eventually allowed fate to take its course. They also believe they had it easier than others because they married in the second decade of this century. They're not wrong.

One of my cousins recently married a Lebanese woman of a different religious background. When singer Tania Kassis opened their elegant Beirut wedding with her famous "Islamo-Christian Ave," a melodic melding of the Muslim call to prayer with Ave Maria, a few of the more conservative Christian guests raised a subtle eyebrow, but no one batted an eye. Many things are different: my cousin is male; he and his wife are just over forty with lucrative careers; she shares educational institutions with our family; the extended families' social circles share status and political history; our grandparent's generation has all passed on; and it has been well over twenty years since I opened the door.

In 2010, when Rita returned to her village after being the first to break the marriage rules, everyone stared at her, their whispers palpable on her skin. Then a "very Christian" cousin whispered a quiet "Well done" in her ear. "You are very brave, and this village should respect that." When a female elder began scolding Rita, her husband interrupted: "What are you talking about? Your father didn't want me to marry you, and you married me anyway, so you did the same thing! Let the girl do whatever she wants with her life." Other cousins thanked Rita, saying she gave them the courage to challenge their parents.

Serene credits her elopement in 2010 for changing how her parents think about sect. She sees positive reverberations in her Druze village, where she has become a respected member of the community. "People saw that life continued normally," she told me. "They were freed from a social constraint. It is as though they were enslaved, and someone freed them. They needed time to adapt. Maybe this is what I did, this small thing. I made a very personal decision, but it's a decision that affected the people around me."

Many others also described watching their families grow less sectarian after their mixed marriage. While not everyone I interviewed embraced the same vision of social change, many shared the belief that their marriages challenged social norms, personal status laws, and the idea that sect or religion made someone too different to marry. They pointed to how their choices affected people around them, describing their marriages as "an enriching experience" or "a challenge to reality" for their families. "The way to make change is to start from yourself as an individual," one person told me, "and then it's like a snowball. It grows around you and has an impact around you. I really believe this. Because in my own society, my small social world, I think I had an influence. My marriage had an influence. Even if it was 1 percent, I'm really proud of it."

Whether straight-faced or with a wink, some even suggested their marriages were a model for a better Lebanon. "I think we're improving society with our marriage," said several. One chuckled, "If they make a rule in Lebanon that everyone has to marry interreligiously, we will obliterate sectarianism. Just force everyone to marry someone different. A few generations will go by, everyone will be mixed, that's it, no more problems!"

Couples' children were often the vehicles for hope: "In the end, these kids won't be like me or like him. They're going to be something we can't even comprehend right now. Something new." Conversations I had with children of mixed couples reflected social change. People over thirty said they had often felt like an outlier, what one described as "a floating species." Children and teenagers I spoke with described their lives as "normal." One ten-year-old asked me why I was interviewing her mother, and when I replied that it was because her parents were from different religions, she rolled her eyes and snorted, "*'Aadi,*" which means, "It's normal, so what?"

People who saw our conversation as an opportunity to change ideas about mixed marriage asked me to share advice with my readers. Parents who had opposed their children's mixed marriages advised others in their shoes to learn from their mistakes and accept the match as long as the couple loved each other. Couples shared advice as well: Have good social support. Do your legal research. Find other mixed couples to be friends with. Don't involve your partner in "the noise and details" of your extended family. Take the time to get to know your partner before telling anyone. Be sure you're really in love and they are worth the fight. And most of all, be patient and stick to your path. One person shared, "I always tell people, 'Listen, they're going to make it look impossible, like the worst problem you'll ever face, until you just do it. It's going to be hard. They're not going to talk to you. And then, later, it will be phenomenal. You'll see the change.'"

And some interviewees tried to use their marriage to change people's minds. Upon hearing his barber talk about preventing his daughter's mixed marriage, one man shared his story, prompting the barber to ask a lot of questions about how mixed marriage worked in Lebanon. "Maybe I helped him change his mind," he told me. Another explained both her mixed identity and her civil marriage to her longtime butcher. "I felt I took a small chance telling him, but I wanted to show him I'm normal. Here I am, a mixed person with a civil marriage who buys meat from you." These open conversations with acquaintances mark a sea change from earlier eras. Remember, interreligious marriage did not become the main frontier at the edge of marital choice for Lebanese until the 1990s. Given all this contextual evidence of change, what do the numbers tell us?

Numbers and Other Metrics of Change

"So how many mixed marriages are there in Lebanon today?" That's the first thing people usually ask me. How common is it? How many people are we talking about? My initial response is always, "There are no good numbers." The Ministry of Interior contains records for civil marriages registered with the state,[3] and each of the fifteen personal status courts contains records for marriages officiated by their clerics, with different rules and methods of recordkeeping. In theory, one could go to each court and count the marriage records, most of which are not digitized. I hope some tenacious future scholar does so.

In the absence of government statistics, a research group in Lebanon called Information International created a method for counting mixed marriages using the 2011 electoral registration records and published their results in 2013.[4] They counted 10,797 Muslim-Christian marriages, but headlines reporting this study in major Lebanese papers used the phrase "173,000 mixed marriages." The larger number includes intersectarian marriages—Christians marrying other Christians and Muslims marrying other Muslims.[5] That 173,000 represented about 15 percent of all Lebanese marriages. Within that 15 percent, only about 6 percent were *interreligious*.

In other words, according to the 2011 electoral registration records, 0.9 percent of Lebanese marriages were interreligious without conversion.

Enter my brilliant research assistant, Muhammad Zamzam. He learned the method Information International used to extract mixed marriages from electoral registration records. The method relies on the patriarchal default of the Lebanese state: When female citizens are married, their family registration number is changed from that of their father to that of their husband. This means that their registration moves to their husband's region.[6] By looking at those regional lists and counting women listed with a different sect than everyone else with their family registration number, one can reasonably approximate mixed marriages where no one converted. I obtained the 2018 electoral registration lists,[7] and Muhammad worked his magic. He found that in 2018, 1.31 percent of Lebanese marriages were interreligious without conversion.

These numbers are flawed, not least because the electoral registration lists on which they rely are themselves flawed.[8] They leave out mixed marriages where someone converted or where anyone is under twenty-one years old (voting age). The count also includes unmarried women who converted out of conviction and officially changed their sect. Despite its limitations, this method gives us the best approximation of how many mixed marriages are registered in Lebanon. If anything, we are likely undercounting mixed marriages for two reasons. Our count does not include marriages involving conversion or marriages that were not registered with the Lebanese state.

Nevertheless, because our numbers for 2013 and 2018 were generated using the same method, I can confidently say that mixed marriages increased over that five-year time period, from at least 0.9 percent to at least 1.31 percent. That's a 43 percent increase. The numbers may be small, even if we estimate 2 to 5 percent of marriages to be mixed to compensate for undercounting, but we see a steady rise.

We can also measure the increase in mixed marriage by using civil marriage as an imperfect proxy. Let's assume that some significant proportion of civil marriages are mixed couples.[9] We know civil marriages abroad have increased since the end of the civil war. Recent estimates suggest that in the twenty-first century, between 1,200 and 2,500 of the 40,000 Lebanese marriages annually are civil marriages,[10] with between 560 and 700 of them conducted in Cyprus,[11] the closest and cheapest option.[12] We know the Cyprus wedding industry has grown exponentially.[13] Evidence for an increase in civil marriage is, in this mental exercise, evidence for an increase in mixed marriage as well. We also know that social concern about both civil marriage and mixed marriage has exploded. A quick Google search brings up at least fifty Arabic language articles about them between 2007 and 2019. Some worry about children raised in mixed families;[14] others interview couples marrying in Cyprus. Some relay the opinions of prominent religious leaders, politicians, or celebrities, while others poll the public. Moments of both dramatic violence and romantic coexistence have set off media flurries.[15]

Not all civil marriages are mixed, but as people think about civil marriage, mixed marriage is the elephant in the room. Dramatic talk show circles bring mixed couples face-to-face with clerics—social issue entertainment, Lebanese style. Films, like Nadine Labaki's 2012 *Where to Now?*, include interreligious romance, as do television serials, like "Ahmad and Christina." Even without looking at the numbers, I can confidently say that in the twenty-first century, many Lebanese have had mixed marriage on the mind.

Similarity and Difference, Revisited

Throughout this book, we've seen that mixed couples agree with their parents that similarity or affinity is key to a good marriage and a harmonious household but define similarity differently. Many saw this revision of what counts as similar or different as a way they practiced antisectarianism. My interviewees found commonality in their mutual refusal to relate sect to social hierarchies. Some upheld legal and patriarchal norms by prioritizing the husband's traditions. Others embraced hybrid or creative family practices. Some treasured their differences, each maintaining their own faith. Others insisted on mutual secularism. No matter their approach, sect was not an important criterion in their assessments of compatibility with their partner.

Despite their general disavowal that sectarian difference matters, mixed couples still cared about social difference, whether it was class, politics, national identity, or values. If these couples serve as a sign that society is moving away from divisions, then they should be open to their children marrying whomever they want to marry, right? To test this idea, I often concluded interviews by asking people whom they would *not* want their own kids to marry.

At first, most people replied that they hoped to raise their children to make good choices and therefore trusted that they would choose someone who shared their values and views. Quite a few said, "Of course I would not interfere," or "Of course they can marry whomever they want." They talked about the importance of the potential spouse's character: "I don't give a shit who they marry as long as they are good to my children. No one who hurts them, is an asshole, cheats on them, you know, *real* problems." Most also said they would express their opinions without opposing potential partners. They preemptively called out the hypocrisy that opposing their own child's marital choice would require, saying, "How could I argue? Look at us!"

As they continued to mull over my question, people's initial responses became nuanced by specific characteristics they would find unacceptable or concerning in a son- or daughter-in-law. The most commonly mentioned potential problem was someone "super religious," "fanatic," or "extremist" with regard to any religion. One father told me, "If my son or daughter comes home with someone who is very religious, that will completely break my heart, and I will not be okay with it, and I will fight it, and if they stop talking to me I don't care. Everybody says that they won't do this, but later on they'll change their mind, so I'll say it up front, I have no shame in being honest." Others were more tentative: "I would be a little disconcerted if my child married someone religious, but I wouldn't, like, be awful about it. At least I *hope* not." Others explained that as long as the spouse didn't impose their beliefs on others, they would deal with it. A woman whose son was in his twenties at the time said, "Oh my god, I have thought about this so many times. It is possible that in the future, he might come and say that he wants to marry a woman who wears the headscarf, for example, so I have thought about how I would be about it. And I decided that as long as he is happy, he can do whatever he wants." People also mentioned political redlines, perspectives held by a son- or daughter-in law that were incompatible with their values. Most common among these were: "A right-wing evangelical anything—insert the religion of your choice." "A Zionist, a Nazi, a colonialist, a racist." Others added "Christian supremacy in Lebanon" to the list. And quite a few parents simply couldn't imagine their child wanting to be with someone whose religious or political views differed from their own. One woman kept saying,

"It would be impossible for my daughter to want to marry someone that different from us," until her husband pointed out that her own parents had thought that what she did in marrying him was equally "impossible."

For the most part, the concerns my interviewees shared diverged from the opposition they had faced from their families. They expressed worries about differences of belief and value but were careful to separate those values from sect as a label or category. To the extent that they are judging potential spouses by the content of their beliefs rather than their identity characteristics, this marks a change of perspective. The fundamental change mixed couples signal is that they do not rely on sect to explain how they see social differences. Their perspective challenges the hardening of sect into a social and legal category that people use to determine who will be like them and who will be different.

There are, however, limits to this social change. As forests of relationality grow more diverse, human-made structures still curb the path of new branches and roots. As the concentric circles of social worlds expand to include Lebanese of all sects as appropriate marriage partners, other possibilities remain out of bounds.

Collateral Pitfalls

The pitfalls that appear in my interviewees' imaginations of social change and a nonsectarian world are often unintentional, the consequences of rewriting one social script for difference without eliminating hierarchal difference overall. Sexuality and race are the most obvious limits. Very few people eschewed all identity-based criteria when describing whom their children could marry. Interviewees varied on the question of whether they would embrace a child's same-sex partner. For some, it was a limit. For others, a struggle. "Even if my child was gay, I would work on myself to accept their partner."

And while a few interviewees, mostly in diaspora, bashfully admitted that they would be upset if their child wanted to marry someone Black or South Asian, most were silent about racial difference. That silence doesn't mean they would happily suture an interracial couple into their family. It suggests that interracial marriage—other than marriage to white people of European ancestry—is utterly unimaginable and reminds us that fighting one form of discrimination doesn't mean that a person is working against all forms of discrimination. For example, most interviewees in Lebanon who could afford it had a live-in domestic worker. Even if they found it distasteful or treated their domestic worker well, they were still participating in an abusive racialized labor system.

The limits of sexuality and race come together in the idea that mixed couples' children are the key to social change. By reinforcing the idea that heterosexual marriage and biological reproduction are the only way to create a family in Lebanon, the focus on mixed children excludes queer Lebanese from the country's future. Not only same-sex couples, but also heterosexual couples who aren't legally married, couples who don't have biological children, and any other family formations are denied the power to take part in making social change. The idea of "mixed children" also excludes the children of mixed-race couples and of Lebanese women married to non-Lebanese men. While the children of Lebanese men are always granted citizenship, the race and nationality of their mother condition their acceptance into the idea of a Lebanese nation.

Fighting sectarianism by highlighting a Lebanese national identity in its place gets us to nationalism, and from there it's an easy slide into chauvinism. That shared Lebanese national identity banishes sect as a category of difference by embracing a biologically reproduced combination of race, class, and nationality in its stead. Yet in moments when families discover similarity, when new grafts on family trees thrive, we see assumptions about social difference unmade. In the best of worlds, when the changes wrought by mixed marriage break open sect only to reveal other layers of discrimination, we turn our attention to dismantling those as well.

Dismantling Sectarianism

Sectarianism is Lebanon's Ouroboros, the personal and the political feeding one another in a seemingly endless loop. If you give constructed social categories long enough, and do enough damage with them, separating people through law, violence, differential resources, and geography, people imagine that the categories were there all along, inextricable from their lives. Sectarian discourse doesn't tell us that sect is natural; it tells us how well the institutions and structures and politicians have done their work, how successful sectarianism has been in Lebanon as a social, political, and economic project benefiting the elite.

As the empty category of sect has been filled with meaning over decades—meaning related to status, class, politics, region, and fear—it has solidified into something people use to make quick judgments about one another. Layers of sediment have built sect into something that matters for many Lebanese. Sect-based personal status laws and the lack of any civil family law adds a layer. Opposition to mixed marriage that relies on the language of sect adds another. And at its core is Lebanon's political-sectarian government system, with its concomitant corruption and sect-based resource distribution, with political elites fanning the flames of sectarianism to mine the ashes for wealth, to line their own protected bank accounts, to prevent people from unifying against them. Sect is pushed to the foreground again and again, in multiple realms of life, making it the most salient form of social difference in Lebanese society.

This idea that sect is Lebanon's most salient form of social difference gives us insight into the problem of social change. Parents use sectarianism to oppose mixed marriage because it's easy, the most readily available script for explaining what upsets them about another person. And couples use antisectarianism to counter it. At least two consequences to this dynamic come to mind. First, the space sect takes up suggests that there are other social divides that are hidden, more difficult to discuss. Some appear if we scratch the surface, such as class, status, and geography, which have emerged in the chapters of this book. Others, like race, are so deeply entrenched that they appear in violence and blatant discrimination, with the counterscripts to fight against them still limited to only the most progressive social circles and activist groups. Second, if people practice sectarianism so overtly and with such public ease, perhaps this signals that we are over its peak, moving toward its decline. What is made can always be unmade.

In a demonstration during Lebanon's October 2019 uprising, women living along a former civil war fault line evoked a wedding. A video of this event begins with a woman saying, "When the barricades went up, we stepped on them, and we came together, and we built a family."[16] Women of all ages, some marked by their dress as Muslim or Christian and others unidentifiable, carry white roses as they walk their streets. "No to sectarianism, we want national unity" dominates the soundscape until it is broken by loud *zaghroutas*, a celebratory ululation. A man smoking on a balcony tosses rice down on the marchers. And two women, perhaps of different religious backgrounds, lift a single white rose to the sky together. Through the roses, rice, and ululations, this protest weds two neighborhoods that exemplify sectarian difference.

For over a decade, marriage has been both symbol and demand at antisectarian and secular protests in Lebanon. Most concretely, mixed marriage is one driver behind efforts—in 1957, 1972, 1976, 1977, 1985, 1996, 2011, 2013, and 2014—to push a civil marriage law through parliament.[17] Thus far, all have succumbed to clerical and political pressure. A civil marriage law would be a step toward dismantling sectarianism and would make things easier for mixed couples, but it won't automatically change how families respond to them. In 1967, when the Lovings, who were sentenced to a year in prison for their interracial marriage in Virginia, fought that decision all the way to the Supreme Court and won, laws restricting interracial marriage in the US were overturned. Social norms were not. Similarly, despite the US Supreme Court decision upholding the right to marriage for same-sex couples in 2015, many people continue to oppose these unions. At the same time, neither of these court decisions took place in a vacuum. They rested on social movements that nurtured space for them on the ground.

In Lebanon, mixed marriage has served for many as a part of that social movement, a symbol of or evidence for people's antisectarian commitments, made real through their intimate ties. Many hoped the 2019 revolution would lead to the dismantling of sectarianism, including in relation to kinship. Some scholars, reporters, pundits, and observers were quick to diagnose the uprisings as evidence that Lebanese society is not sectarian. Their claims highlight the idea, supported by this book, that sectarianism is a political, economic, and social structure rather than an inherent or essential characteristic of society. But the creation and reinforcement of sectarianism in nearly every domain of Lebanese life for well over a century has embedded it in both the material and affective soil of the country. Removing sectarianism from the political system will kill a key vector in the continual reproduction of Lebanon's Ouroboros. But structural and institutional inequalities and discrimination, including on an interpersonal level, won't magically vanish.

———

Much has changed in Lebanon since I completed the interviews for this book. Many of my interviewees have moved, whether seeking a more affordable apartment, a better generator setup for electricity, fewer stairs to walk up because elevators no longer function regularly, or a more economically feasible life outside the country altogether. Sectarian political discourses have grown more shrill, lines of antipathy etched deeper and deeper as people seek answers to why things have deteriorated so badly. The corrupt system of criminal politicians strangling Lebanon right now is the same corrupt system that has consistently refused to release the constraints of sect-based personal status law and that upholds a system where people are legally linked to a sect determined for them by the state based on their paternal line. The spaces created by the 2019 uprisings were crushed by their violent suppression by state security forces. Economic collapse, the devastating port explosion, and the global Covid-19 pandemic have rearranged the conditions for encounter and possibility. As the currency devaluation institutes a dollarized economy that exacerbates already high poverty rates, sect-based networks facilitate access to basic needs, as resources like fuel for cars and generators are distributed through sectarian patronage systems. When I began writing this book, the poverty rate in Lebanon was around 20 percent; as I finish, it is over 80 percent.[18] And as the book moves through production, southern Lebanon is once again under regular Israeli bombardment as the world watches Israel carry out a genocide of Palestinians in Gaza with impunity.

Marriage is an act of hope and future building. How do changing expectations of how one can make a life under these circumstances change decisions about whom to marry? How does the hopelessness that many Lebanese young people feel affect their choices? Many of the dynamics I have written about here continue. People continue to meet one another, fall in love, and marry, sometimes across the lines of religion and sect. Families continue to object, to argue, to reconcile, to comment, or to accept mixed marriage, opening up new spaces of similarity and kinship in the process. Leaving the country for a civil marriage is now prohibitively expensive for most Lebanese. It's possible the new option to have an online civil marriage,[19] officiated by someone sitting in Utah while you sit at home in Lebanon, will make it more accessible. As the economic collapse nurtures yet another moment of increased emigration, diaspora spaces continue to shape ideas about mixed marriage. Economic precarity may change parents' calculations of who will make a good spouse for their child. Marriage among Lebanese minors under the age of eighteen seems to be increasing.[20] Wealth or the ability to leave the country may grow more important than sect.

New frontiers of acceptable love are moving into the spotlight with generational change. Alongside mixed marriage at the frontier of boundary-pushing in the late twentieth and early twenty-first centuries, Lebanon's broader civil rights movements have flourished, whether intertwined or in uncomfortable alliance, including fights for queer rights. Because same-sex couples cannot marry in Lebanon, sect doesn't present a pragmatic legal problem for them, but the few interviews I did with queer couples show that it still matters. One man's mother jested when he told her he was dating a Muslim man: "Look, gay, fine. But Muslim, too much! Couldn't you find some Maronite?!" Her jest held a touch of truth. Queer Lebanese I know who are not out to their families have joked that had their partner been a doctor of the right sect, coming out would be easier. That said, they all emphasized that "being queer was the more critical issue all around." By the time parents accept a queer child's choice of partner, sect is often a moot point. Scholar Sabiha Allouche links these struggles, writing that "intersectarian love is best understood as a queer utopia given its potential to destabilize normative affective attachments in post-civil war Lebanon."[21]

Social change is slow. Describing the effects of the 2019 uprisings, Bassel Salloukh writes that "no matter the short-term outcome . . . something has changed irreversibly in Lebanon."[22] He includes the *affective* achievements of the revolution, "an introspective interrogation" that has broken sectarianism's "monopoly . . . over peoples' modes of mobilization and identification." This book shows seeds of that "introspective interrogation" sprouting. To understand how to move beyond sectarianism, we must understand how it seeps into intimate and familial interactions, decision-making, assumptions, and conflicts. We must consider how the process of marriage has changed and how gender factors into shifting social norms. We must think about how ideas about who counts as different or "too different" are also shifting; as the fault lines move, so do definitions of what makes a marriage "mixed" in the first place. We must acknowledge how people act in "sectarian" ways, aligning with or discriminating against others based on sect. To understand how sect emerges in the social and interpersonal is to know better how to work against it in this imagined future where structural and institutional sectarianism no longer shape life to the same extent.

I have been writing this book during what can only be called dark times for Lebanon and much of the world. Dark times shed light on what Hiba Abu Akar calls the "intertwinement of hope and despair."[23] When faced with the need to end a book on a note of hope, authors sometimes suggest radical forms of relating to one another—and to other species, stretching the idea of difference to include multiple forms of living beings.[24] Ursula K. Le Guin's writings have long grappled with the question of building communities and commonalities through and across differences, human and nonhuman. More recently, Ghassan Hage's solution to racism is to understand that "all social relations are an entanglement of multiplicities," and to recover that multiplicity.[25] We live in a time replete with imagined worlds where a variety of species, humans and nonhumans, organics and inorganics, cyborgs and robots, find ways to live together with difference. Part of that process is about redefining and reimagining whom we count as kin. Perhaps we can view mixed couples as taking a step toward fulfilling Joanne Nucho's proposal to reimagine the labor of "doing collective" to create cross-sect solidarities, forms of community that render sect irrelevant.[26] If the current time of uncertainty in Lebanon is one that creates opportunities to transcend sectarianism in all its guises, including the interpersonal, my interlocutors have shown us one way to do that in practice.

Anything made can be unmade. We can put sect back in its place: one kind of difference among many. We can think of Lebanese society as one that, like other societies, has multiple intersecting social identities, inequalities, and cleavages. Once we understand sect as but one part of a complex constellation of social difference, we will be one step closer to dismantling the hierarchical policing of sect as a category by the state. We will be one step closer to dislodging sect from its position as the keystone of governance and disrupting its deployment by political parties against the public good. At minimum, we will be one step closer to refusing to buy into the sharp cleavages and notions of irreconcilable difference propagated by the political elite in Lebanon as a weapon used to divide us. And if done right, we will be one step closer to working against *all* forms of discrimination and creating a radically inclusive social world.

I leave you with a story about a wedding that encapsulates both an imagined nonsectarian future and its exclusions, the silences marking the forms of difference that must be brought into the fight for social change.

––––––––

The first guests to arrive for the lavish dinner celebrating Nadya and Marwan's wedding were Muslim. The hotel employee staffing the reception desk easily identified them as such. His shift had just begun, and he hadn't paid much attention to who was hosting the party that evening, but two of the women in the group wore designer headscarves as part of their formal attire. Family tended to arrive before friends, so the employee assumed it was a Muslim couple who had married.

A few minutes later, another group walked into the hotel lobby looking for the same party. No headscarves this time. The female elder of the group, clearly important to the family, boasted a perfectly coiffed and highlighted hairstyle and bright lipstick. "Hmm," the employee said under his breath. He was joined by a colleague who stared in open curiosity. "They seem Christian," the first whispered. "Maybe this is a mixed family." Unusual, but not something he hadn't seen before in his years working at this posh Beirut establishment.

The next few guests to arrive confirmed his suspicions. The curious hotel staff at the reception desk, growing in number, continued to watch as they entered, chatting about which side of the family they must be from. Older women in a Chanel scarf or a blondish bob were easier to identify. Men posed a challenge unless their beard was trimmed in a specific way. Younger women might seem similar with elaborate hairstyles, full makeup, and staggering heels flashing red soles, but the staff assumed—not necessarily correctly—that variations in how much skin their dresses revealed identified their sect.

Then a group walked in that befuddled them. The elders were marked by their dress as religious leaders in the Druze community. Everyone knew they were Druze. But why were they going to the same wedding? None of these employees were Druze. They thought Druze didn't marry outside the community and that if they did, it would be a quiet affair in Cyprus.

An hour later, just as the regular guests began to arrive, the hotel employee saw the father of the bride walking through the lobby. He intercepted him, and asked, "This wedding, what *are* you?" Her father smiled and said, "We are mixed! We are Lebanese!"

Acknowledgments

No one thinks or writes in a vacuum. This project has been shaped not only by my own experiences but also by those of countless friends and family members who have shared their stories, friends' stories, and friends of friends' stories. I've been thinking about this book for over twenty years, amassing sedimented layers of ideas, debts, and conversations, some of which I will no doubt forget to mention here. It is a gift to have so many people to thank.

Above all, I've relied on the generosity of the nearly two hundred (mostly) strangers who invited me into their living rooms or met me in cafés or on Skype, offered me coffee and cake, showed me photos, shared emotionally intense aspects of their lives and love stories with me, and then connected me to others who did the same. I really wanted to include every single story in this book—and did in a first draft that was twice as long—but apparently presses have page limits. Even if you don't see your exact words here, your story is part of the ideas that connect it all together. Even if you don't agree with everything I've written, I hope you see yourself in these pages in some way. You all have my deepest gratitude.

So many people helped with the snowballing, word-of-mouth process of finding interviewees—colleagues, friends, cousins, aunts, uncles, friends of friends, and friends of friends of friends, and friends of cousins of friends! Whether you sent an email, made a phone call, forwarded a message or Facebook post, or mentioned someone you thought I should meet, thank you!

I've had the amazing fortune to be able to bounce ideas around, brainstorm, muse, puzzle over conundrums, and learn from many brilliant friends, colleagues, teachers, and people who fit all those categories, including Qutayba Abdullatif, Lila Abu-Lughod, Ziad Abu-Rish, Nada Addoum, Fida Adely, Dina al-Kassim, Lori Allen, Evelyn Alsultany, Gloria Aoun, Sami Atallah, Lara Balaa, Aslı Bali, Amahl Bishara, Hiba Bou Akar, Melani Cammett, Jessica Cattelino, Hadi Deeb, Don Donham, Leila Farsakh, Ilana Feldman, Ghassan Hage, Sondra Hale, Sherine Hamdy, Mona Harb, Ghenwa Hayek, Sami Hermez, Yamila Hussein, Amira Jarmakani, Vienna Khansa, Line Khatib, Haitham Khoury, the late and dearly missed Saba Mahmood, Rima Majed, Ussama Makdisi, Leila Mansouri, Maya Mikdashi, Gabriela Morales, Nadine Naber, Tsolin Nalbantian, Joanne Nucho, Seo Young Park, Wendy Pearlman, Julie Peteet, Fadia Rafeedie, Nadine Samara, Nadya Sbaiti, Sherene Seikaly, Susan Slyomovics, Lisa Wedeen, Jessica Winegar, and Tarek Zeidan. Ghenwa, Mona, Nadya, and Tsolin regularly sent fascinating and relevant articles, excerpts, memes, and videos my way and were always there to text about translations and confusions. Maya helped me decipher the intricacies of Lebanese personal status law. Fida and Amahl helped me think about comparative contexts. Nadine N. and Jessica W. were always there with encouragement when I needed it. Haitham and Tarek, along with the late, gorgeous Luna, plus Fasfas, Gigi, and Kitsu, provided my home in Beirut for years; Mona was a constant rock; Vienna kept me grounded in worlds outside Ras Beirut; and Nada and Johnny ensured game night escapes from fieldwork.

More good fortune took the shape of fantastic research assistants: Malak Al-Afaneh, Lucienne Altman, Lily Hahn, Harriet Lindeman, Christophe Maroun, Samia Rachid, Yusra Scott, Noor Tamari, Franjie Tannous, and, most especially, Nadim El-Kak, Mariana Nakfour, and Mohammad Zamzam.

My incredible colleagues in our "small but mighty" anthropology department at Scripps College, Seo Young Park and Gabriela Morales, make work a joy even when institutional forces do their best to thwart us. Wendy Cheng, Kim Drake (and the late sweet Roxy and the infectiously joyful Wicker), Heather Ferguson, Leila Mansouri, Joanne Nucho, and Sumita Pahwa are stalwart sources of support, laughter, and comradeship who make the small world of the Colleges feel much larger. Heather's commitment to collective labor has transformed the weight of institutional fights into friendship.

I am thankful for the anchors that kept me sane during the year that began in 2020 and kept going and going and going. My sister-cousin Nadine Samara, and pre-academic-life friends Katie Carson, Dorothy McLaughlin, and Sarah Saxer—I really don't know what I would do without you all. Coediting *Practicing Sectarianism* with Tsolin Nalbantian and Nadya Sbaiti during the pandemic kept my thinking sharp and gifted me the camaraderie that only grows from joint labors.

Yelizaveta Renfro's creative nonfiction courses jumpstarted this book and provided feedback that helped me think about broader audiences. A series of virtual writing groups kept me putting words on the page. Thank you to Scripps colleagues Kim Drake, Adam Novy, Gabriela Morales, and Jen Groscup; transnational friends Mona Harb, Tsolin Nalbantian, and Nadya Sbaiti; diaspora friends Ghenwa Hayek, Hiba Bou Aker, and Lara Balaa; and anthropology friends Jessica Winegar, Lori Allen, and Ilana Feldman for the check-ins and encouragement. Lunches with Evelyn Alsultany, Jessica Cattelino, Wendy Cheng, and Joanne Nucho always inspire with conversations about writing's joys and frustrations, plus strategies to preserve it in the face of institutional pressures. Extra shout-out to Evelyn for truly getting the cat thing.

Students in my Middle East Anthropology seminar in spring 2023 read the manuscript and asked excellent questions that prompted some of my revisions. Lena Abed, Serenat Arpat, Nayla Dayal, Marissa Habashy, Melanie Kallah, Scarlette McCullough, Leah McGregor, Liz Messinger, Emily Radner, Sulekha Ram-Junnarkar, Lily Ross, Maddy Wessels, and Carrie Zaremba—thank you! Audiences at the University of Illinois at Chicago; the University of California, Los Angeles; BRISMES; Yale University; Whitman College; Cornell University; and Northwestern University prompted new ideas with their comments. Thank you to everyone who invited me to speak in those venues.

I completed (somehow) the final edits to this manuscript as Israel committed genocide against Palestinians in Gaza. I have so much gratitude and respect for colleagues and friends who are comrades in the struggle for Palestinian liberation and beyond, and who understand that none of us free under we all are, especially the Claremont Faculty for Justice in Palestine and its national network, the AnthroBoycott collective, and the Palestinian Feminist Collective.

As should be obvious by now, I am grateful to have friends who are colleagues, colleagues who are friends, and a social world full of wonderful people who will read my work, debate ideas with me, suggest different approaches (not that I listen), catch confusions or mistranslations, and cheer me on when I need a boost. This book has especially benefited from the sharp eyes and minds of Mona Harb, Joanne Nucho, Maya Mikdashi, Nadya Sbaiti, Seo Young Park, and Gabriela Morales, as well as Kate Wahl and the press reviewers, who all read the full manuscript. Maya's comments in particular pushed me in critically important directions. It feels obvious and weirdly legalistic to add the expected "any remaining errors are my own"— but that is of course the case.

At Stanford University Press, Kate Wahl is more than an editor; she is an interlocutor and a rock star—thank you for encouraging me to write the book I wanted to write, solving an outline problem, and always providing sage counsel. I also thank Thane Hale, David Zielonka, Tiffany Mok, Adriana Smith, and June Sawyers for their labor and care. Maya Seikali and the Kite Creative Studio team produced the perfect maps; Jana Traboulsi's gorgeous drawing graces the cover. I do not take for granted the privileges of funding that allowed me the time and travel necessary to research and write. It was only possible with grants from the Wenner-Gren Foundation, the American Council of Learned Societies, the Ruth Landes Memorial Research Fund of the Reed Foundation, and Scripps College.

Too many losses accompanied finishing this book. I'll never forget how my aunt casually pulled up the contacts on her phone one afternoon after yet another delicious lunch, giving me numbers, and the hilarious connections and conversations that ensued. I miss your smile, Aunti Nelly, and the warm welcome of your home in Beirut. Ammo Ameed also shared contacts and stories, over amazing BBQ and toot; Hamat is missing a key ingredient without you. And Ammo Abdo, you accepted me into your family without question, on merits other than religious conformity; this book is a clue as to how much that meant to me. I hope you would have liked this one as well.

Everyone fighting for civil marriage, for liberation, for queer rights, for feminist change, for antisectarian and antiracist change—activists in Lebanon and elsewhere—you inspire me. Everyone who has married against the grain of their family's desires, fighting for love, you're in this book. Everyone who didn't, breaking their own hearts instead, I see you too.

My parents have always supported my strange career and intellectual adventures . . . though I wonder what they'll think this time. Thank you for all the love and everything you have done for me. Hadi, my stalwart brother, thank you for sharing my love of books—their making and reading. Not all siblings are also friends; I'm lucky that we are. Gadun's purrs and snores have accompanied my writing for, as of this moment, nearly twenty-one years (knock on wood), beginning the moment he curled up on my lap as I frantically finished my dissertation. Flubb provides laughs and amazing hugs (yes, you can hug a cat), and now Lulu the Magical Lynx keeps us elders on our toes (the current score is teenage kitten: 3,724,321; elder humans and felines: 4). And perhaps most obviously, at least to those who know me, and certainly most importantly, Qutayba, *hayati*, love of my life, thank you for everything, but especially for loving me as I am. It helps that we are both cats. This one's for you.

Notes

Introduction

1. Nina later told me she bought the "Muslim painting" from a Syrian antique dealer and the Christian one from a Vienna flea market. She knew the latter was a copy of an "old master" painting. My colleague Luis Salés helped identify it as an inexact copy of Raffaello Sanzio's *Madonna del Prato*, 1506.

2. "Roum Orthodox" officially translates to "Greek Orthodox," but to avoid conflation with Greek ethnicity, I follow their self-identification in Arabic.

3. Whether Druze counts as a sect of Islam depends on whom you ask and for what purpose (marriage, census numbers, etc.). Most Lebanese consider Druze a different religion altogether.

4. I explain how I came to these numbers in the final chapter of the book.

5. McCarthy, *Interfaith Encounters*, 126.

6. Estimates of Christian populations vary widely and are politicized, but it is safe to say that Lebanon has at least three times as many Christians as Egypt or Jordan.

7. Adely, "A Different Kind of Love," 111; Haddad, "Christian Identity."

8. See Mahmood, *Religious Difference*; and Erwin, "Reconciling Conflicting Identities."

9. In "Bargaining with Patriarchy," Deniz Kandiyoti classically terms women's strategizing within the limitations of their social world the "patriarchal bargain."

10. Mikdashi, *Sextarianism*, describes this intersection between sect and sex as "sextarianism."

11. See also Allouche, "Love, Lebanese Style."

12. Merton, "Intermarriage," 362 (emphasis added).

13. Crenshaw, "Mapping the Margins."

14. Mikdashi, *Sextarianism*.

15. Haddad, "'Sectarianism' and Its Discontents," details this lexical confusion around "sectarianism."

16. The largest of these categories are Sunni Islam, Shiʻi Islam, and Maronite Christianity. There are also significant populations of Roum Orthodox Christians, Melkite Roum Catholics, and Druze (counted as Muslim by the state but not always by other Muslim communities). The state also recognizes two additional Muslim groups (ʻAlawites and Ismaʻilis), nine Christian ones (Roman Catholicism, Syriac Orthodox, Syriac Catholicism, Assyrian or Nestorian, Armenian Orthodox, Armenian Catholicism, Chaldean Catholic, Coptic Orthodox, and Protestants/Evangelicals), and Judaism.

17. There are fifteen of these personal status laws; three sects follow close approximations.

18. The French, with local elites, established this system during their post–World War I mandate to give Maronite Christians political dominance. The quotas are based on a questionable, politically motivated 1932 census. See Maktabi, "The Lebanese Census."

19. Scholars have thoroughly debunked the ideas that sect and sectarianism are primordial and explain all conflict in the Middle East. See, inter alia, Beydoun, *Al-Jumhuriyya al-mutaqattiʻa*; Gökarıksel and Secor, "Uneasy Neighbors"; Haddad, "'Sectarianism' and Its Discontents"; Harik, *Politics and Change*; Hurd, "Politics of Sectarianism"; Joseph, "Politicization of Religious Sects"; Kern, *Imperial Citizen*; Makdisi, *Culture of Sectarianism*; Traboulsi, *History of Modern Lebanon*; and Weiss, *Shadow of Sectarianism*.

20. Makdisi, *Culture of Sectarianism*.

21. On how sectarianism is maintained and reproduced in the civil, political, legal, religious, and economic realms, see Bou Akar, *For the War Yet to Come*; Cammett, *Compassionate Communalism*; Clark and Salloukh, "Elite Strategies"; Deeb and Harb, *Leisurely Islam*; Joseph, *Gender and Citizenship*; Kingston, *Reproducing Sectarianism*; Nucho, *Everyday Sectarianism*; Majed, "In Defense of Intra-sectarian Divide"; Mikdashi, *Sextarianism*; Monroe, *Insecure City*; Salloukh et al., *Politics of Sectarianism*; and Salti and Chaaban, "Role of Sectarianism."

22. Deeb, Nalbantian, and Sbaiti, *Practicing Sectarianism*.

23. Hage, *Is Racism an Environmental Threat?*, 98.

24. These were mainly Catholic schools but included Orthodox and Protestant schools. For 2023–24, Beirut Baptist College tuition is $2,000, and Saint Coeur Catholic School tuition is between $1,650 and $1,900. The latter can be paid in Lebanese lira, making it more accessible for families without access to dollars. A Human Rights Watch January survey completed in 2022 found that the median

household income in Lebanon was $122 per month ($1,464 annually). See Human Rights Watch, "Lebanon: Events of 2022."

25. Local private school tuition for 2023–24 ranged from $1,500 to $4,000. Schools like Rawda ($5,000), Sagesse, and Ahliyyeh were more expensive. The most popular elite schools among interviewees were International College (IC) and Collège Protestant (CP), followed by Collège Louise Wegmann, the American Community School (ACS), and Brummana High School. In 2023–24, ACS cost $11,000. IC lowered its tuition after the economic collapse to $7,000, matching CP.

26. Gandhi, *Collected Works*, 35.

27. Chopra and Punwani, "Discovering the Other."

28. Gupta, "Hindu Women, Muslim Men"; Rao, "Love Jihad."

29. Leonard, "It's Better to Stick to Your Own Kind," estimates that 2 to 10 percent of all marriages are mixed in Northern Ireland.

30. Stoltzfus, *Resistance of the Heart*.

31. Kandido-Jakšić, "Social Distance."

32. Leonard, "It's Better to Stick to Your Own Kind," 99.

33. Cromer, "Intermarriage Handbooks"; Campbell and Putnam, "America's Grace."

34. Dainius, "Moving Statues of a Man and Woman."

35. Karam and Majed, *The Lebanon Uprising of 2019*.

36. Human Rights Watch, "Lebanon: Events of 2022."

Chapter One

1. Khater, *Inventing Home*, 141–43.

2. Khater, *Inventing Home*; Doumani, *Family Life*.

3. Khlat, "Consanguineous Marriage; Barbour and Salameh, "Consanguinity in Lebanon."

4. Obeid, *Border Lives*.

5. Makdisi, *Culture of Sectarianism*, 35.

6. Jawhariyyeh, *Storyteller of Jerusalem*, 239. Thanks to Lori Allen for bringing this to my attention.

7. Suad Joseph's surveys with one hundred households in a mixed Beirut suburb showed sect endogamy until the mid-twentieth century. Both intersectarian and interreligious marriage rates increased between 1945 and 1975 (Joseph, "The Politicization of Religious Sects"). Weber, "Briser et suivre," cites a 1971 survey statistic that 91.3 percent of marriages were within sect, and the vast majority within religion. Another study followed one Sunni Beiruti family over time and found sect endogamy until 1958, then a major shift to 35 percent within sect, 27 percent within religion, and 38 percent married to Christian Lebanese (Al-Bayadi, "Al-zawaj al-mukhtalat"). Even in Saida, a more conservative city, marriages between Muslims and Christians increased between 1970 and 1980 (Bou Harb, "Mushkilat al-zawaj al-mukhtalat").

8. On this graph, marriages lag behind political events or periods by a few years. For example, a person who comes of age or falls in love during the late 1960s might not marry until the 1970s, and the latter point is seen on the graph. It remains to be seen if the post-2005 political tensions in Lebanon will create another lull in mixed marriage rates or change this terrain in ways not yet visible.

9. Ziadah, "Al-zawaj al-mukhtalat"; Alamuddin and Starr, *Crucial Bonds*, found that Druze were more sect endogamous than other Lebanese groups between 1930 and 1980.

10. On Lebanese University and its changing role in society, see Kabbanji, "Heurs et malheurs."

11. Kabbanji, "Heurs et malheurs."

12. Kern, *Imperial Citizen*.

13. Semerdjian, "Armenian Women."

14. Deringil, *Conversion and Apostasy*.

15. Makdisi, *Culture of Sectarianism*, 163.

16. Weiss, *Shadow of Sectarianism*.

17. Donham, *Violence in a Time of Liberation*, 7.

18. Throughout her work, Suad Joseph has underscored the material consequences of socially constructed differentiations of sect.

19. Harrison, "The Persistent Power of 'Race.'"

20. Jackson Jr., *Real Black*, 17 (emphasis added).

21. Hall, "Ethnicity," 16.

22. Hage calls this "turning difference into a polarity" (*Is Racism an Environmental Threat?*, 22).

23. For more on this racist labor system called *kafala*, see Kassamali, "Migrant Worker Lifeworlds."

24. Thank you to then-director of the LCPS Sami Atallah for sharing this data with me.

25. Alamuddin and Starr, *Crucial Bonds*; Tarabey, *Family Law in Lebanon*.

26. For more on Druze beliefs, including reincarnation, see Tarabey, *Family Law in Lebanon*.

27. For more on the importance of endogamy and marriage rituals for maintaining a sense of sectarian identity among Druze in Syria, see Kastrinou, *Power, Sect and State*.

28. Tarabey notes that in the early 1970s, 28 percent of Druze marriages were within families and 38 percent within villages. By the early 2000s, it was 10 percent and 19 percent (*Family Law in Lebanon*, 75).

29. See also Radwan, "Economic Adversities," 115; and Harik, "Perceptions of Community."

30. Druze children are generally taught to believe in God, but there are no obligatory rituals or prayers, and only one major holiday, Eid al-Adha. At age forty, one may choose to study the sacred texts.

31. See Semerdjian, *"Off the Straight Path"*, for more on how Armenian canon law worked to separate communities during the Ottoman Empire.

32. Alajaji, *Music and the Armenian Diaspora*.

33. For ethnographic analyses of "minority fears," see Connolly, "Forbidden Intimacies"; and Vardar, "Inter-religious Marriage."

34. Suny, *They Can Live in the Desert*.

35. Rubaii, "Tripartheid," 125. People have also told me that Sunni-Shi'i marriage among Iraqis of similar class status has grown more fraught since 2003.

36. For more on the post-2005 emergence of a Sunni-Shi'a fault line, see Majed, "In Defense of Intra-sectarian Divide."

37. See Hovsepian, *The War on Lebanon*.

Chapter Two

1. See, for example, Chong, *Love across Borders*.

2. Hirsch and Wardlow, *Modern Loves*.

3. Abu-Lughod, "Introduction."

4. Abu-Lughod, *Remaking Women*.

5. Hart, "Love by Arrangement."

6. Schielke, *Egypt in the Future Tense*.

7. Adely, "A Different Kind of Love."

8. The rise of companionate marriage as an ideal in eighteenth-century England is linked to new value placed on individual emotions and desires (Stone, *Family*).

9. Joseph, "Connectivity and Patriarchy."

10. Joseph, "Gender and Relationality," 470.

11. Obeid, *Border Lives*.

12. A 2011 report found that in Lebanon, youth are "increasingly" making "the final decision" regarding marriage. See Khouri and Lopez, *A Generation on the Move*.

13. Pew Forum on Religion & Public Life, *The World's Muslims*. The poll also found that Lebanese Muslim families are more open to mixed marriages than other Arab Muslim families.

14. Among interviewees, the range of marriage age for women between 1960 and 1975 was fourteen to twenty-six; from 1975 to 1990 it was eighteen to thirty-two; from 1990 to 2005 it was eighteen to thirty-seven; and from 2005 to 2018 it was twenty-three to forty-five.

15. Riley, *'Til Faith Do Us Part*, also suggests that religious people who won't marry outside their faith are more likely to marry young.

Chapter Three

1. Women vote in their husband's district, which some interviewees found alienating. See also Talhouk, "Parliamentary Elections."

2. El Hage, "Online Civil Marriage Ceremonies."

3. In 2012, legal activists found a loophole allowing Lebanese to marry civilly in the country by deleting sect from their state identity documents. Many couples did so, but they and their children remain mired in legal uncertainty as a result.

4. Mikdashi, *Sextarianism*.

5. See Mikdashi, *Sextarianism*, on these personal status laws and their impact.

6. Frontiers Ruwad Association, *Marriage Registration in Lebanon*.

7. Mikdashi, *Sextarianism*.

8. Maya Mikdashi shared that court records mention the Orthodox bishop granting waivers for mixed marriage.

9. The name of the group translates loosely to "We married civilly . . . and we hope that you will enjoy a similar happy occasion in the future."

10. Article 25 of Decree 60LR; see Human Rights Watch, *Unequal and Unprotected*.

11. Lebanese Code of Civil Procedure, article 79. See also Dabbous-Sensenig, "Mixed Marriages."

12. Al-Hasbani, "Referential Set of Social Knowledge."

13. See also Allouche, "Love, Lebanese Style."

14. Harb, *Describing the Lebanese Youth*. This was confirmed by an unpublished LCPS survey from 2018 shared by then-director Sami Atallah. See also Makarem, "We Talked to People."

Chapter Four

1. Yahya and Boag, "My Family Would Crucify Me!"; Driscoll, Davis, and Lipetz, "Parental Interference."

2. See Obeid, *Border Lives*, on twenty-first-century elopements in Arsal, a rural area of Lebanon.

3. Alexander, "Elopements Are on the Rise."

4. Similarly, Chowdhry, *Contentious Marriages*, suggests that youth in India challenge senior male patriarchy by eloping.

5. Baydoun, *Cases of Femicide*.

6. Lewis et al., "Femicide in the United States."

7. In 2019, 747 domestic violence reports were filed with Lebanon's Internal Security Forces; in 2020, there were 1,468. Assume underreporting and note that sexual assault within marriage or against domestic workers is not reportable and therefore uncounted. The Resource Center for Gender Equality's helpline fielded 1,375 calls in 2019 and 4,127 in 2020 (Houssari, "Domestic Violence").

Chapter Five

1. On the coproduction of sect and class, see Deeb and Harb, *Leisurely Islam*; Farsoun, "E Pluribus Plura"; Joseph, "Working-Class Women's Networks"; Majed, "The Political (or Social) Economy"; Salloukh et al., *Politics of Sectarianism*; and Traboulsi, *History of Modern Lebanon*.

2. On stereotypes about Shi'a as lower class, see Deeb and Harb, *Leisurely Islam*.

Chapter Six

1. Harb, "Professor Mona Harb: What is Urban Planning?"

2. Hage, *Diasporic Condition*.

3. Cheng, *The Changs Next Door to the Díazes*, 10.

4. The data for both these figures came from the 2018 electoral registration records; however dubious, they are consistent for the purposes of comparison.

5. Some people moved their registrations to Beirut both recently and in earlier eras as it grew into the hub of the nation-state.

6. Nasr, "New Social Realities."

7. Peleikis, "Shifting Identities," shows how sect, linked to class and neighborhood, gained importance in a village during the war.

8. See Hourani, "Ideologies of the Mountain," 170–78.

9. Deeb and Harb, *Leisurely Islam*, chapter 3.

10. Mermier, "The Frontiers of Beirut," 379.

11. Obeid, *Border Lives*.

12. Fregonese argues that Beirut's "double imaginary of openness and closure" stems from Lebanon's colonial beginnings ("Between a Refuge and a Battleground," 318).

13. Hayek, *Beirut*.

14. Davie, "Demarcation Lines"; El-Hibri, *Visions of Beirut*; Nasr, "New Social Realities"; Yahya, "Reconstituting Space."

15. Deeb and Harb, *Leisurely Islam*.

16. Deeb and Harb, *Leisurely Islam*, 25.

17. Bou Akar, *For the War Yet to Come*.

18. Cheng, *The Changs Next Door to the Díazes*, 10.

19. Gökarıksel and Secor, "Uneasy Neighbors"; Shirlow, "Ethno-sectarianism."

20. Deeb, *An Enchanted Modern*; Deeb and Harb, *Leisurely Islam*. Bou Akar, *For the War Yet to Come*, adds the key point that *bi'a* links the political and natural in ways that entrench sectarian boundaries in space.

21. Comfort also relates to Hage's concept of "home" in *Is Racism an Environmental Threat?*

22. Hafeda, *Negotiating Conflict*, describes myriad bordering practices in Beirut. See also the Beirut Urban Lab's mapping projects at https://beiruturbanlab.com/.

23. Seurat, "Le quartier de Bâb Tebbâné à Tripoli."

24. See Shaery-Yazdi, "Rethinking Sectarianism," for an analysis of how discourse about this castration revealed the assumption that this violence was sectarianism.

25. Hage, *The Diasporic Condition*, 60.

26. Leichtman, "From the Cross (and Crescent)," reports that 25 percent of Lebanese marriages in Senegal are interreligious.

27. Naber, *Arab America*.

28. Exceptions include a Christian SSNP leader who opposed his daughter's marriage to a Muslim a generation ago.

Chapter Seven

1. On the headscarf as symbol of alleged Muslim sexism, see Abu-Lughod's now classic corrective "Do Muslim Women Really Need Saving?"

2. Kassem connects Lebanese ideas of Maronite supremacy to Europe-centered Islamophobia and white supremacy in *Islamophobia and Lebanon*.

3. Makdisi, *Age of Coexistence*, 132–33.

4. See Mamdani's classic *Good Muslim, Bad Muslim*.

5. See Deeb and Harb, *Leisurely Islam*.

6. Asad, *Formations of the Secular*.

7. On French secularism and its contradictions, see Fernando, *Republic Unsettled*.

8. Ussama Makdisi has described a history of secularist antisectarian discourse and practice beginning in at least 1860 in the Levant (*Age of Coexistence*). See also Bardawil, *Revolution and Disenchantment*; and Farha, *Lebanon*.

9. On secularism and the Lebanese left, see Haugbolle, "Social Boundaries and Secularism."

10. Some fit Mikdashi's description in *Sextarianism* of "evangelical secularists" who "believe that cultural and ethical change must precede political change" (16).

11. Mikdashi, "Sex and Sectarianism," notes that focusing on making the state secular misses the point, as the Lebanese state is already secular. On the secular logics of the state, see also Moumtaz, *God's Property*.

12. On Hizbullah and related political-religious movements, see Deeb, *An Enchanted Modern*; and Norton, *Hezbollah*.

13. A few recent examples: Alsultany, *Broken*; Aziz, *The Racial Muslim*; Naber, "Look, Mohammed the Terrorist Is Coming"; Rana et al., "Pedagogies of Resistance"; and Rana and Daulatzai, "Writing the Muslim Left."

14. Gualtieri, *Between Arab and White*, 146–47.

15. Rana, "The Story of Islamophobia."

16. Chan-Malik, *Being Muslim*; Jackson, "Islam, Muslims and the Wages of Racial Agnosia."

17. See Korkman, "(Mis)Translations," for a trenchant analysis of this problem in relation to Turkey.

18. See Majed, "Sectarian Neoliberalism," 78.

19. Kassamali, "Migrant Worker Lifeworlds," 32.

20. Mikdashi, "Sex and Sectarianism," 43.

21. Masuzawa, *Invention of World Religions*, describes the history of this idea.

22. Kassem, *Islamophobia and Lebanon*.

23. Elhassan, *Ninety-Ninth Floor*, 58.

24. Elhassan, 100.

25. Elhassan, 264.

26. Elhassan, 286.

27. Meier, "Matrimonial Strategies," estimates that there are several hundred such marriages annually.

28. By 1970, one-third of the Lebanese workforce was Syrian (Chalcroft, *Invisible Cage*, 79).

29. Mikdashi, "Sex and Sectarianism."

Chapter Nine

1. Paler, Marshall, and Atallah, *Fear of Supporting Political Reform.*

2. See also Radwan, "Economic Adversities," 110.

Chapter Ten

1. Volk, "Missing the Nation."

2. I didn't ask about circumcision because until recently, babies with penises of all sects born in urban Lebanon were circumcised as a common medical practice related to ideas about hygiene. These ideas continue to inform most parents' decisions about circumcision.

3. Mikdashi, "Notes on Understanding."

Conclusion

1. The wedding is that of Lebanese Instagram model Serena Mamlouk.

2. This quote encapsulates what Mikdashi, *Sextarianism*, calls "evangelical secularism."

3. I filed the appropriate forms to request these numbers twice with no response.

4. Information International, *Istitlaa ra'y bayn al-zawaj al-dini wal-madani.*

5. Akiki, "Bayn al-zawaj al-mukhtakat wa al-insihar al-watani"; *As-Safir*, "173 alf zawaj mukhtalat" [170,000 mixed marriages], February 4, 2013, 5.

6. Moawad, "The Bigger Struggle."

7. Gratitude to Sami Atallah for making this happen!

8. Salame, "Mapping Lebanon."

9. Indeed, a study that reports that between 1943 and 1975 there were approximately 25,000 Muslim-Christian marriages registered in Lebanon seems to be based on a journalistic estimation of Cyprus marriages during that time (Ziadah, "Al-zawaj al-mukhtalat").

10. Jammal, "Al-zawaj al-madani fi Lubnan"; Tarabey, "'Aras fi qubrus." Even the higher estimate is still only 6 percent of Lebanese marriages.

11. Chamas, "When Weddings Become Protests."

12. See De Giacometti, "Island of Love," on these Cyprus civil weddings.

13. Cyprus has been marrying foreigners—especially Lebanese and Israelis—in civil ceremonies since 1923. The earliest Cyprus wedding among my interviewees was in 1975 (and the earliest civil marriage in 1970 in Paris), but no doubt there were quite a few earlier ones.

14. Ajab, "Kayf ya'ish."

15. Bazzi, "Ma'sa rabi'"; Awada, "Muhajjaba wa zawaj knisi."

16. "From Ain El-Rummaneh to Chiyah, you [feminine plural, *antunna*] are the revolution."

17. Some of these proposed laws would have added a civil personal status option; others would have created a single unified civil personal status law for all citizens. See Hyndman-Rizk, "A Question of Personal Status."

18. Human Rights Watch, "Lebanon: Events of 2022."

19. We don't know whether these marriages can be registered in Lebanon, and one needs to know enough English to navigate the US civil marriage system and the wedding.

20. Hammoud, "20% zawaj al-muqasarat fi Lubnan."

21. Allouche, "Queering Heterosexual (Intersectarian) Love," 547.

22. Salloukh, "The Autumn of Sectarianism."

23. Bou Akar, "The Search for Hope."

24. See Haraway, *Staying with the Trouble* and Tsing, *Mushroom at the End of the World* for just two of many examples.

25. Hage, *Is Racism an Environmental Threat?*, 123.

26. Nucho, "Inequality and Identity."

Bibliography

Abdullahi A. An-Na'im, ed. *Inter-religious Marriage among Muslims*. Atlanta, GA: Emory Law School, 2005.

Abu-Lughod, Lila. "Do Muslim Women Really Need Saving? Anthropological Reflections on Cultural Relativism and Its Others." *American Anthropologist* 104, no. 3 (2002): 783–90.

———. "Introduction: Feminist Longings and Postcolonial Conditions." In Abu-Lughod, *Remaking Women*, 3–31.

———, ed. *Remaking Women: Feminism and Modernity in the Middle East*. Princeton, NJ: Princeton University Press, 1999.

Adely, Fida. "A Different Kind of Love: Compatibility (Insijam) and Marriage in Jordan." *Arab Studies Journal* 24, no. 2 (2016): 102–27.

Ajab, Nisreen. "Kayf ya'ish abna' al-zawaj al-mukhtalat fi Lubnan?" [How do children of mixed marriages live in Lebanon?]. *Elaph*, August 11, 2009. https://elaph.com/Web/Youth/2009/8/470671.htm.

Akiki, Vivienne. "Bayn al-zawaj al-mukhtakat wa al-insihar al-watani" [Between mixed marriage and national unity]. *An-nahar*, August 8, 2014. https://tinyurl.com/4983s8ba.

Alajaji, Sylvia Angelique. *Music and the Armenian Diaspora: Searching for Home in Exile*. Bloomington: Indiana University Press, 2015.

Alamuddin, Nura S., and Paul D. Starr. *Crucial Bonds: Marriage among the Lebanese Druze*. Delmar, NY: Caravan Books, 1980.

Al-Bayadi, Safwat. "Al-zawaj al-mukhtalat wa tawabi'hu" [Mixed marriage and its accompaniments]. In Majlis kana'is al-sharq al-awsat, *Andhima al-ahwal alshakhsiyya*, 187–98.

Alexander, Ella. "Elopements Are on the Rise: Why Modern Couples Are Running Away from Lavish Weddings." *Harper's Bazaar*, April 5, 2019. https://www.harpersbazaar.com/uk/bazaar-brides/a27054966/elopements-are-on-the-rise/.

Al-Hasbani, Mariam. "Referential Set of Social Knowledge and the Choice of Type of Marriage among Lebanese Couples." Master's thesis, Lebanese University, 2009.

Allouche, Sabiha. "Love, Lebanese Style: Toward an Either/and Analytic Framework of Kinship." *Journal of Middle East Women's Studies* 15, no. 2 (2019): 157–78.

———. "Queering Heterosexual (Intersectarian) Love in Lebanon." *International Journal of Middle East Studies* 51 (2019): 547–65.

Alsultany, Evelyn. *Broken: The Failed Promise of Muslim Inclusion*. New York: New York University Press, 2022.

Asad, Talal. *Formations of the Secular: Christianity, Islam, Modernity*. Cultural Memory in the Present. Stanford, CA: Stanford University Press, 2003.

Awada, Ali. "Muhajjaba wa zawaj knisi . . . qusa Butrus wa Marwa" [A woman wearing a headscarf and a church wedding . . . Boutrus and Marwa's story]. *An-nahar*, August 11, 2017. https://tinyurl.com/yc22jcan.

Aziz, Sahar. *The Racial Muslim: When Racism Quashes Religious Freedom*. Oakland: University of California Press, 2021.

Barbour, Bernadette, and Pascale Salameh. "Consanguinity in Lebanon: Prevalence, Distribution and Determinants." *Journal of Biosocial Science* 41, no. 4 (2009): 505–17.

Bardawil, Fadi. *Revolution and Disenchantment: Arab Marxism and the Binds of Emancipation*. Durham, NC: Duke University Press, 2020.

Baydoun, Azza Charara. *Cases of Femicide before Lebanese Courts*. Beirut: KAFA (Enough) Violence and Exploitation, 2011. https://kafa.org.lb/en/node/152.

Bazzi, Jihad. "Ma'sa Rabi' tiftah al-sijal hawl al-Druz wa rafaq al-zawaj min al-tawaif al-ukhra" [Rabi's tragedy opens debate about the Druze refusal to marry from other sects]. *Radio Sawa*, July 31, 2013. https://tinyurl.com/5n983f3x.

Beydoun, Ahmad. *Al-jumhuriyya al-mutaqatti'a: Masa'ir al-sigha al-Lubnaniyya ba'd ittifaq al-taef* [The fractured republic: The fates of Lebanon's formula after Ta'if]. Beirut: Dar an-nahar, 1999.

Bou Akar, Hiba. *For the War Yet to Come: Planning Beirut's Frontiers*. Stanford, CA: Stanford University Press, 2018.

———. "The Search for Hope." *Society and Space*, August 30, 2020. https://www.societyandspace.org/articles/the-search-for-hope.

Bou Harb, Noha. "Mushkilat al-zawaj al-mukhtalat fi Saida wa-al-dawahi" [Problems of mixed marriage in Saida and its suburbs]. In Majlis kana'is al-sharq al-awsat, *Andhima al-ahwal alshakhsiyya*, 237–58.

Cammett, Melani. *Compassionate Communalism: Welfare and Sectarianism in Lebanon*. Ithaca, NY: Cornell University Press, 2014.

Campbell, D. E., and Putnam, R. D. "America's Grace: How a Tolerant Nation Bridges Its Religious Divides." *Political Science Quarterly* 126 (2011): 611–40.

Chalcroft, John. *The Invisible Cage: Syrian Migrant Workers in Lebanon.* Stanford, CA: Stanford University Press, 2009.

Chamas, Sophie. "When Weddings Become Protests: The Debate over Civil Marriage in Lebanon." *Deseret News*, March 18, 2015. https://www.deseret.com/2015/3/18/20560939/when-weddings-become-protests-the-debate-over-civil-marriage-in-lebanon.

Chan-Malik, Sylvia. *Being Muslim: A Cultural History of Women of Color in American Islam.* New York: New York University Press, 2018.

Cheng, Wendy. *The Changs Next Door to the Díazes: Remapping Race in Suburban California.* Minneapolis: University of Minnesota Press, 2013.

Chong, Kelly H. *Love across Borders: Asian Americans, Race, and the Politics of Intermarriage and Family-Making.* New York: Routledge, 2021.

Chopra, Rohit, and Jyoti Punwani. "Discovering the Other, Discovering the Self: Inter-religious Marriage among Muslims in the Greater Bombay Area, India." In An-Na'im, *Inter-religious Marriage among Muslims*, 45–161.

Chowdhry, Prem. *Contentious Marriages, Eloping Couples: Gender, Caste, and Patriarchy in Northern India.* Oxford: Oxford University Press, 2007.

Clark, Janine A., and Bassel F. Salloukh. "Elite Strategies, Civil Society, and Sectarian Identities in Postwar Lebanon." *International Journal of Middle East Studies* 45, no. 4 (2013): 731–49.

Connolly, Jennifer. "Forbidden Intimacies: Christian-Muslim Intermarriage in East Kalimantan, Indonesia." *American Ethnologist* 36, no. 3 (2009): 492–506.

Crenshaw, Kimberlé. "Mapping the Margins: Intersectionality, Identity Politics, and Violence against Women of Color." *Stanford Law Review* 43 (1991): 1241–99.

Cromer, Gerald. "Intermarriage Handbooks: Ensuring Jewish Survival." *Jewish Journal of Sociology* 47, no. 1–2 (2005): 48–53.

Dabbous-Sensenig, Dima. "Mixed Marriages and Interlocking Forms of Discrimination in Lebanon." *Al-Raida* 18–19, no. 93–94 (2001): 5–6.

Dainius, "Moving Statues of a Man and Woman Pass Through Each Other Daily, Symbolizing Tragic Love Story." *Bored Panda*, 2015, https://www.boredpanda.com/metal-statue-love-story-ali-nino-tamara-kvesitadze-georgia/?utm_source=google&utm_medium=organic&utm_campaign=organic.

Davie, Michael F. "Demarcation Lines in Contemporary Beirut." *The Middle East and North Africa: World Boundaries*, vol. 2. Edited by Clive H. Schofield and Richard N. Schofield. London: Routledge, 2012.

Deeb, Lara. *An Enchanted Modern: Gender and Public Piety in Shi'i Lebanon.* Princeton, NJ: Princeton University Press, 2006.

Deeb, Lara, and Mona Harb. *Leisurely Islam: Negotiating Geography and Morality in South Beirut.* Princeton, NJ: Princeton University Press, 2013.

Deeb, Lara, Tsolin Nalbantian, and Nadya Sbaiti, eds. *Practicing Sectarianism: Archival and Ethnographic Interventions on Lebanon.* Stanford, CA: Stanford University Press, 2022.

Deringil, Selim. *Conversion and Apostasy in the Late Ottoman Empire.* Cambridge: Cambridge University Press, 2012.

Di Giacometti, Michela. "'The Island of Love': (Civil) Marriage Ceremonies of Middle East Nationals in the Republic of Cyprus." *Bulletin de correspondance helle'nique moderne et contemporain*, December 2019. https://doi.org/10.4000/bchmc.300.

Donham, Donald L. *Violence in a Time of Liberation: Murder and Ethnicity at a South African Gold Mine, 1994.* Durham, NC: Duke University Press, 2011.

Doumani, Beshara. *Family Life in the Ottoman Mediterranean: A Social History.* Cambridge: Cambridge University Press, 2017.

Driscoll, Richard, Keith E. Davis, and Milton E. Lipetz. "Parental Interference and Romantic Love: The Romeo and Juliet Effect." *Journal of Personality and Social Psychology* 24, no. 1 (1972): 1–10.

El Hage, Anne-Marie. "Online Civil Marriage Ceremonies, a New Pressure Tactic for Lebanese Couples." *L'Orient Today*, July 19, 2022. https://today.lorientlejour .com/article/1306143/online-civil-marriage-ceremony-a-new-pressure-tactic -for-lebanese-couples.html.

Elhassan, Jana Fawaz. *The Ninety-Ninth Floor.* Translated by Michelle Hartman. Northhampton, MA: Interlink Books, 2017. Originally published as *Tabiq 99* (Beirut: Difaf Publishing, 2014).

El-Hibri, Hatim. *Visions of Beirut: The Urban Life of Media Infrastructure.* Durham, NC: Duke University Press, 2021.

Erwin, Courtney P. "Reconciling Conflicting Identities: How National and Religious Identities Influence the Decision to Marry in Egypt." *Law and Identity* 3, no. 2 (2005): 675–709.

Farha, Mark. *Lebanon: The Rise and Fall of a Secular State under Siege.* Cambridge: Cambridge University Press, 2019.

Farsoun, Samih K. "E Pluribus Plura or E Pluribus Unum? Cultural Pluralism and Social Class in Lebanon." In *Toward a Viable Lebanon*, edited by Halim Barakat, 99–130. Washington, DC: Center for Contemporary Arab Studies, Georgetown University, 1988.

Fernando, Mayanthi. *The Republic Unsettled: Muslim French and the Contradictions of Secularism.* Durham, NC: Duke University Press, 2014.

Fregonese, Sara. "Between a Refuge and a Battleground: Beirut's Discrepant Cosmopolitanisms." *Geographical Review* 102, no. 3: 316–36.

Frontiers Ruwad Association. *Marriage Registration in Lebanon: A Guide to Procedure and Practices.* Accessed March 31, 2024. https://docplayer.net/47767445 -Marriage-registration-in-lebanon-a-guide-to-procedures-and-practices.html.

Gandhi, Mahatma. *The Collected Works of Mahatma Gandhi*. New Delhi: Publications Division, Government of India, 1999. https://www.gandhiashramsevagram .org/gandhi-literature/mahatma-gandhi-collected-works-volume-35.pdf.

Gökarıksel, Banu, and Anna J. Secor. "Uneasy Neighbors: The Making of Sectarian Difference and Alevi Precarity in Urban Turkey." *International Journal of Middle East Studies* 54 (2022): 243–59.

Gualtieri, Sarah M. *Between Arab and White: Race and Ethnicity in the Early Syrian American Diaspora*. Berkeley: University of California Press, 2009.

Gupta, Charu. "Hindu Women, Muslim Men: Love Jihad and Conversions." *Economic and Political Weekly* 44, no. 51 (2009): 13–15.

Haddad, Fanar. "'Sectarianism' and Its Discontents in the Study of the Middle East." *Middle East Journal* 71, no. 3 (2017): 363–82.

Haddad, Mohanna. "Christian Identity in the Jordanian Arab Culture: A Case Study of Two Communities in North Jordan." *Journal of Muslim Minority Affairs* 20, no. 1 (2000): 137–46.

Hafeda, Mohamad. *Negotiating Conflict in Lebanon: Bordering Practices in a Divided Beirut*. London: I. B. Tauris, 2019.

Hage, Ghassan. *The Diasporic Condition: Ethnographic Explorations of the Lebanese in the World*. Chicago: University of Chicago Press, 2021.

———. *Is Racism an Environmental Threat?* Cambridge: Polity Press, 2017.

Hall, Stuart. "Ethnicity: Identity and Difference." *Radical America* 23, no. 4 (1989): 9–20.

Hammoud, Zaynab. "20% zawaj al-muqasarat fi Lubnan" [20% marriage of minors in Lebanon]. *Al-Akbar*, March 14, 2024. https://tinyurl.com/a5ycm9bx.

Haraway, Donna. *Staying with the Trouble: Making Kin in the Chthulucene*. Durham, NC: Duke University Press, 2016.

Harb, Charles. *Describing the Lebanese Youth: A National and Psycho-Social Survey*. Beirut: Issam Fares Institute for Public Policy and International Affairs, July 2010.

Harb, Mona. "Professor Mona Harb: What Is Urban Planning?" In *Reflections with Jad Ghosn*, 2021. Podcast audio, 1:49:00. https://podcasts.apple.com/us/podcast/ reflections-with-jad-ghosn/id1539873270?i=1000543061308.

Harik, Iliya. *Politics and Change in a Traditional Society, Lebanon 1711–1845*. Princeton, NJ: Princeton University Press, 1968.

Harik, Judith P. "Perceptions of Community and State among Lebanon's Druze Youth." *Middle East Journal* 47, no. 1 (1993): 41–62.

Harrison, Faye. "The Persistent Power of 'Race' in the Cultural and Political Economy of Racism." *Annual Review of Anthropology* 24 (1995): 47–74.

Hart, Kimberly. "Love by Arrangement: The Ambiguity of 'Spousal Choice' in a Turkish Village." *Journal of the Royal Anthropological Institute* 13, no. 2 (2007): 345–62.

Haugbolle, Sune. "Social Boundaries and Secularism in the Lebanese Left." *Mediterranean Politics* 18, no. 3 (2013): 427–43.

Hayek, Ghenwa. *Beirut, Imagining the City: Space and Place in Lebanese Literature.* I. B. Tauris, 2014.

Hirsch, Jennifer S., and Holly Wardlow, eds. *Modern Loves: The Anthropology of Romantic Courtship and Companionate Marriage.* Ann Arbor: University of Michigan Press, 2006.

Hourani, Albert. "Ideologies of the Mountain and the City: Reflections on the Lebanese Civil War." In *The Emergence of the Modern Middle East*, edited by Albert Hourani. London: Macmillan Press, 1981.

Houssari, Najia. "Domestic Violence Doubles in Lebanon." *Arab News*, February 11, 2021. https://arab.news/5xqfv.

Hovsepian, Nubar, ed. *The War on Lebanon: A Reader.* New York: Olive Branch Press, 2007.

Human Rights Watch. "Lebanon: Events of 2022." *World Report 2023.* Accessed December 9, 2023. https://www.hrw.org/world-report/2023/country-chapters/lebanon.

———. *Unequal and Unprotected: Women's Rights under Lebanese Personal Status Laws.* January 19, 2015. https://www.hrw.org/report/2015/01/19/unequal-and-unprotected/womens-rights-under-lebanese-personal-status-laws.

Hurd, Elizabeth Shakman. "Politics of Sectarianism: Rethinking Religion and Politics in the Middle East." *Middle East Law and Governance* 7 (2015): 61–75.

Hyndman-Rizk, Nelia. "A Question of Personal Status: The Lebanese Women's Movement and Civil Marriage Reform." *Journal of Middle East Women's Studies* 15, no. 2 (2019): 179–98.

Information International. *Istitlaa ra'y bayn al-zawaj al-dini wal-madani* [Survey about religious and civil marriage]. 2013.

Jackson, John L., Jr. *Real Black: Adventures in Racial Sincerity.* Chicago: University of Chicago Press, 2005.

Jackson, Sherman A. "Islam, Muslims and the Wages of Racial Agnosia in America." *Journal of Islamic Law and Culture* 13, no. 1 (2011): 1–17.

Jammal, Rita. "Al-Zawaj al-madani fi Lubnan . . . Zawaj qanuni wa 'irqala waq'iyya" [Civil marriage in Lebanon . . . Legalities and obstacles]. *Al-Araby*, February 24, 2019. https://tinyurl.com/dc7cnxpa.

Jawhariyyeh, Wasif. *The Storyteller of Jerusalem: The Life and Times of Wasif Jawhariyyeh, 1904–1948.* Edited by Issam Nassar. Translated by Nada Elzeer. Northampton, MA: Olive Branch Press, 2013.

Joseph, Suad. "Connectivity and Patriarchy among Urban Working-Class Arab Families in Lebanon." *Ethos* 21, no. 4 (1993): 452–84. http://www.jstor.org/stable/640580.

———, ed. *Gender and Citizenship in the Middle East.* Syracuse, NY: Syracuse University Press, 2000.

———. "Gender and Relationality among Arab Families in Lebanon." In "Who's East? Whose East?" Special issue, *Feminist Studies* 19, no. 3 (1993): 465–86. http://www.jstor.org/stable/3178097.

———. "The Politicization of Religious Sects in Borj Hammoud, Lebanon." PhD diss., Columbia University, 1975.

———. "Working-Class Women's Networks in a Sectarian State: A Political Paradox." *American Ethnologist* 10, no. 1 (1983): 1–22.

Kabbanji, Jacques. "Heurs et malheurs du système universitaire Libanais: À l'heure de l'homogénéisation et de la marchandisation de l'enseignement supérieur." *Revue du monde musulman et de la Méditerranée* 131 (2012): 127–45.

Kandido-Jakšić, Maja. "Social Distance and Attitudes towards Ethnically Mixed Marriages." *Psihologija* 41, no. 2 (2008): 149–62.

Kandiyoti, Deniz. "Bargaining with Patriarchy." *Gender and Society* 2, no. 3 (1988): 274–90.

Karam, Jeffrey G., and Rima Majed, eds. *The Lebanon Uprising of 2019: Voices from the Revolution*: I. B. Tauris, 2022.

Kassamali, Sumayya. "Migrant Worker Lifeworlds of Beirut." PhD diss., Columbia University, 2017.

Kassem, Ali. *Islamophobia and Lebanon: Visibly Muslim Women and Global Coloniality*. I. B. Tauris, 2023.

Kastrinou, Maria A. *Power, Sect and State in Syria: The Politics of Marriage and Identity amongst the Druze*. London: I. B. Tauris, 2016.

Kern, Karen M. *Imperial Citizen: Marriage and Citizenship in the Ottoman Frontier Provinces of Iraq*. Syracuse, NY: Syracuse University Press, 2011.

Khalaf, Samir, and Philip S. Khoury, eds. *Recovering Beirut: Urban Design and Postwar Reconstruction*. Leiden: E. J. Brill, 1993.

Khater, Akram Fouad. *Inventing Home: Emigration, Gender, and the Middle Class in Lebanon, 1870–1920*. Berkeley, CA: University of California Press, 2001.

Khlat, M. "Consanguineous Marriage and Reproduction in Beirut, Lebanon." *American Journal of Human Genetics* 43 (1988): 188–96.

Khouri, Rami G., and Vivian M. Lopez, eds. *A Generation on the Move: Insights into the Conditions, Aspirations and Activism of Arab Youth*. Beirut: Issam Fares Institute for Public Policy and International Affairs, 2011.

Kingston, Paul. *Reproducing Sectarianism: Advocacy Networks and the Politics of Civil Society in Postwar Lebanon*. Albany, NY: State University of New York Press, 2013.

Korkman, Zeynep K. "(Mis)Translations of the Critiques of Anti-Muslim Racism and the Repercussions for Transnational Feminist Solidarities." *Meridians* 22, no. 2 (2023): 267–96.

Lebanese Code of Civil Procedure, article 79 (1983). In Special Tribunal for Lebanon, *Selected Articles: Lebanese Criminal Code 2009*. February 2010. https://www.legal-tools.org/doc/d0f1c2/pdf.

Leichtman, Mara A. "From the Cross (and Crescent) to the Cedar and Back Again: Transnational Religion and Politics among Lebanese Christians in Senegal." *Anthropological Quarterly* 86, no. 1 (2013): 35–76.

Leonard, Madeleine. "'It's Better to Stick to Your Own Kind': Teenagers' Views on Cross-Community Marriages in Northern Ireland." *Journal of Ethnic and Migration Studies* 35, no. 1 (2009): 97–113.

Lewis, Patricia C., Nadine J. Kaslow, Yuk Fai Cheong, Dabney P. Evers, and Kathryn M. Yount. "Femicide in the United States: A Call for Legal Codification and National Surveillance." *Frontiers in Public Health* 12 (2024). https://doi.org/10.3389/fpubh.2024.1338548.

Mahmood, Saba. *Religious Difference in a Secular Age: A Minority Report.* Princeton, NJ: Princeton University Press, 2016.

Majed, Rima. "In Defense of Intra-sectarian Divide: Street Mobilization, Coalition Formation, and Rapid Realignments of Sectarian Boundaries in Lebanon." *Social Forces*, no. 1 (2020): 1–27.

———. "The Political (or Social) Economy of Sectarianism in Lebanon." Middle East Institute, November 7, 2017. https://www.mei.edu/publications/political-or -social-economy-sectarianism-lebanon.

———. "'Sectarian Neoliberalism' and the 2019 Uprisings in Lebanon and Iraq." In Karam and Majed, *The Lebanon Uprising of 2019*, 76–88.

Majlis kana'is al-sharq al-awsat. *Andhima al-ahwal alshakhsiyya: Abhath wa-khibrat fi qawanin al-'a'ila wa-alzawaj al-mukhtalat wa-al-tabani* [Personal status laws: Research on and experiences with family law, mixed marriage, and adoption]. Beirut: Majlis kana'is al-sharq al-awsat, 1990.

Makarem, Nadine. "We Talked to People about Inter-sectarian Marriages in Lebanon." *Step Feed*, April 24, 2017. https://stepfeed.com/we-talked-to-people-about -inter-sectarian-marriages-in-lebanon-5689.

Makdisi, Ussama. *Age of Coexistence: The Ecumenical Frame and the Making of the Modern Arab World.* Oakland: University of California Press, 2019.

———. *The Culture of Sectarianism: Community, History, and Violence in Nineteenth-Century Ottoman Lebanon.* Berkeley: University of California Press, 2000.

Maktabi, Rania. "The Lebanese Census of 1932 Revisited: Who Are the Lebanese?" *British Journal of Middle Eastern Studies* 26, no. 2 (1999): 219–41.

Mamdani, Mahmood. *Good Muslim, Bad Muslim: America, the Cold War, and the Roots of Terror.* New York: Random House, 2004.

Masuzawa, Tomoko. *The Invention of World Religions.* Chicago: University of Chicago Press, 2005.

McCarthy, Kate. *Interfaith Encounters in America.* New Brunswick, NJ: Rutgers University Press, 2007.

Meier, Daniel. "Matrimonial Strategies and Identity Relations between Palestinian Refugees and Lebanese after the Lebanese Civil War." *Journal of Refugee Studies* 23, no. 2 (2010): 111–33.

Mermier, Franck. "The Frontiers of Beirut: Some Anthropological Observations." *Mediterranean Politics* 18, no. 3 (2013): 376–93.

Merton, Robert K. "Intermarriage and the Social Structure: Fact and Theory." *Psychiatry* 4 (1941): 361–74.

Mikdashi, Maya. "Notes on Understanding a Viral Video and Child Custody in Lebanon." *Jadaliyya*, June 21, 2018. https://www.jadaliyya.com/Details/37677.

——. "Sex and Sectarianism: The Legal Architecture of Lebanese Citizenship." *Comparative Studies of South Asia, Africa, and the Middle East* 34, no. 2 (2014): 279–93.

——. *Sextarianism: Sovereignty, Secularism, and the State in Lebanon.* Stanford, CA: Stanford University Press, 2022.

Moawad, Nadine. "The Bigger Struggle for Women in Municipalities." *Sawt al niswa*, 2016. http://sawtalniswa.com/article/557.

Monroe, Kristin V. *The Insecure City: Space, Power, and Mobility in Beirut.* New Brunswick, NJ: Rutgers University Press, 2016.

Moumtaz, Nada. *God's Property: Islam, Charity, and the Modern State.* Berkeley, CA: University of California Press, 2021.

Naber, Nadine. *Arab America: Gender, Cultural Politics, and Activism.* New York: New York University Press, 2012.

——. "'Look, Mohammed the Terrorist Is Coming!': Cultural Racism, Nation-Based Racism, and the Intersection of Oppressions after 9/11." In *Race and Arab Americans before and after 9/11*, edited by Amaney Jamal and Nadine Naber, 276–304. Syracuse: Syracuse University Press, 2008.

Nasr, Salim. "New Social Realities and Post-War Lebanon: Issues for Reconstruction." In Khalaf and Khoury, *Recovering Beirut*, 63–80.

Norton, Augustus Richard. *Hezbollah.* Princeton, NJ: Princeton University Press, 2007.

Nucho, Joanne R. *Everyday Sectarianism in Urban Lebanon: Infrastructures, Public Services, and Power.* Princeton, NJ: Princeton University Press, 2016.

——. "Inequality and Identity: Social Class, Urban Space, and Sect." In Deeb, Nalbantian, Sbaiti, *Practicing Sectarianism*, 138–56.

Obeid, Michelle. *Border Lives: An Ethnography of a Lebanese Town in Changing Times.* Leiden: Brill, 2019.

Paler, Laura, Leslie Marshall, and Sami Atallah. "The Fear of Supporting Political Reform." Lebanese Center for Policy Studies, January 5, 2018.

Peleikis, Anja. "Shifting Identities, Reconstructing Boundaries: The Case of a Multi-confessional Locality in Post-War Lebanon." *Die Welt des Islams* 41, no. 3 (2001): 400–29.

Pew Forum on Religion & Public Life. *The World's Muslims: Religion, Politics and Society*. Pew Research Center, April 30, 2013.

Radwan, Chad K. "Economic Adversities and Cultural Coping Strategies: Impacts on Identity Boundaries among Druzes in Lebanon." *Economic Anthropology* 5 (2018): 110–22.

Rana, Junaid. "The Story of Islamophobia." *Souls* 9, no. 2 (2007): 148–61.

Rana, Junaid, Evelyn Alsultany, Lara Deeb, Carol Fadda, Su'ad Abdul Khabeer, Arshad Ali, Sohail Daulatzai, et al. "Pedagogies of Resistance: Why Anti-Muslim Racism Matters." *Amerasia Journal* 46, no. 1 (2020): 57–62.

Rana, Junaid, and Sohail Daulatzai. "Writing the Muslim Left: An Introduction to Throwing Stones." In *With Stones in Our Hands: Writings on Muslims, Racism, and Empire*, edited by Sohail Daulatzai and Junaid Rana, ix–xxii. Minneapolis: University of Minnesota Press, 2018.

Rao, Mohan. "Love Jihad and Demographic Fears." *Indian Journal of Gender Studies* 18, no. 3 (2011): 425–30.

Riley, Naomi Schaefer. *'Til Faith Do Us Part: How Interfaith Marriage Is Transforming America*. Oxford: Oxford University Press, 2013.

Rubaii, Kali J. "Tripartheid: How Sectarianism Became Internal to Being in Anbar, Iraq." *PoLAR: Political and Legal Anthropology Review* 42, no. 1 (2019): 125–41.

Salame, Richard. "Mapping Lebanon I: An Interactive Map Showing Registered Voter Data by District." *L'Orient Today*, May 2, 2022. https://today.lorientlejour .com/article/1298296/mapping-lebanon-i-an-interactive-map-showing -registered-voter-data-by-district.html.

Salloukh, Bassel F. "The Autumn of Sectarianism." Lebanese Center for Policy Studies, February 3, 2020. https://www.lcps-lebanon.org/articles/details/1802/ the-autumn-of-sectarianism.

Salloukh, Bassel F., Rabie Barakat, Jinan S. Al-Habbal, Lara W. Khattab, and Shoghig Mikaelian. *The Politics of Sectarianism in Postwar Lebanon*. London: Pluto Press, 2015.

Salti, Nisreen, and Jad Chaaban. "The Role of Sectarianism in the Allocation of Public Expenditures in Postwar Lebanon." *International Journal of Middle East Studies* 42 (2010): 637–55.

Schielke, Samuli. *Egypt in the Future Tense: Hope, Frustration, and Ambivalence before and after 2011*. Bloomington: Indiana University Press, 2015.

Semerdjian, Elyse. "Armenian Women, Legal Bargaining, and Gendered Politics of Conversion in Seventeenth- and Eighteenth-Century Aleppo." *Journal of Middle East Women's Studies* 12, no. 1 (2016): 1–30.

———. *"Off the Straight Path": Illicit Sex, Community, and Law in Ottoman Aleppo*. New York: Syracuse University Press, 2008.

Seurat, Michel. "Le quartier de Bâb Tebbâné à Tripoli (Liban): Étude d'une 'asabi-yya urbaine." In *Mouvements communautaires et espaces urbains au Machreq*, edited by Mona Zakaria and Bachchâr Chbarou, 45–86. Beirut: Presses de l'Ifpo, 1985.

Shaery-Yazdi, Roschanack. "Rethinking Sectarianism: Violence and Coexistence in Lebanon." *Islam and Christian-Muslim Relations* 31, no. 3 (2020): 325–340. https://doi.org/10.1080/09596410.2020.1780408.

Shirlow, Peter. "Ethno-Sectarianism and the Reproduction of Fear in Belfast." *Capital & Class* 27, no. 2 (2003): 77–93.

Stoltzfus, Nathan. *Resistance of the Heart: Intermarriage and the Rosenstrasse Protest in Nazi Germany*. New York: W. W. Norton, 1996.

Stone, Lawrence. *Family, Sex, and Marriage in England, 1500–1800*. New York: Harper and Row, 1977.

Suny, Ronald Grigor. *"They Can Live in the Desert but Nowhere Else": A History of the Armenian Genocide*. Princeton, NJ: Princeton University Press, 2015.

Talhouk, Joumana. "Parliamentary Elections, Civil Society, and Barriers to Political Change." *Kohl Journal* 4, no. 1 (2018): 24–29.

Tarabey, Carine. "'Aras fi Qubrus fi intidhar iqrar al-zawaj al-madani fi Lubnan' [Cyprus weddings awaiting civil marriage decision in Lebanon]. *BBC Arabic*, February 22, 2019. https://www.bbc.com/arabic/middleeast-47317502.

Tarabey, Lubna. *Family Law in Lebanon: Marriage and Divorce among the Druze*. London: I. B. Tauris, 2013.

Traboulsi, Fawwaz. *A History of Modern Lebanon*. Pluto Press, 2007.

Tsing, Anna Lowenhaupt. *The Mushroom at the End of the World: On the Possibility of Life in Capitalist Ruins*. Princeton, NJ: Princeton University Press, 2021.

Vardar, Somnur. "Inter-religious Marriage in the Greater Istanbul Municipality, Turkey." In An-Na'im, *Inter-religious Marriage among Muslims*, 217–92.

Volk, Lucia. "Missing the Nation: Lebanon's Post-War Generation in the Midst of Reconstruction." PhD diss., Harvard University, 2001.

Weber, Anne Françoise. "Briser et suivre les normes : Les couples islamochrétiens au Liban." In *Les métamorphoses du mariage au Moyen-Orient*, edited by Barbara Drieskens, 1–10. Beyrouth: Presses de l'Ifpo, 2008.

Weiss, Max. *The Shadow of Sectarianism: Law, Shi`Ism, and the Making of Modern Lebanon*. Cambridge: Harvard University Press, 2010.

Yahya, Maha. "Reconstituting Space: The Aberration of the Urban in Beirut." In Khalaf and Khoury, *Recovering Beirut*, 128–66.

Yahya, Siham, and Simon Boag. "My Family Would Crucify Me!': The Perceived Influence of Social Pressure on Cross-cultural and Interfaith Dating and Marriage." *Sexuality & Culture* 18 (2014): 759–72.

Ziadah, Tarek. "Al-zawaj al-mukhtalat baina al-fiqh wa-alwaqi'" [Mixed marriage between jurisprudence and reality]. In Majlis kana'is al-sharq al-awsat, *Andhima al-ahwal alshakhsiyya*, 173–86.

Index